SUPER CHILL

SUPER CHILL

A Year of Living Anxiously

Adam Ellis

Andrews McMeel

PUBLISHING®

This book is
dedicated to
Missy Elliott

FORTUNE TELLER

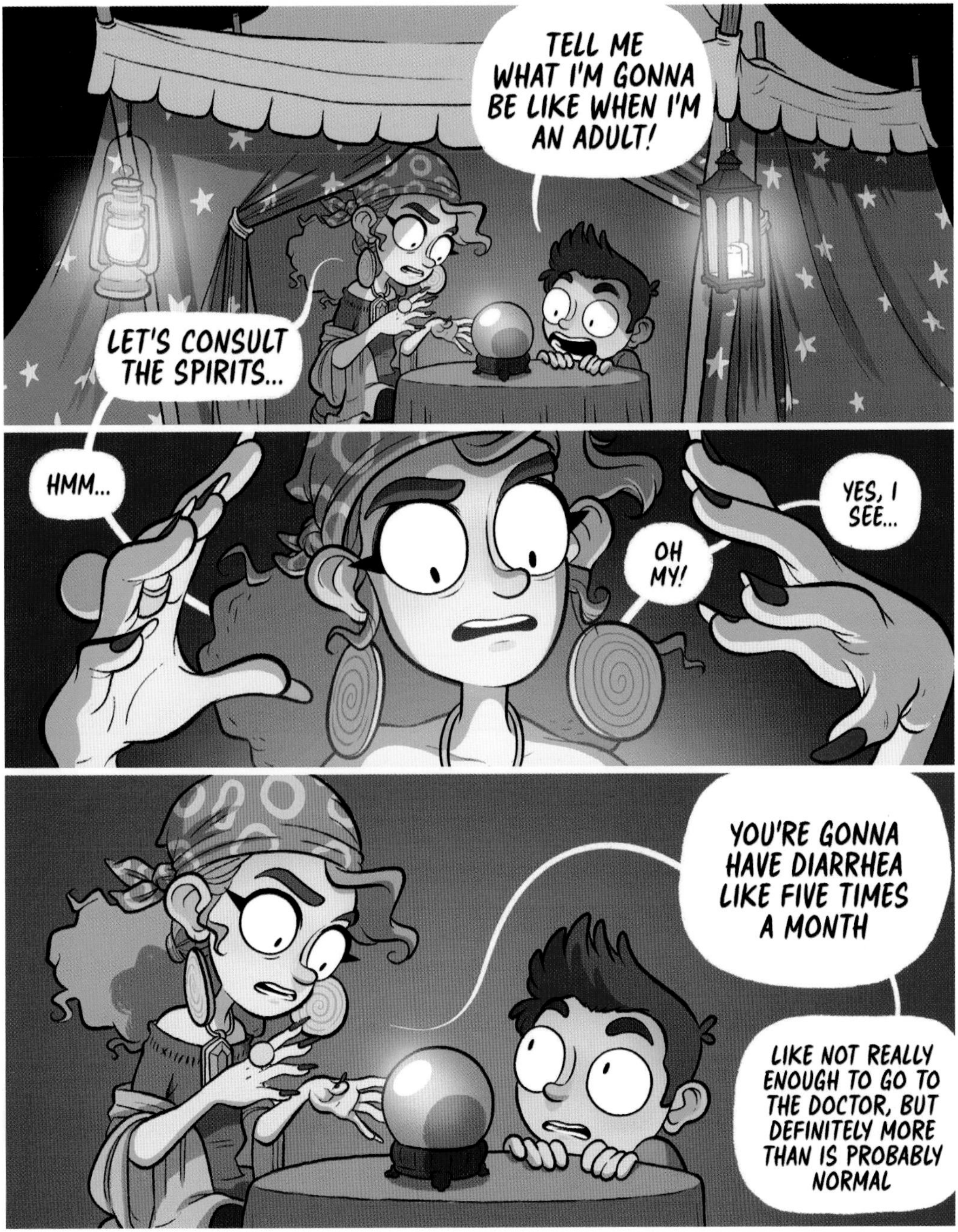
TELL ME WHAT I'M GONNA BE LIKE WHEN I'M AN ADULT!
LET'S CONSULT THE SPIRITS...
HMM...
YES, I SEE...
OH MY!
YOU'RE GONNA HAVE DIARRHEA LIKE FIVE TIMES A MONTH
LIKE NOT REALLY ENOUGH TO GO TO THE DOCTOR, BUT DEFINITELY MORE THAN IS PROBABLY NORMAL

THE PEOPLE'S PRINCESS

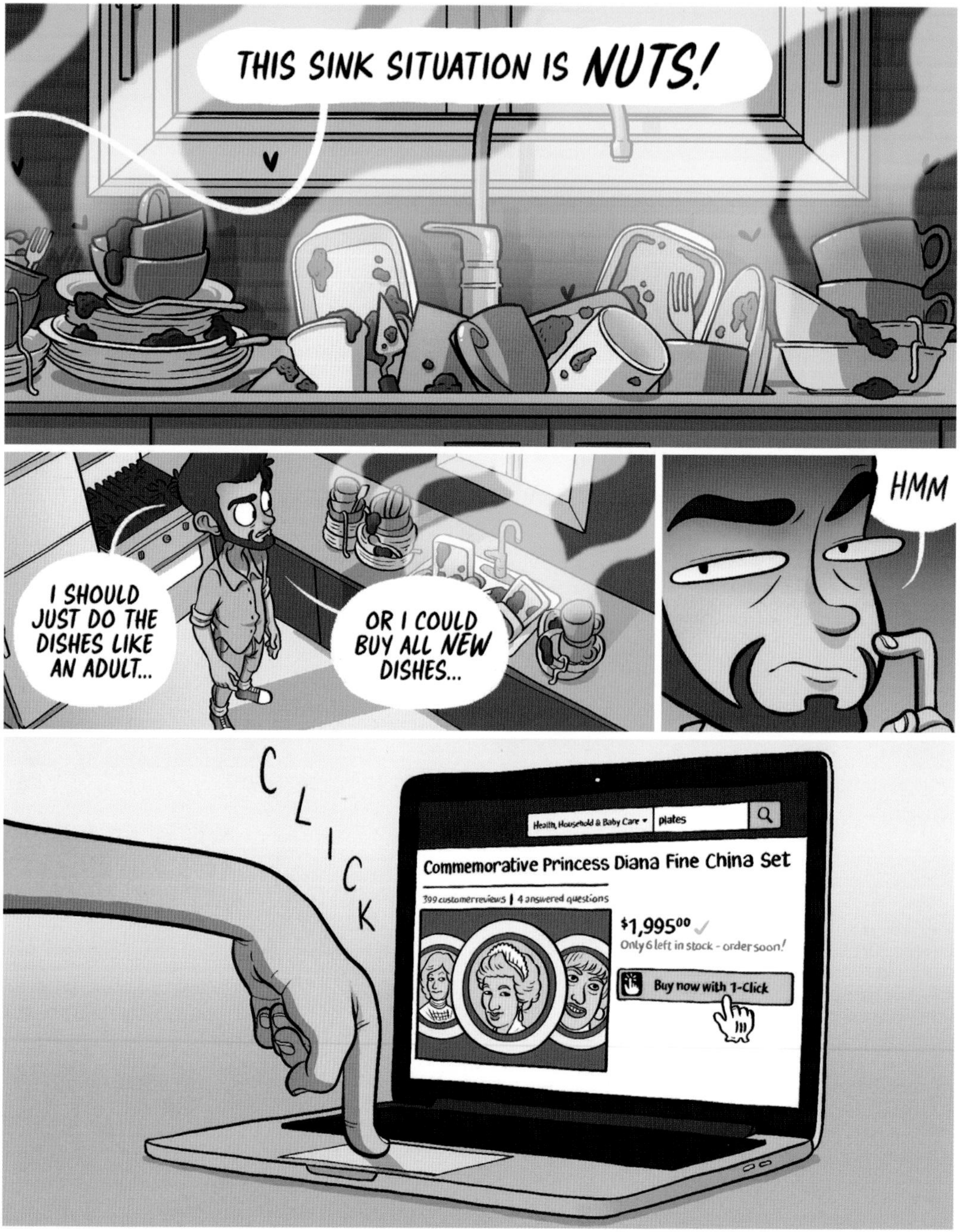
THIS SINK SITUATION IS NUTS!
I SHOULD JUST DO THE DISHES LIKE AN ADULT...
OR I COULD BUY ALL NEW DISHES...
HMM
CLICK
Health, Household & Baby Care
plates
Commemorative Princess Diana Fine China Set
399 customer reviews | 4 answered questions
$1,995.00
Only 6 left in stock - order soon!
Buy now with 1-Click

ANCESTRY RESULTS

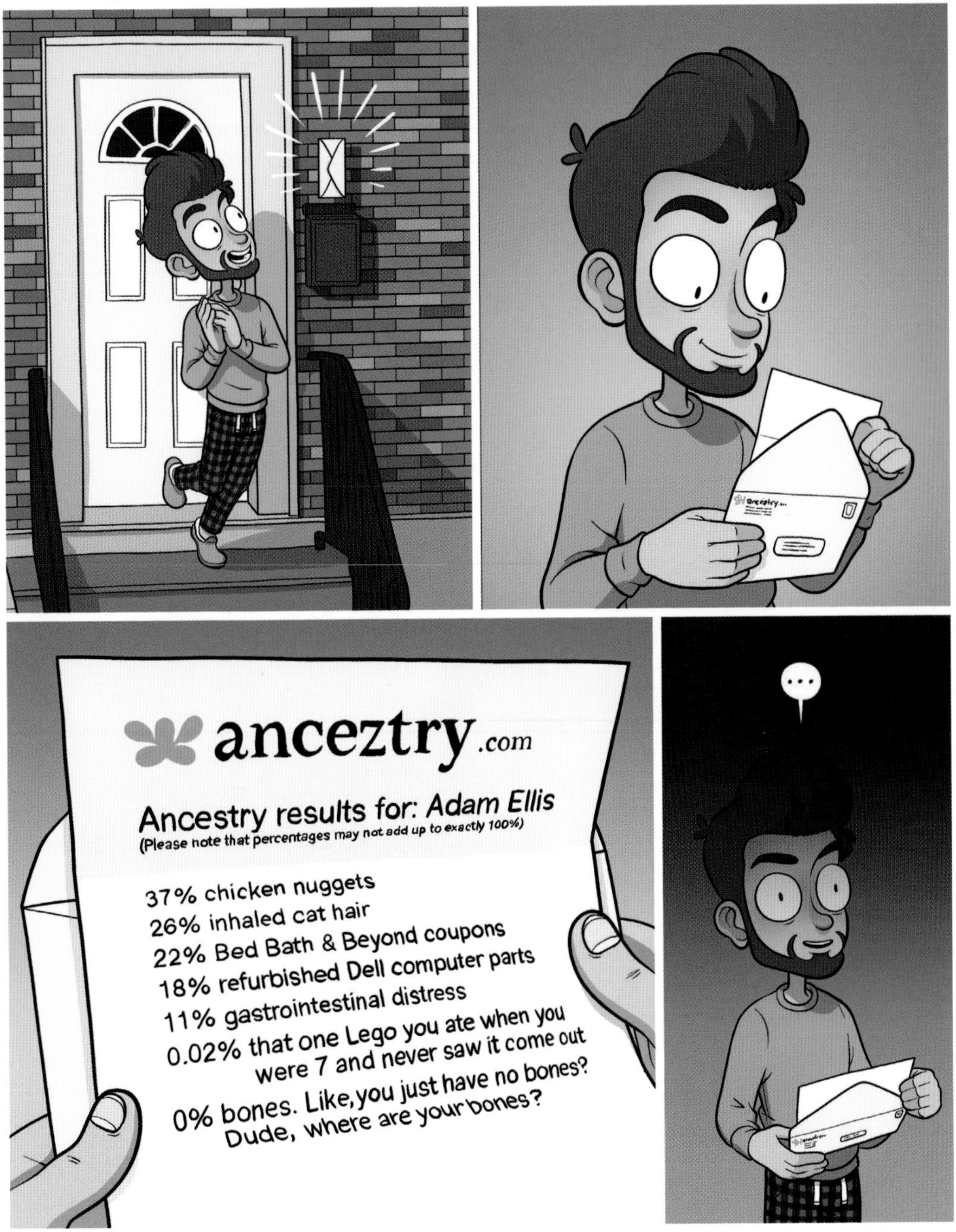

anceztry.com
Ancestry results for: Adam Ellis
(Please note that percentages may not add up to exactly 100%)
37% chicken nuggets
26% inhaled cat hair
22% Bed Bath & Beyond coupons
18% refurbished Dell computer parts
11% gastrointestinal distress
0.02% that one Lego you ate when you were 7 and never saw it come out
0% bones. Like, you just have no bones? Dude, where are your bones?
...

CENTER OF ATTENTION

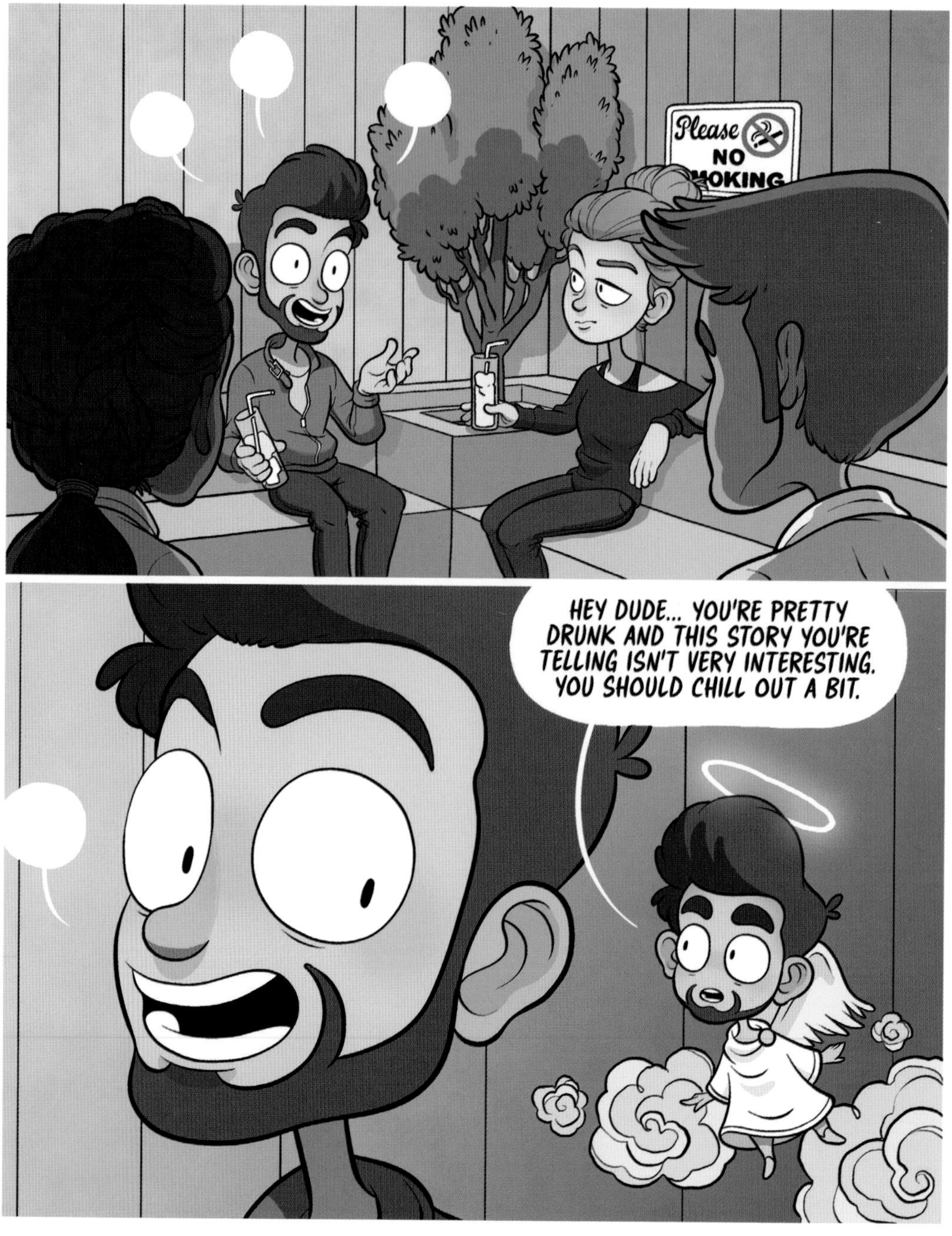
Please NO SMOKING
HEY DUDE... YOU'RE PRETTY DRUNK AND THIS STORY YOU'RE TELLING ISN'T VERY INTERESTING. YOU SHOULD CHILL OUT A BIT.

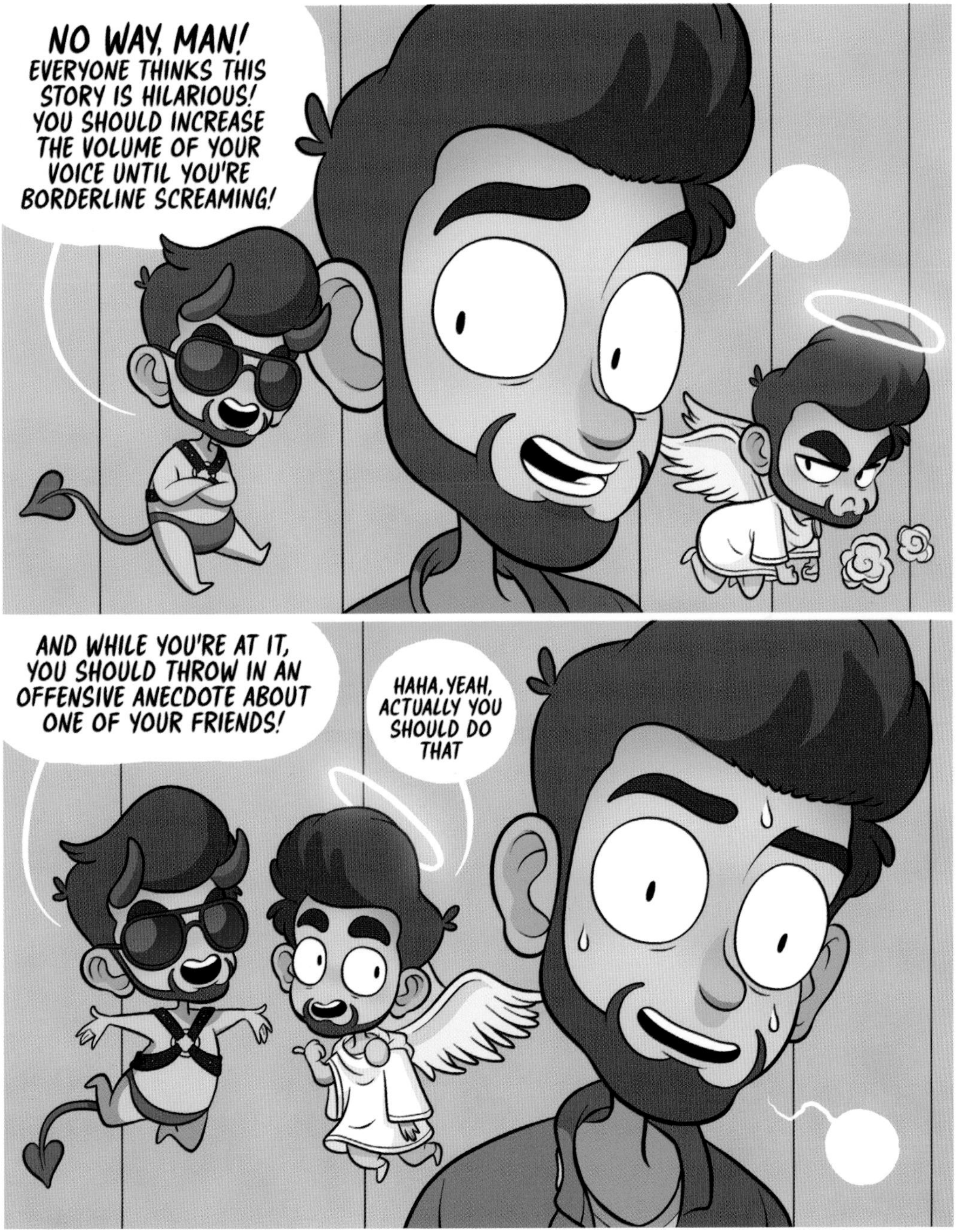
NO WAY, MAN! EVERYONE THINKS THIS STORY IS HILARIOUS! YOU SHOULD INCREASE THE VOLUME OF YOUR VOICE UNTIL YOU'RE BORDERLINE SCREAMING!
AND WHILE YOU'RE AT IT, YOU SHOULD THROW IN AN OFFENSIVE ANECDOTE ABOUT ONE OF YOUR FRIENDS!
HAHA, YEAH, ACTUALLY YOU SHOULD DO THAT

WHEN OTHER PEOPLE GET SICK:

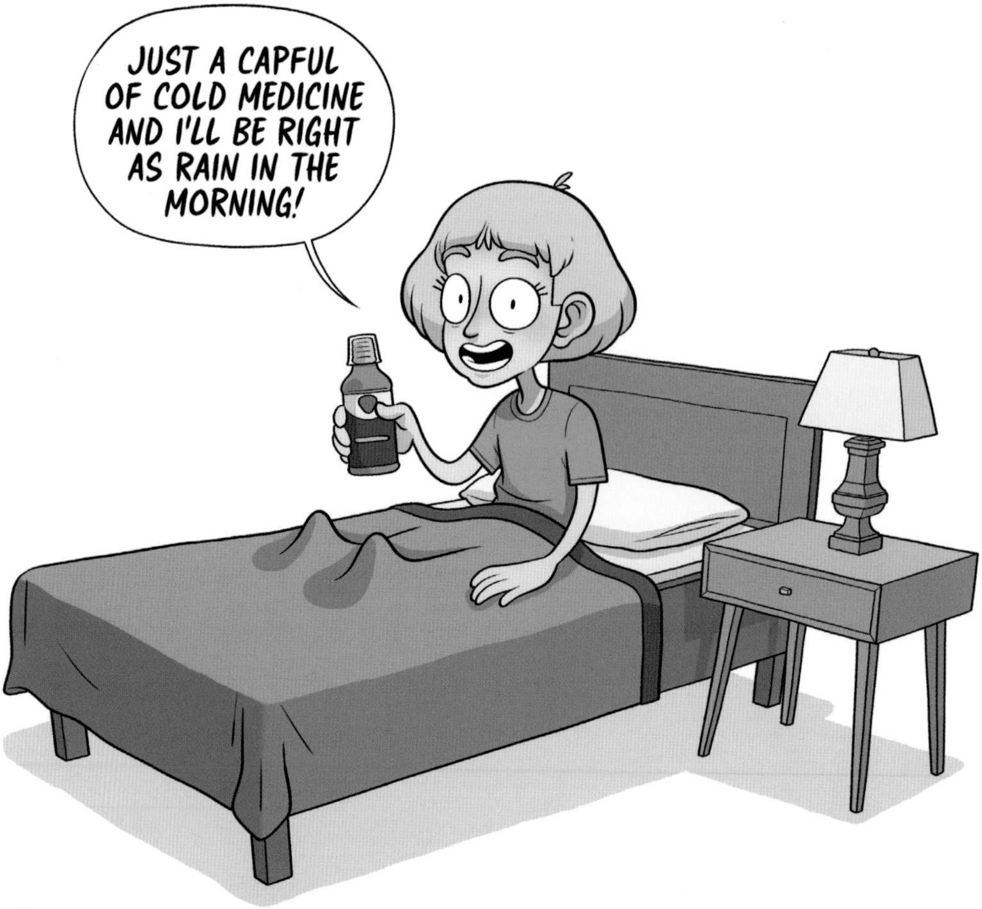
JUST A CAPFUL OF COLD MEDICINE AND I'LL BE RIGHT AS RAIN IN THE MORNING!

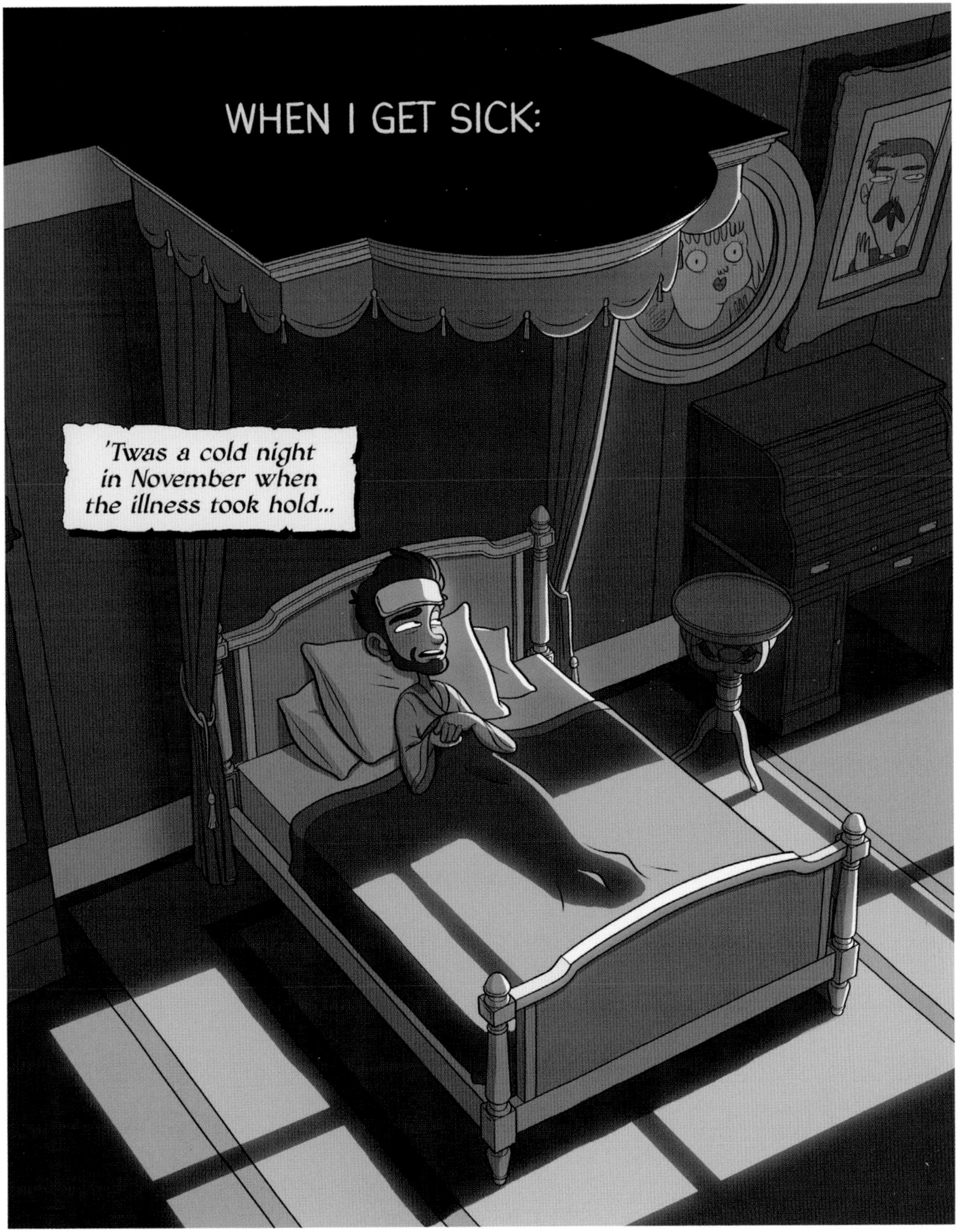
WHEN I GET SICK:
'Twas a cold night in November when the illness took hold...

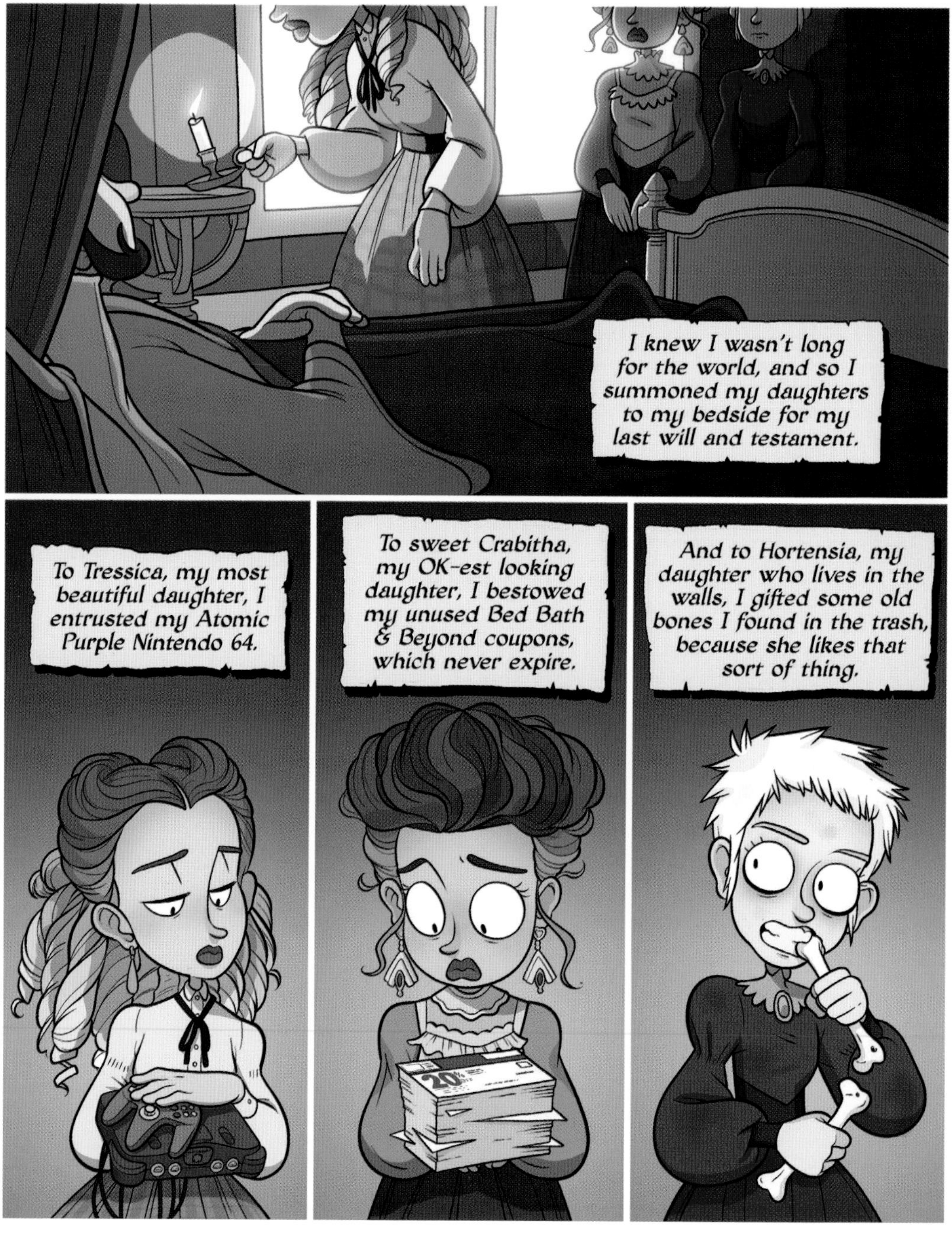
I knew I wasn't long for the world, and so I summoned my daughters to my bedside for my last will and testament.
To Tressica, my most beautiful daughter, I entrusted my Atomic Purple Nintendo 64.
To sweet Crabitha, my OK-est looking daughter, I bestowed my unused Bed Bath & Beyond coupons, which never expire.
20%
And to Hortensia, my daughter who lives in the walls, I gifted some old bones I found in the trash, because she likes that sort of thing.

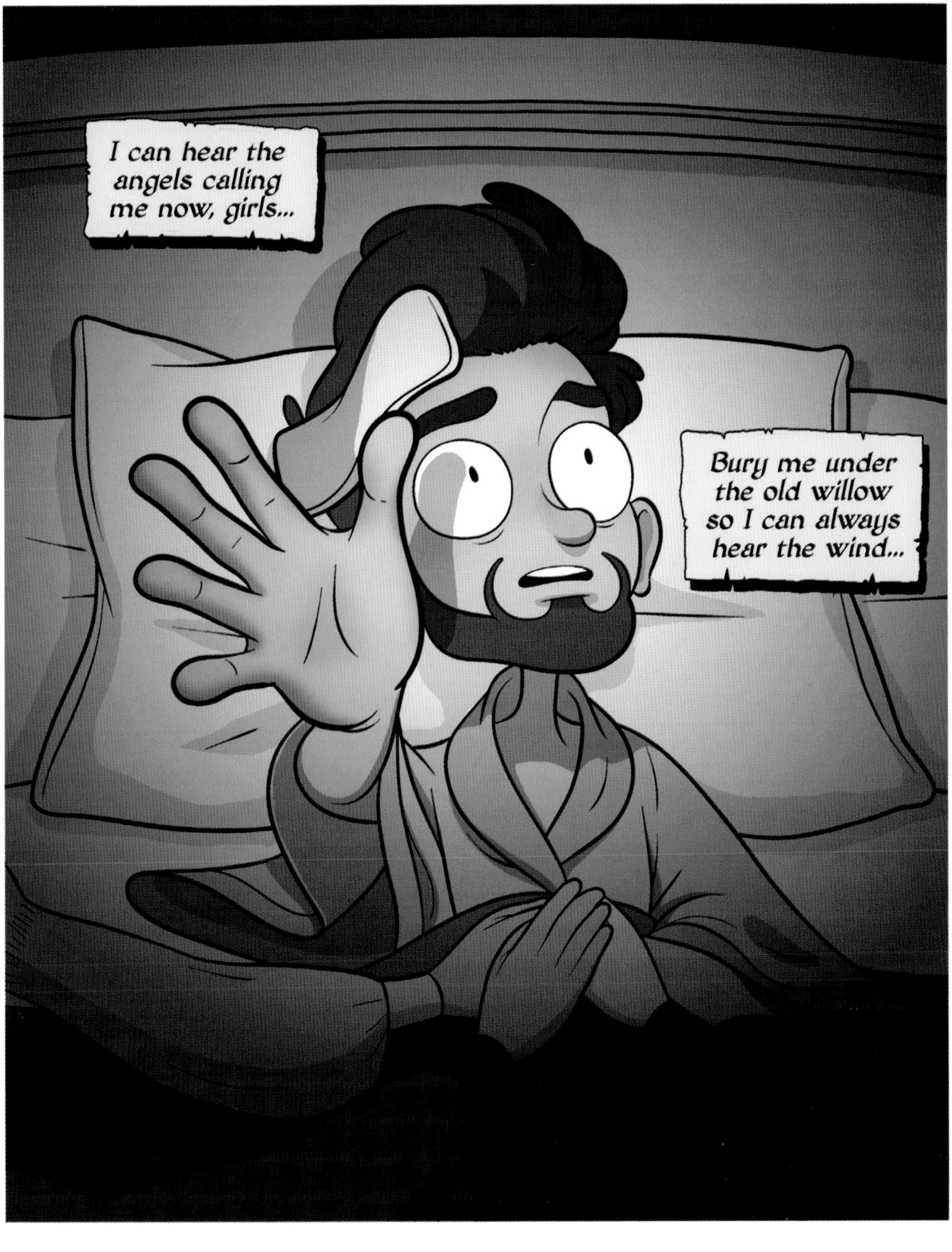
I can hear the angels calling me now, girls...
Bury me under the old willow so I can always hear the wind...

EXCUSES, EXCUSES

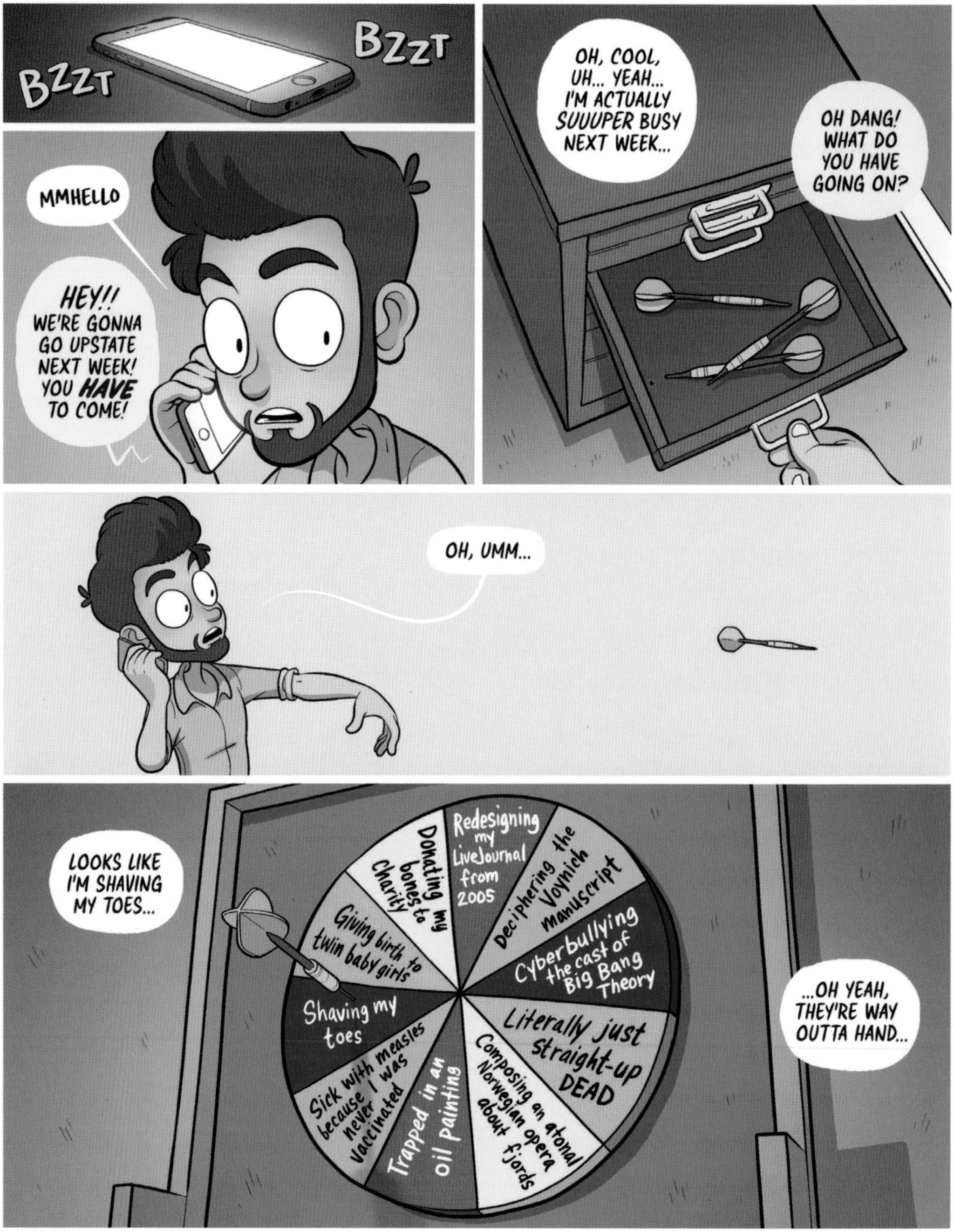
BZZT
BZZT
MMHELLO
HEY!! WE'RE GONNA GO UPSTATE NEXT WEEK! YOU HAVE TO COME!
OH, COOL, UH... YEAH... I'M ACTUALLY SUUUPER BUSY NEXT WEEK...
OH DANG! WHAT DO YOU HAVE GOING ON?
OH, UMM...
LOOKS LIKE I'M SHAVING MY TOES...
Redesigning my LiveJournal from 2005
Deciphering the Voynich manuscript
Cyberbullying the cast of Big Bang Theory
Literally just straight-up DEAD
Composing an atonal Norwegian opera about fjords
Trapped in an oil painting
Sick with measles because I was never vaccinated
Shaving my toes
Giving birth to twin baby girls
Donating my bones to Charity
...OH YEAH, THEY'RE WAY OUTTA HAND...

MY BIRTH

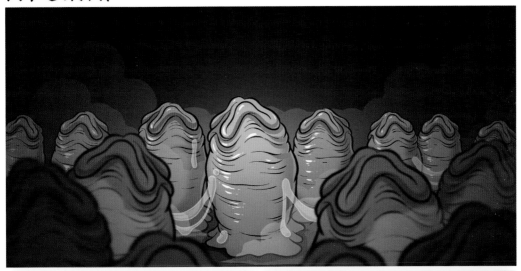

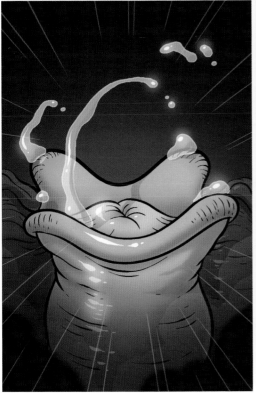

GETTING READY

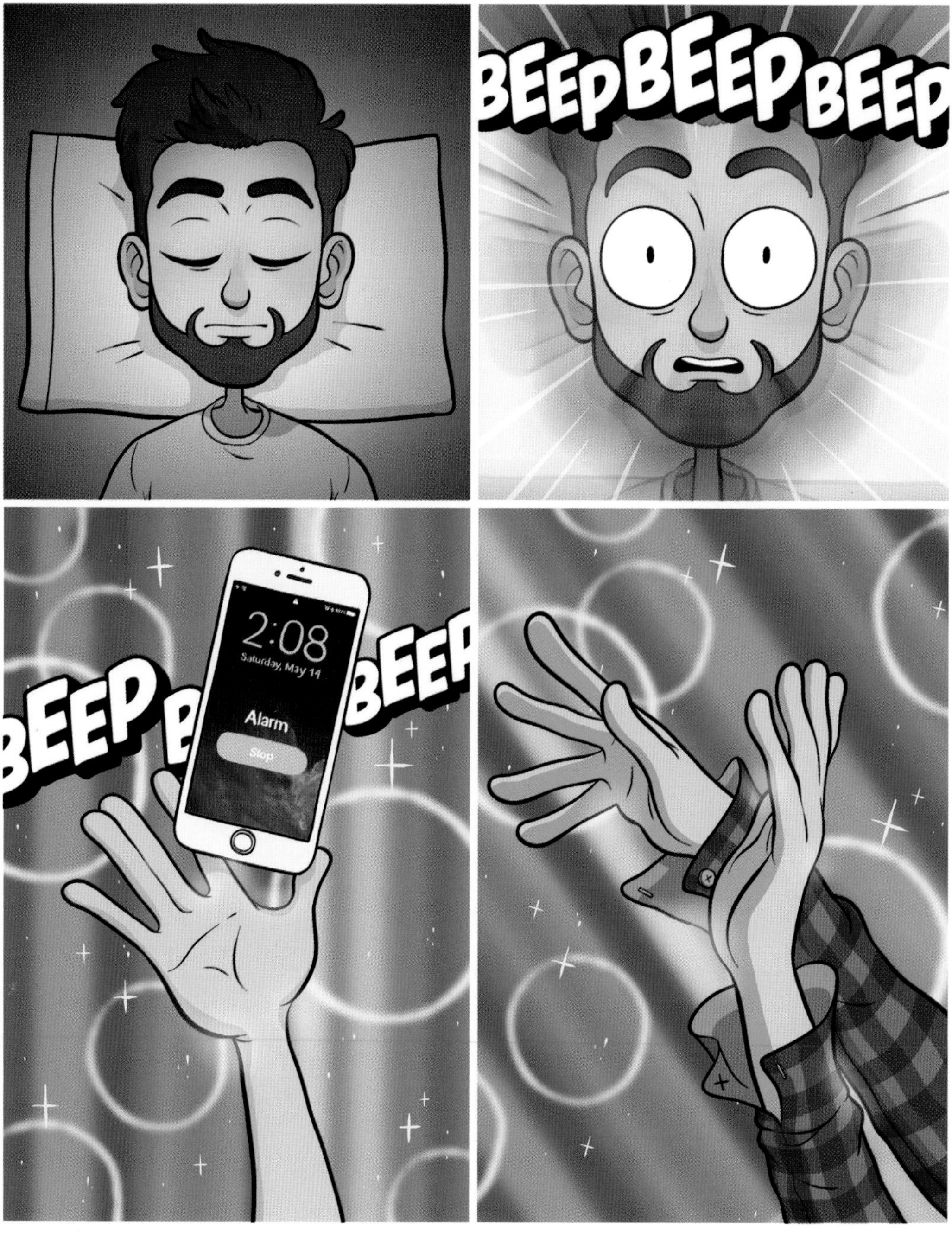

BEEPBEEPBEEP
BEEP
2:08
Saturday, May 14
Alarm
Stop

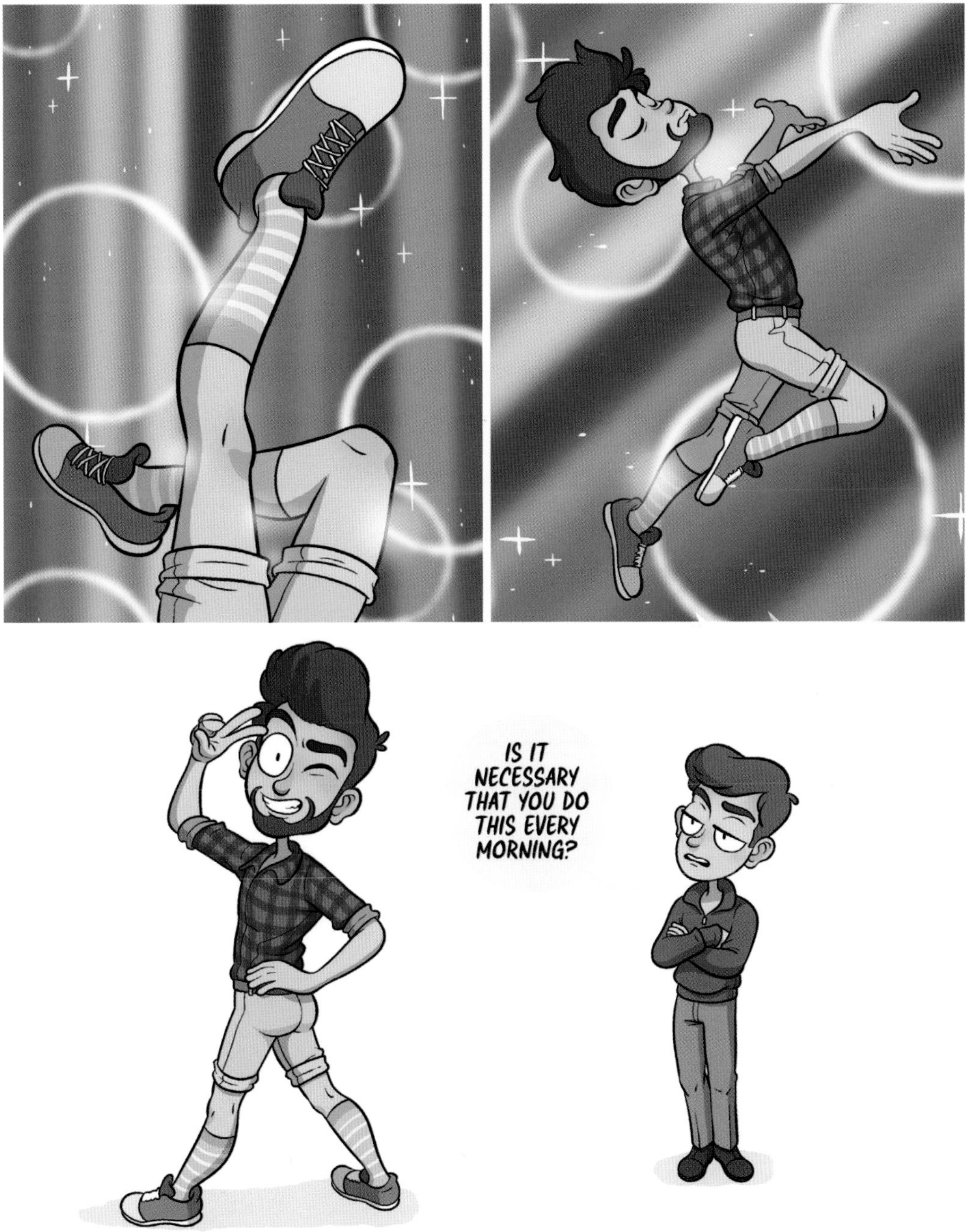
IS IT NECESSARY THAT YOU DO THIS EVERY MORNING?

CH-CH-CHANGES

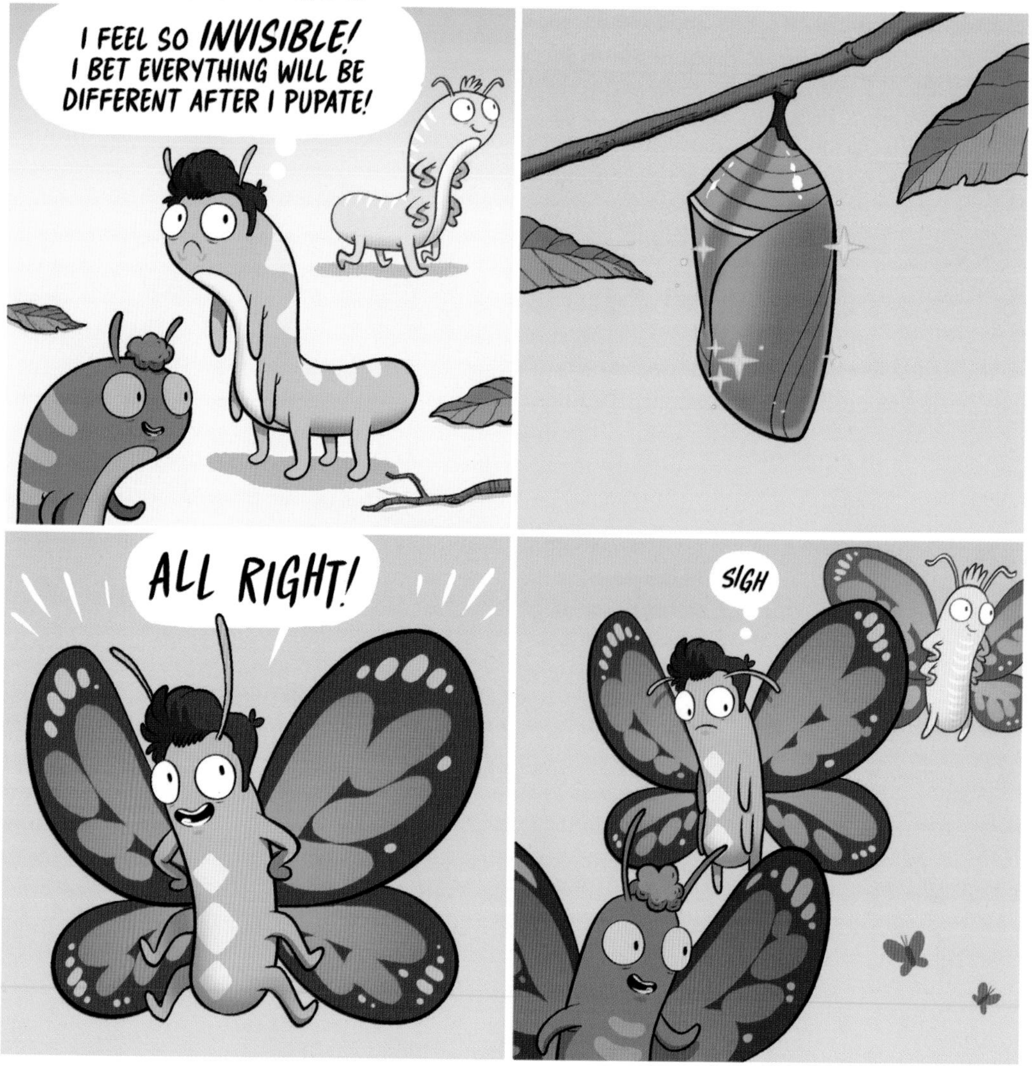
I FEEL SO *INVISIBLE!* I BET EVERYTHING WILL BE DIFFERENT AFTER I PUPATE!
ALL RIGHT!
SIGH

MEMORY FOAM

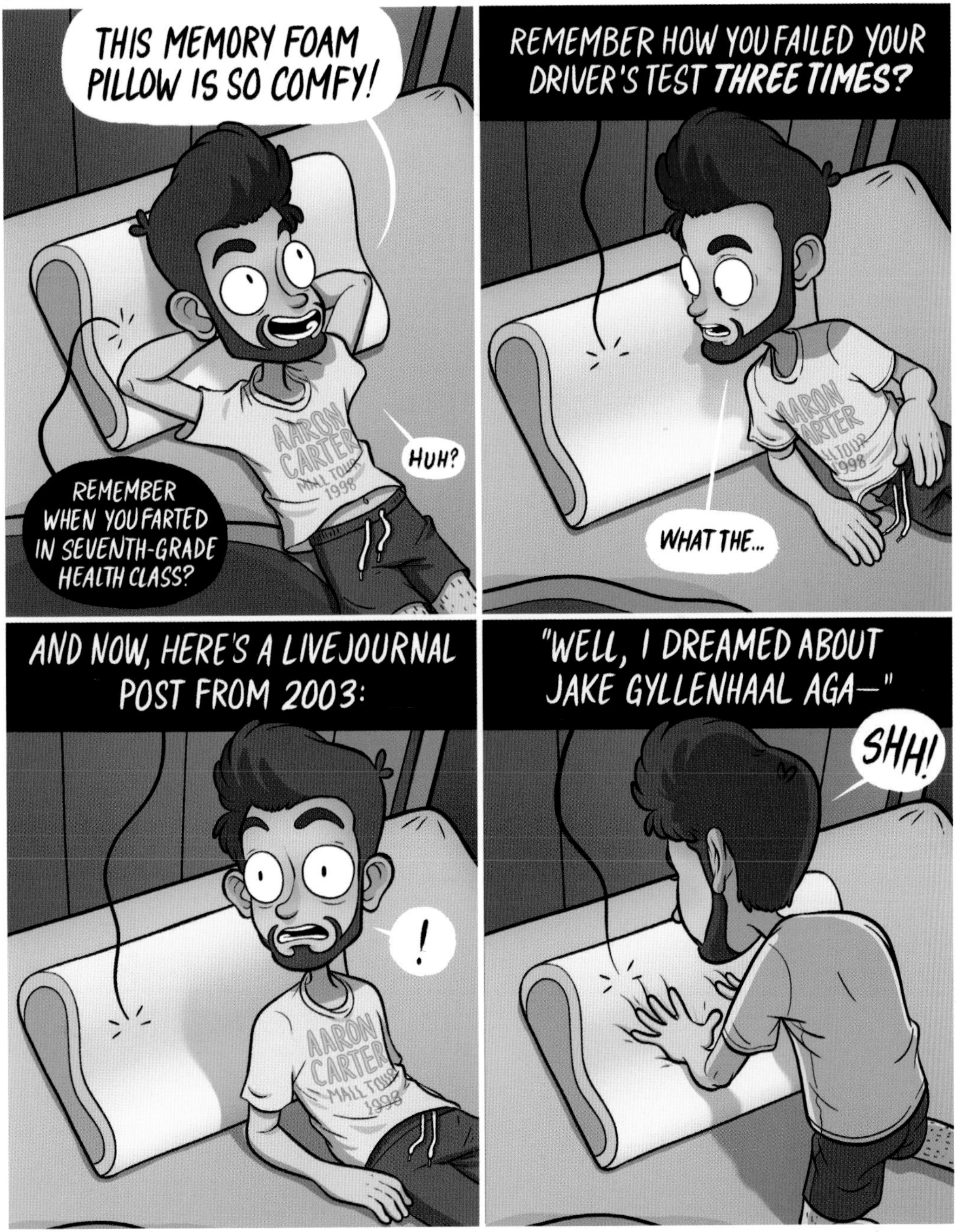
THIS MEMORY FOAM PILLOW IS SO COMFY!
HUH?
REMEMBER WHEN YOU FARTED IN SEVENTH-GRADE HEALTH CLASS?
AARON CARTER MALL TOUR 1998
REMEMBER HOW YOU FAILED YOUR DRIVER'S TEST THREE TIMES?
WHAT THE...
AND NOW, HERE'S A LIVEJOURNAL POST FROM 2003:
!
"WELL, I DREAMED ABOUT JAKE GYLLENHAAL AGA—"
SHH!

TAROT READING

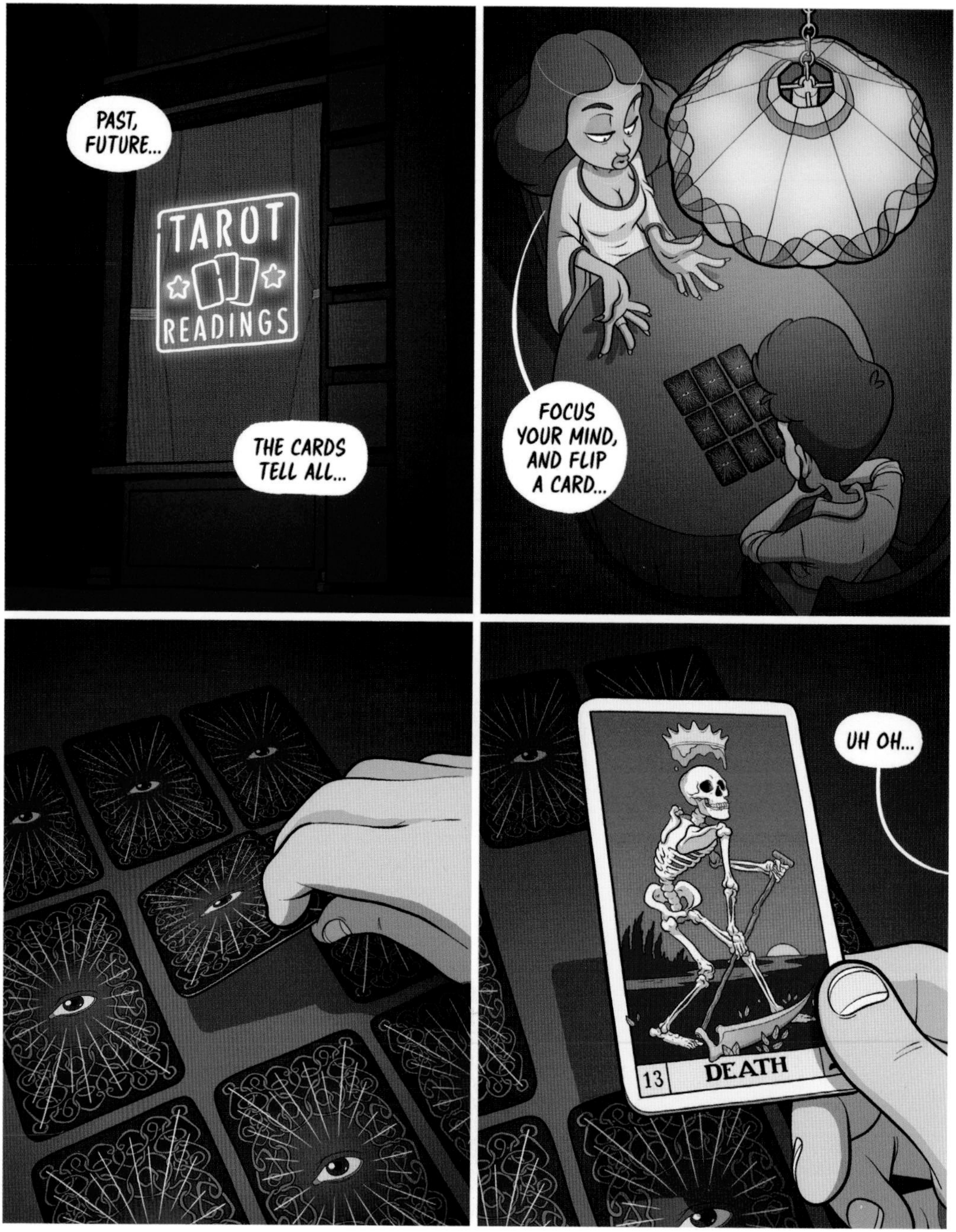
PAST, FUTURE...
TAROT READINGS
THE CARDS TELL ALL...
FOCUS YOUR MIND, AND FLIP A CARD...
13 DEATH
UH OH...

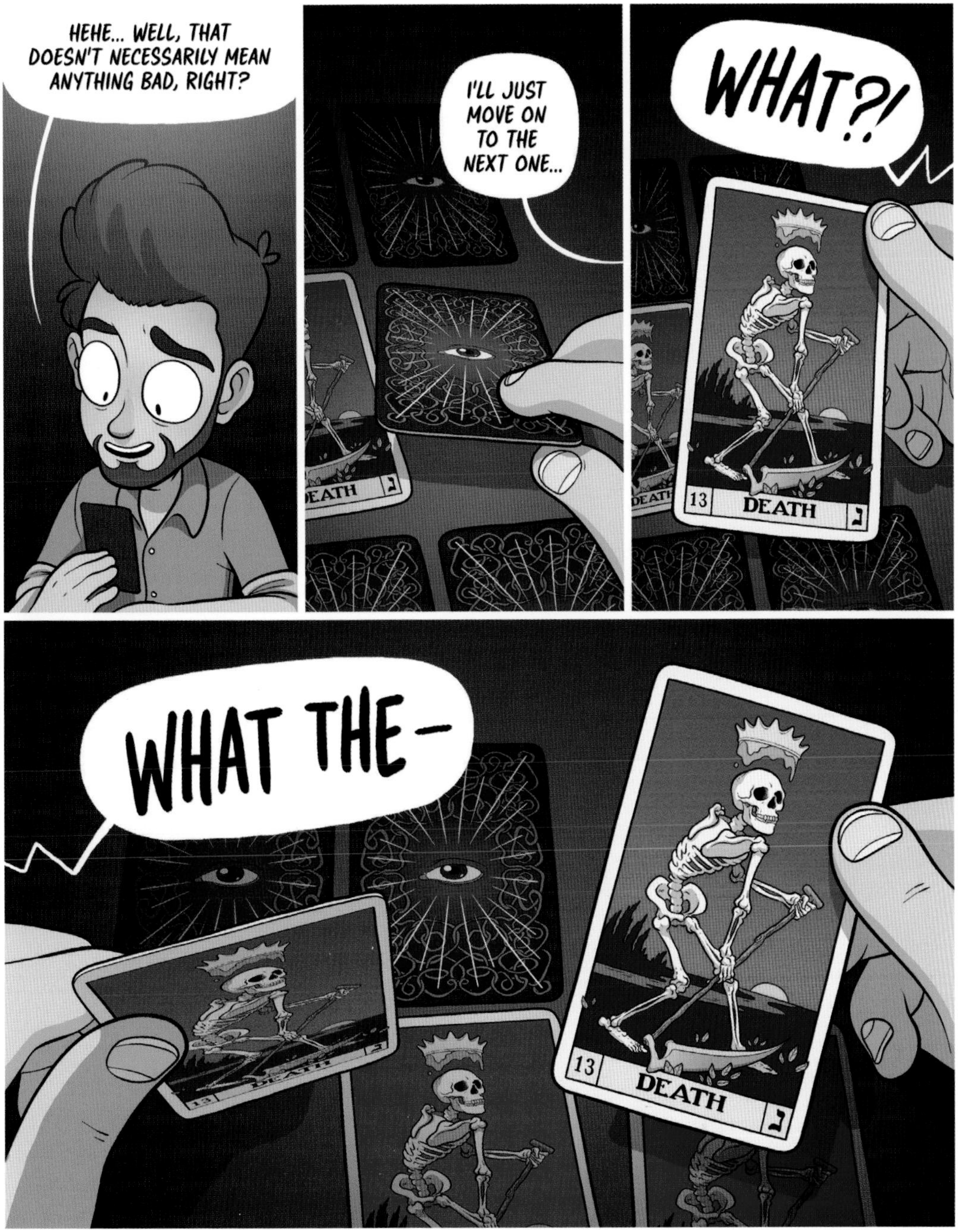
HEHE... WELL, THAT DOESN'T NECESSARILY MEAN ANYTHING BAD, RIGHT?
I'LL JUST MOVE ON TO THE NEXT ONE...
WHAT?!
13
DEATH
WHAT THE-
13
DEATH

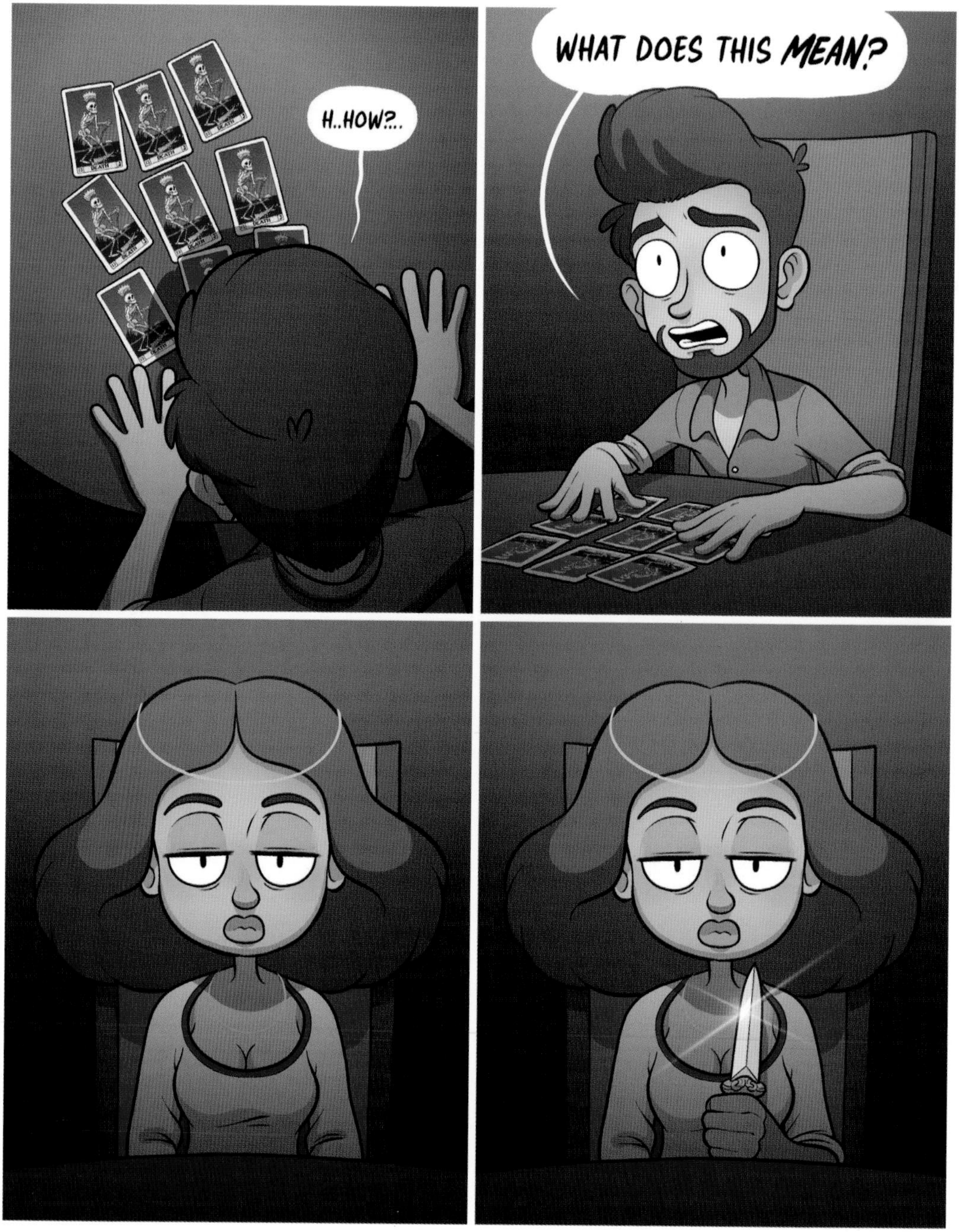
H..HOW?...
WHAT DOES THIS MEAN?

THE CALL

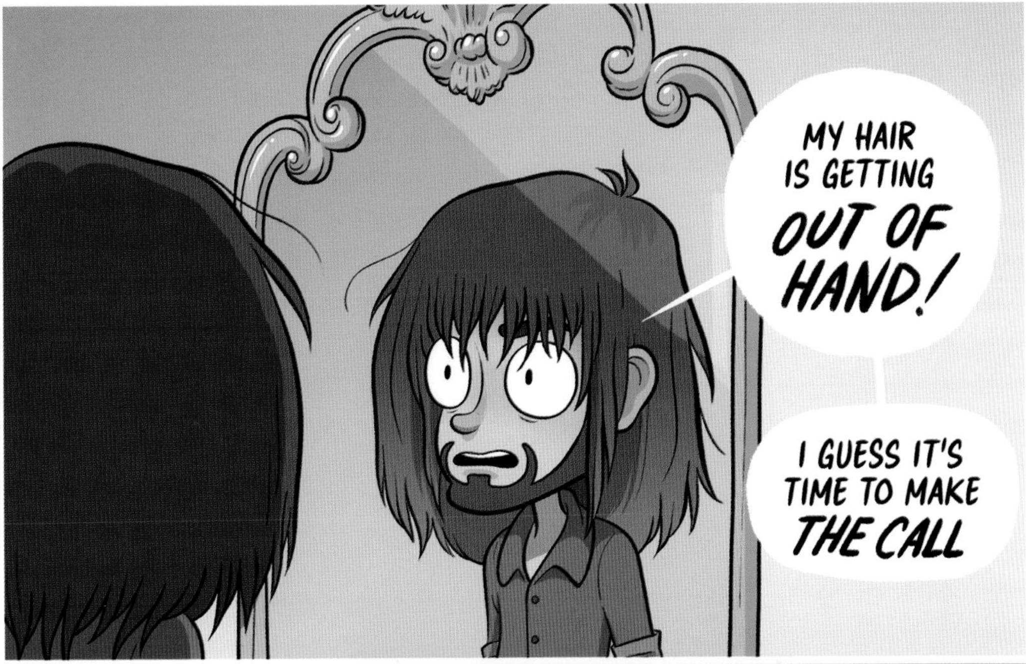
MY HAIR IS GETTING OUT OF HAND!
I GUESS IT'S TIME TO MAKE THE CALL

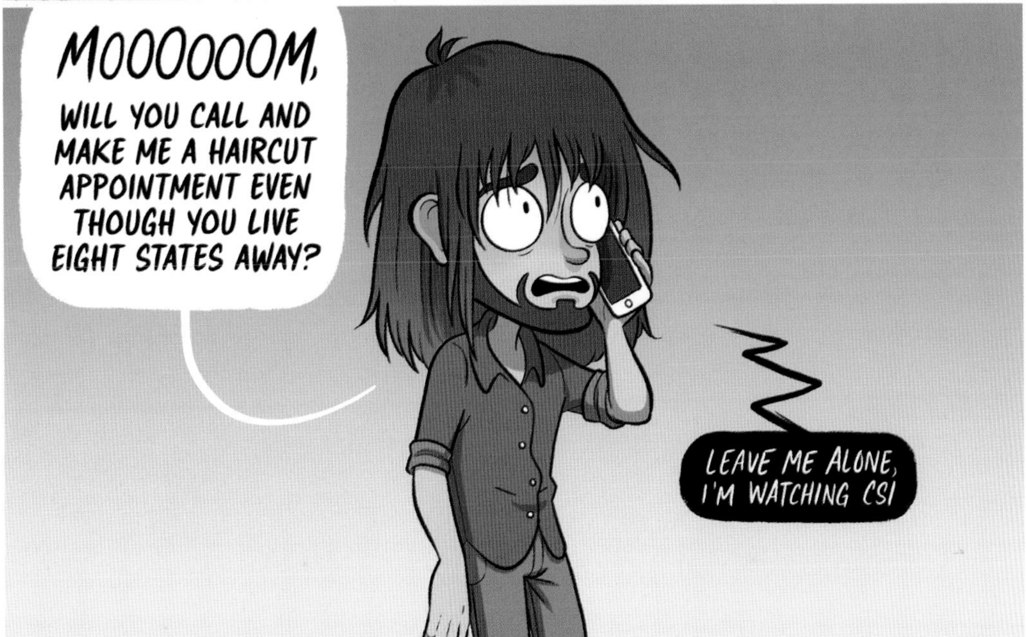
MOOOOOOM, WILL YOU CALL AND MAKE ME A HAIRCUT APPOINTMENT EVEN THOUGH YOU LIVE EIGHT STATES AWAY?
LEAVE ME ALONE, I'M WATCHING CSI

SNIP SNIP

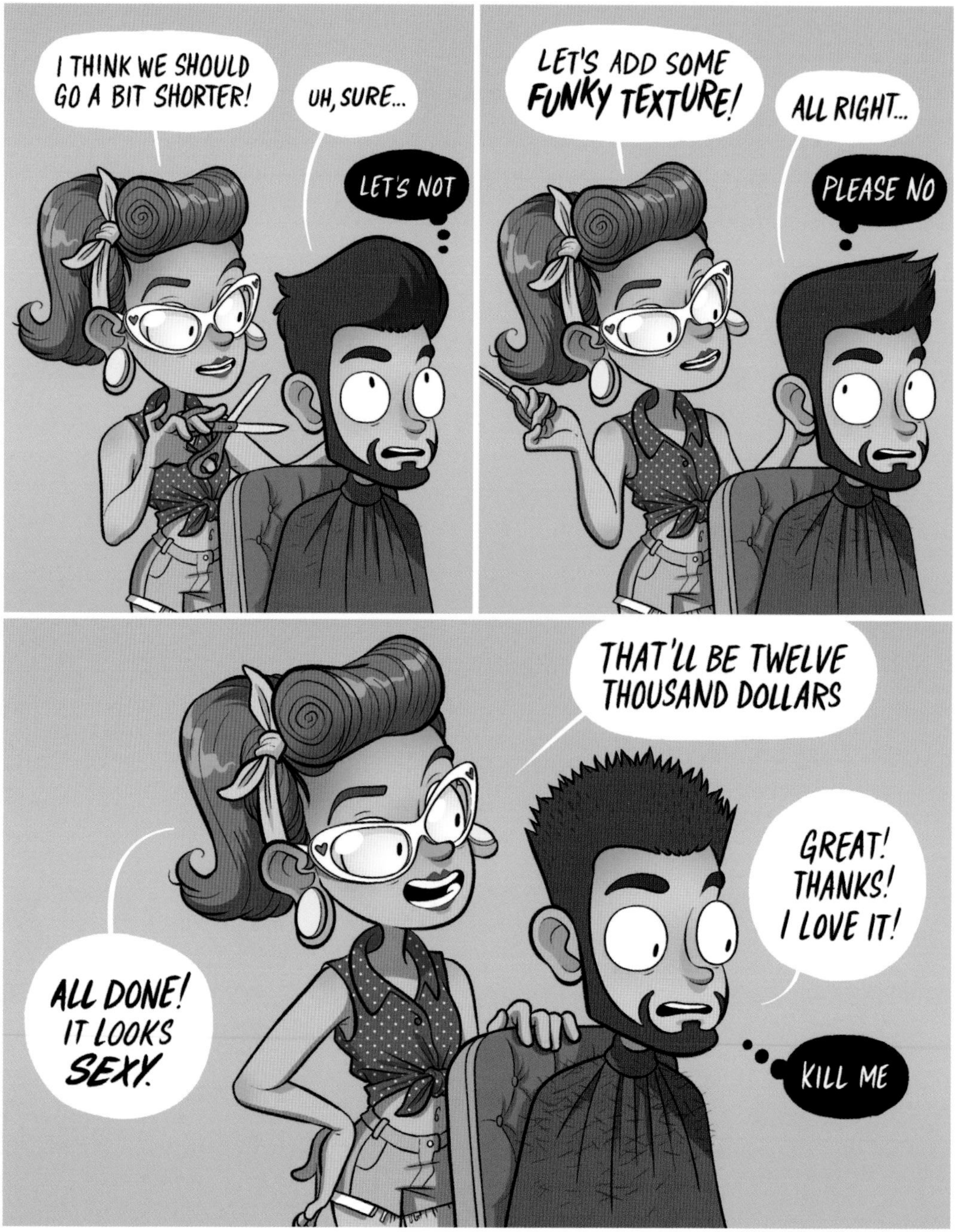
I THINK WE SHOULD GO A BIT SHORTER!
UH, SURE...
LET'S NOT
LET'S ADD SOME FUNKY TEXTURE!
ALL RIGHT...
PLEASE NO
THAT'LL BE TWELVE THOUSAND DOLLARS
ALL DONE! IT LOOKS SEXY.
GREAT! THANKS! I LOVE IT!
KILL ME

DR. FEELBAD

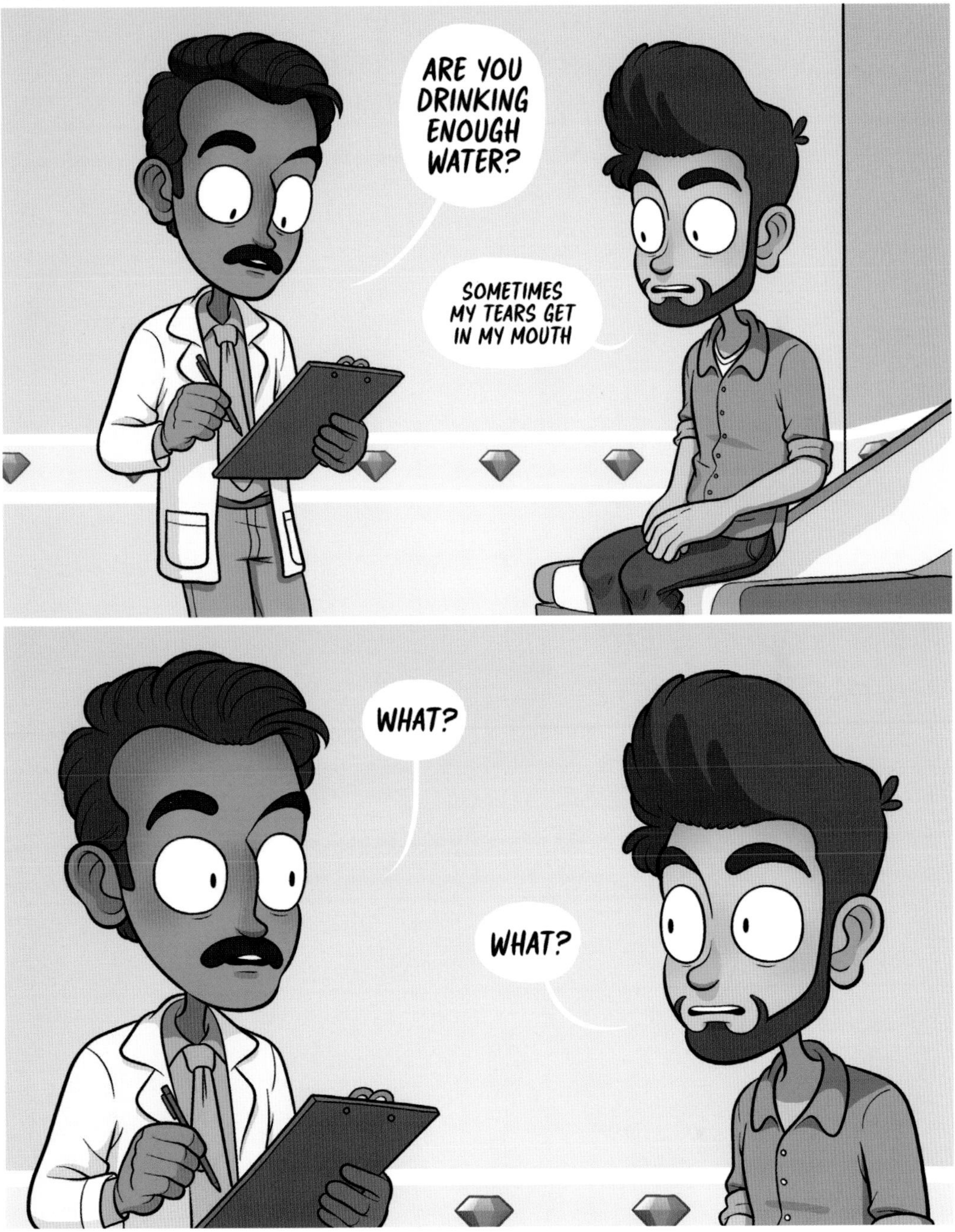
ARE YOU DRINKING ENOUGH WATER?
SOMETIMES MY TEARS GET IN MY MOUTH
WHAT?
WHAT?

FAVOR

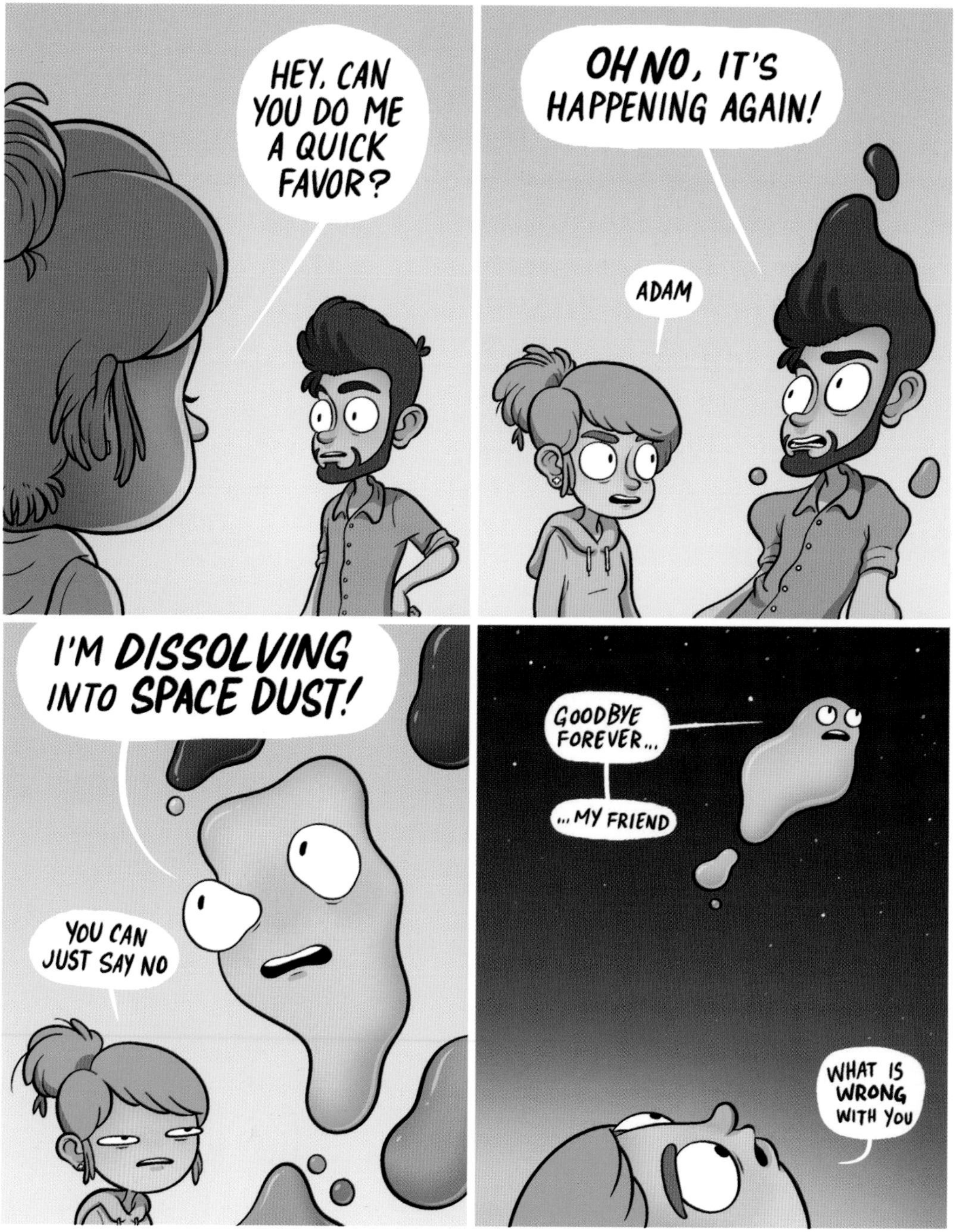

HEY, CAN YOU DO ME A QUICK FAVOR?
OH NO, IT'S HAPPENING AGAIN!
ADAM
I'M DISSOLVING INTO SPACE DUST!
YOU CAN JUST SAY NO
GOODBYE FOREVER...
... MY FRIEND
WHAT IS WRONG WITH YOU

TEETH

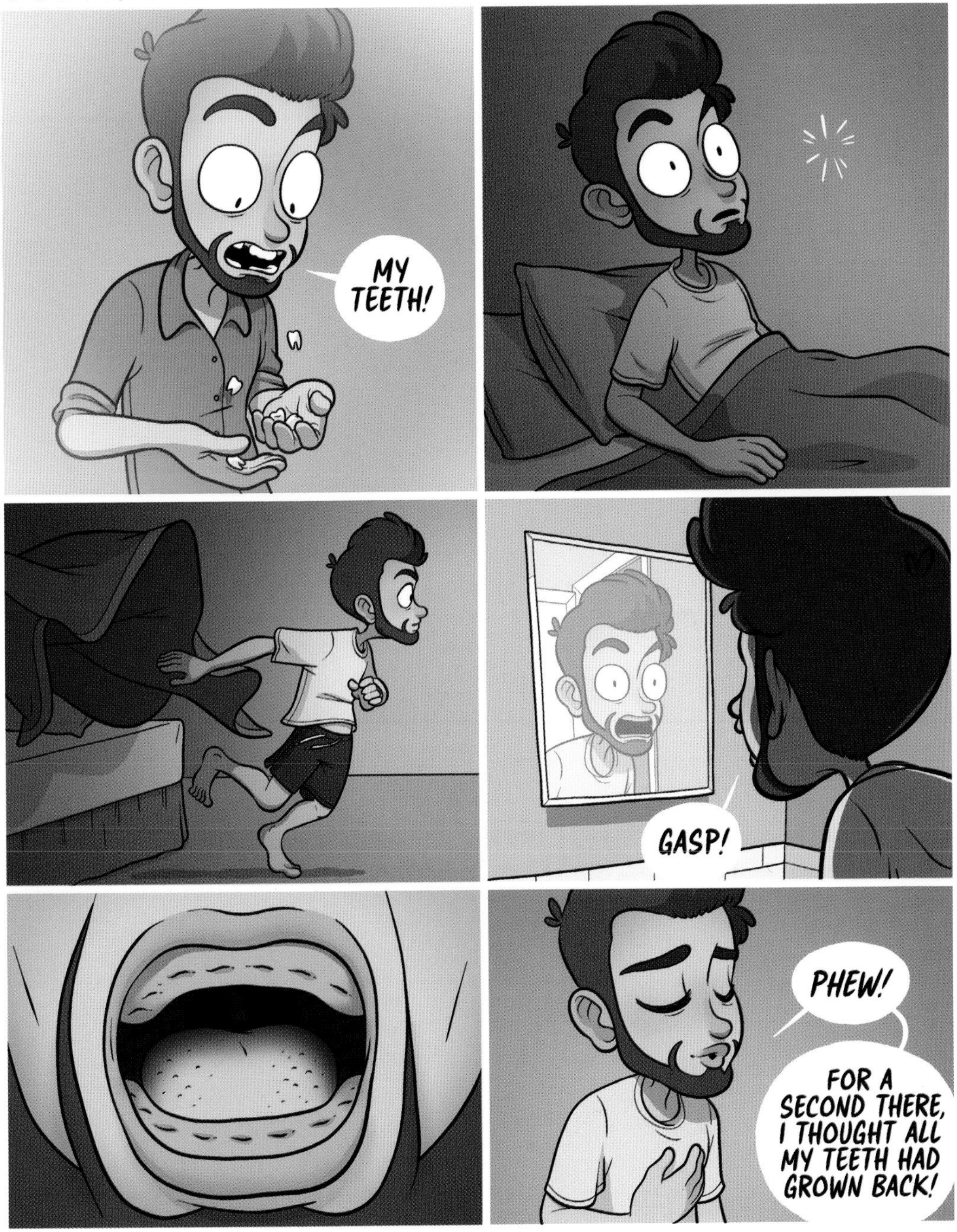

MY TEETH!
GASP!
PHEW!
FOR A SECOND THERE, I THOUGHT ALL MY TEETH HAD GROWN BACK!

RUNNING ON EMPTY

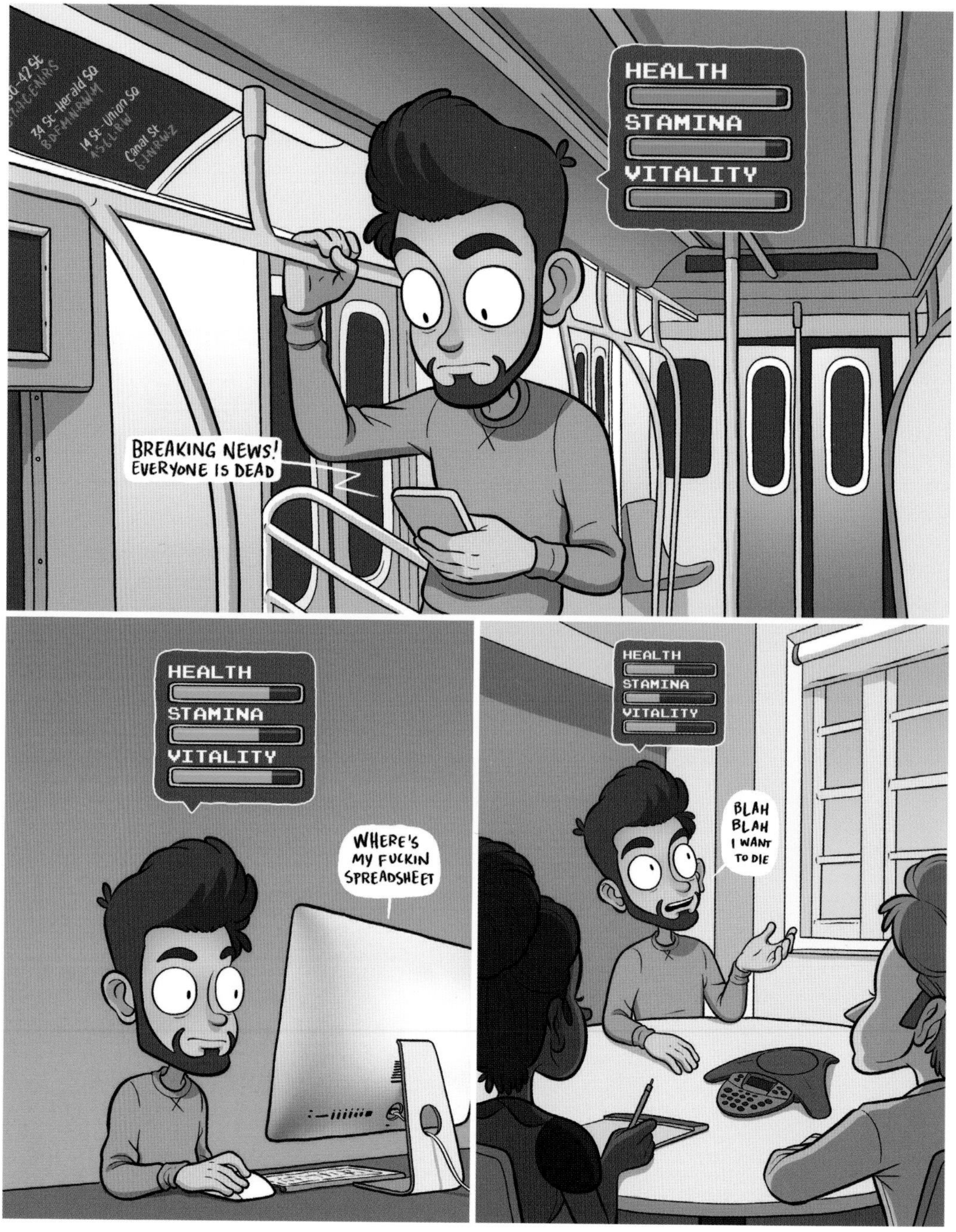

34 St-Herald Sq
14 St-Union Sq
Canal St
HEALTH
STAMINA
VITALITY
BREAKING NEWS! EVERYONE IS DEAD
HEALTH
STAMINA
VITALITY
WHERE'S MY FUCKIN SPREADSHEET
HEALTH
STAMINA
VITALITY
BLAH BLAH I WANT TO DIE

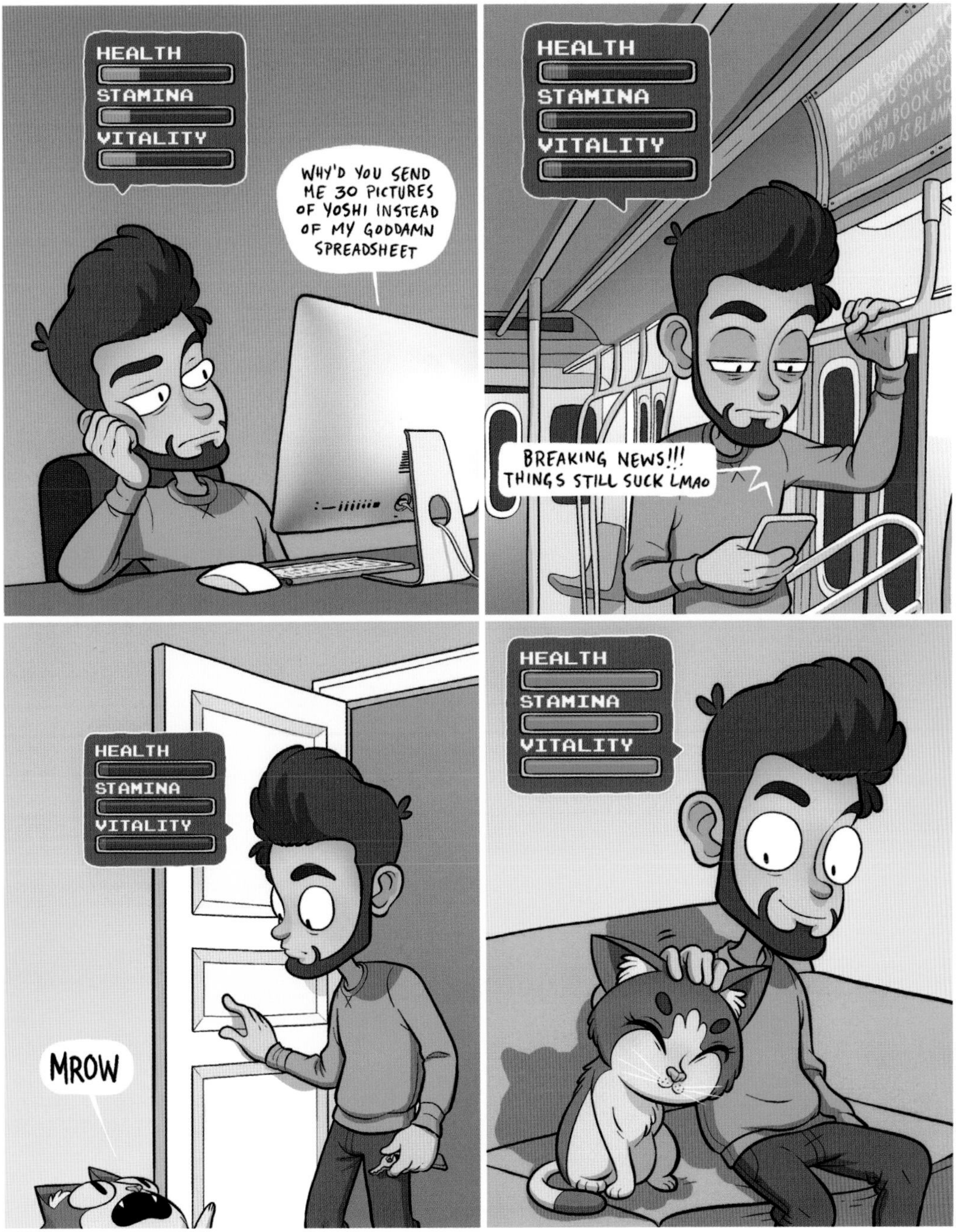
HEALTH
STAMINA
VITALITY
WHY'D YOU SEND ME 30 PICTURES OF YOSHI INSTEAD OF MY GODDAMN SPREADSHEET
HEALTH
STAMINA
VITALITY
NOBODY RESPONDED
MY OFFER TO
THEM IN MY BOOK
THIS FAKE AD IS
BREAKING NEWS!!! THINGS STILL SUCK LMAO
HEALTH
STAMINA
VITALITY
MROW
HEALTH
STAMINA
VITALITY

BUTTERFLY IN THE SKY

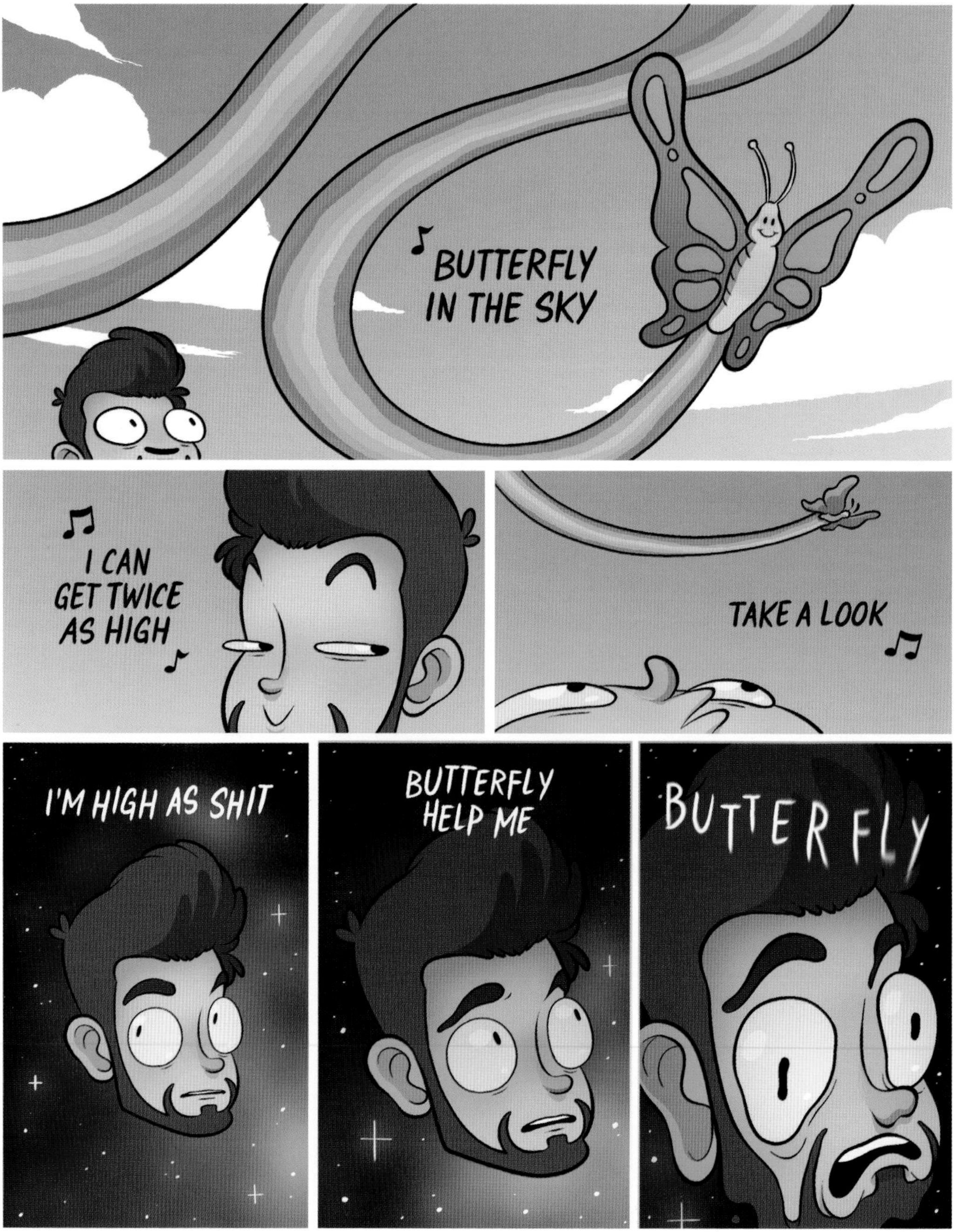

BUTTERFLY IN THE SKY
I CAN GET TWICE AS HIGH
TAKE A LOOK
I'M HIGH AS SHIT
BUTTERFLY HELP ME
BUTTERFLY

TRANSLATION

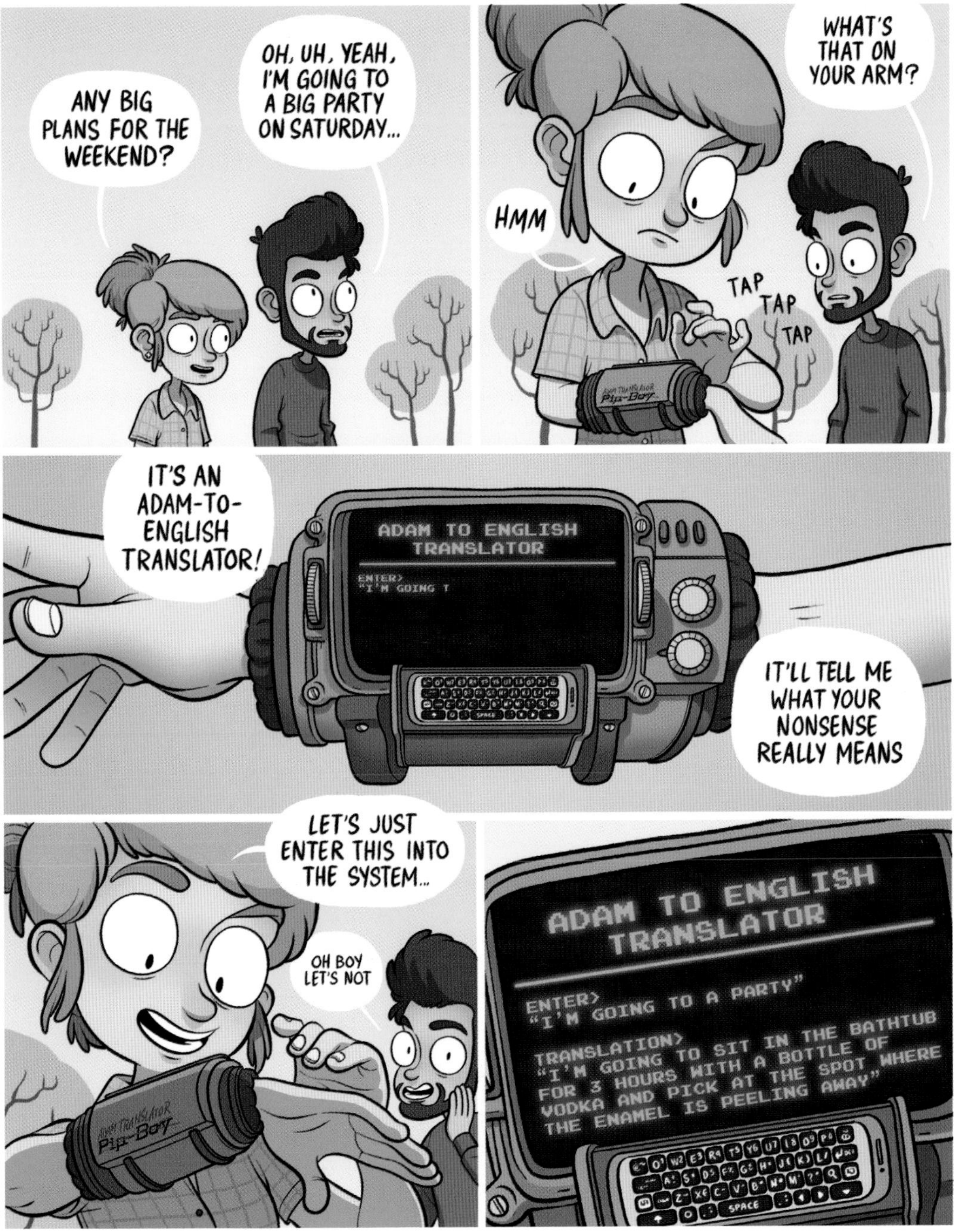

ANY BIG PLANS FOR THE WEEKEND?
OH, UH, YEAH, I'M GOING TO A BIG PARTY ON SATURDAY...
WHAT'S THAT ON YOUR ARM?
HMM
TAP TAP TAP
IT'S AN ADAM-TO-ENGLISH TRANSLATOR!
ADAM TO ENGLISH TRANSLATOR
ENTER> "I'M GOING T
IT'LL TELL ME WHAT YOUR NONSENSE REALLY MEANS
LET'S JUST ENTER THIS INTO THE SYSTEM...
OH BOY LET'S NOT
ADAM TO ENGLISH TRANSLATOR
ENTER> "I'M GOING TO A PARTY"
TRANSLATION> "I'M GOING TO SIT IN THE BATHTUB FOR 3 HOURS WITH A BOTTLE OF VODKA AND PICK AT THE SPOT WHERE THE ENAMEL IS PEELING AWAY"

WHISKER

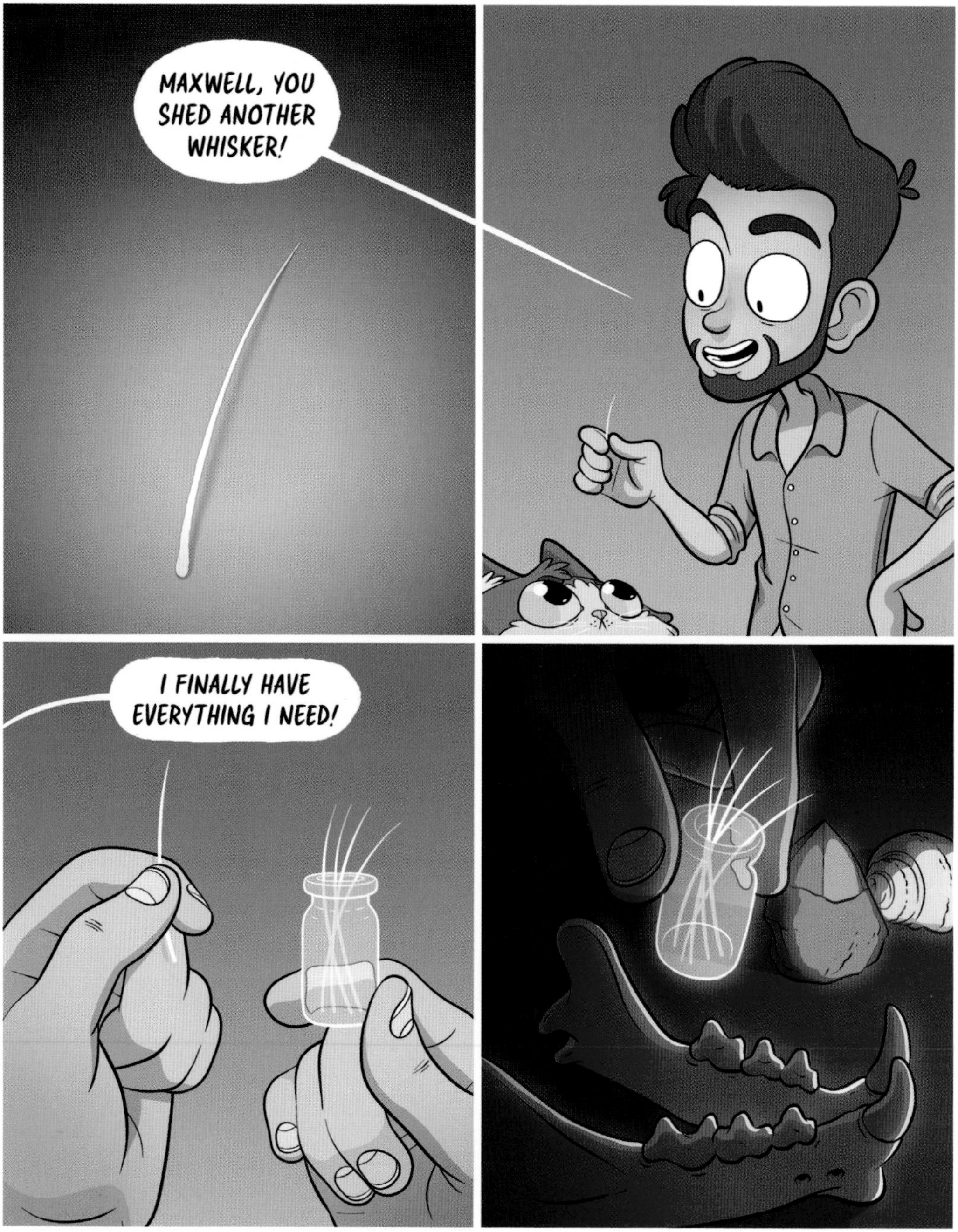
MAXWELL, YOU SHED ANOTHER WHISKER!
I FINALLY HAVE EVERYTHING I NEED!

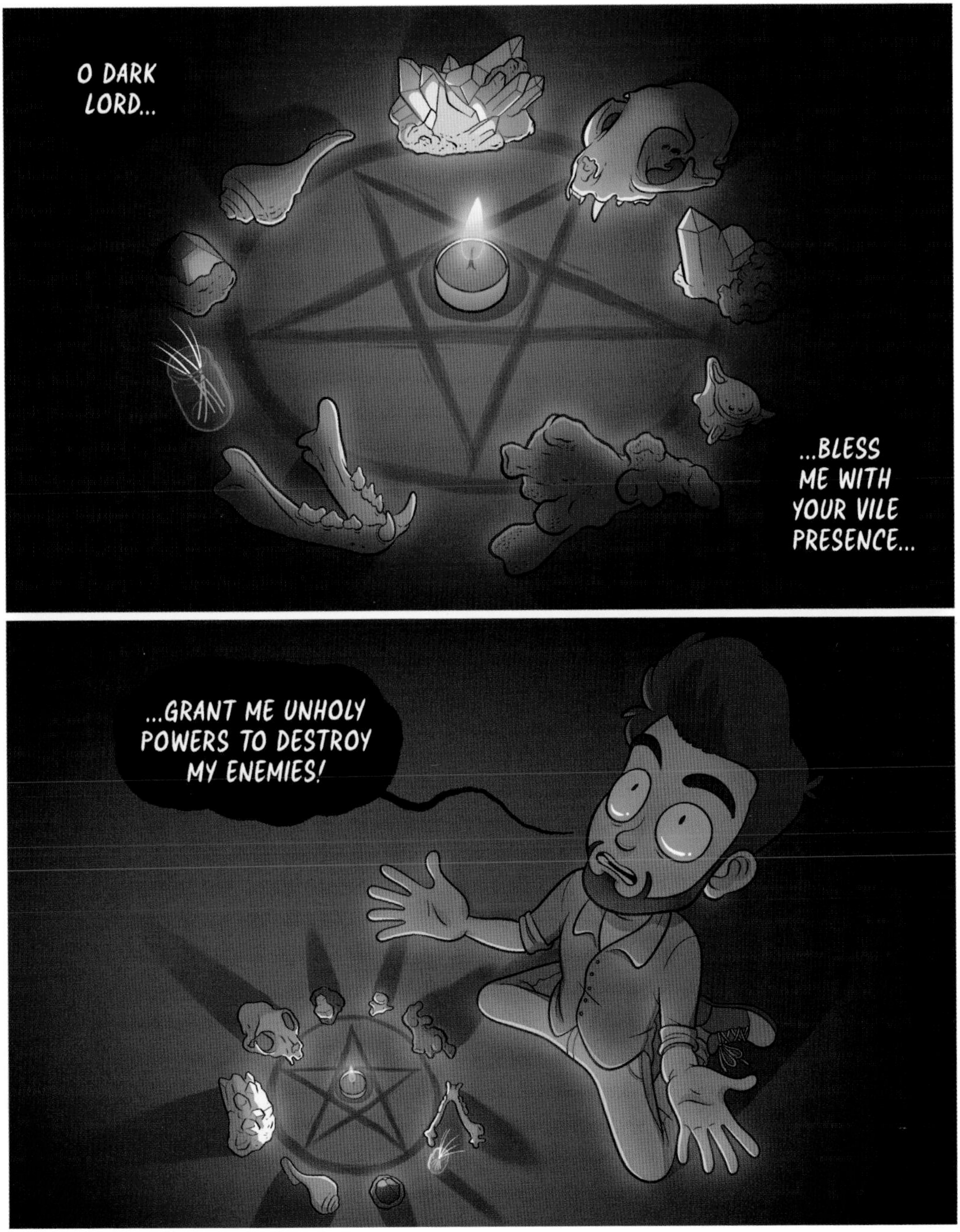
O DARK LORD...
...BLESS ME WITH YOUR VILE PRESENCE...
...GRANT ME UNHOLY POWERS TO DESTROY MY ENEMIES!

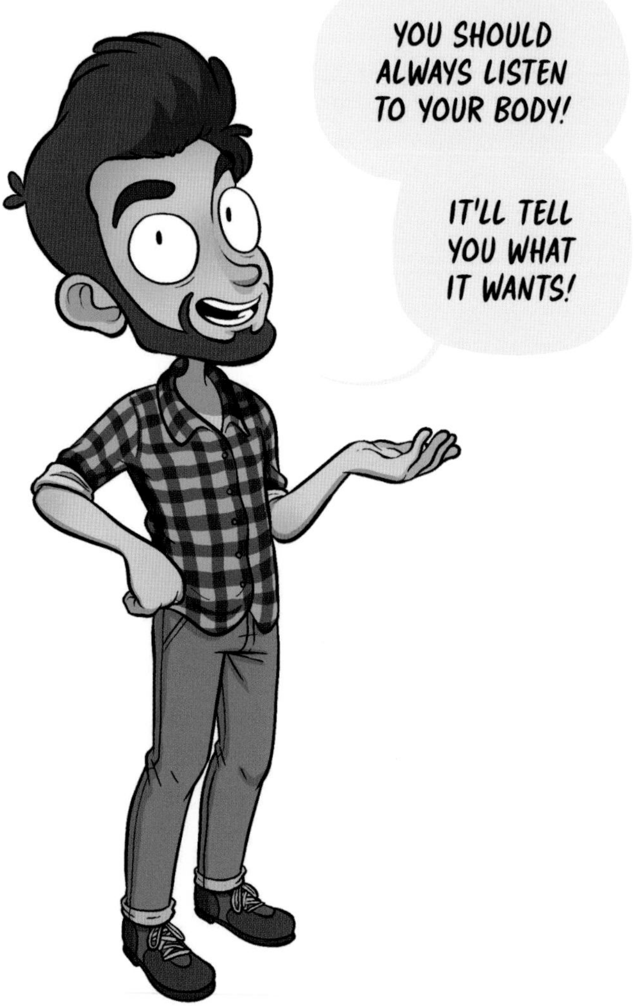
YOU SHOULD ALWAYS LISTEN TO YOUR BODY!
IT'LL TELL YOU WHAT IT WANTS!

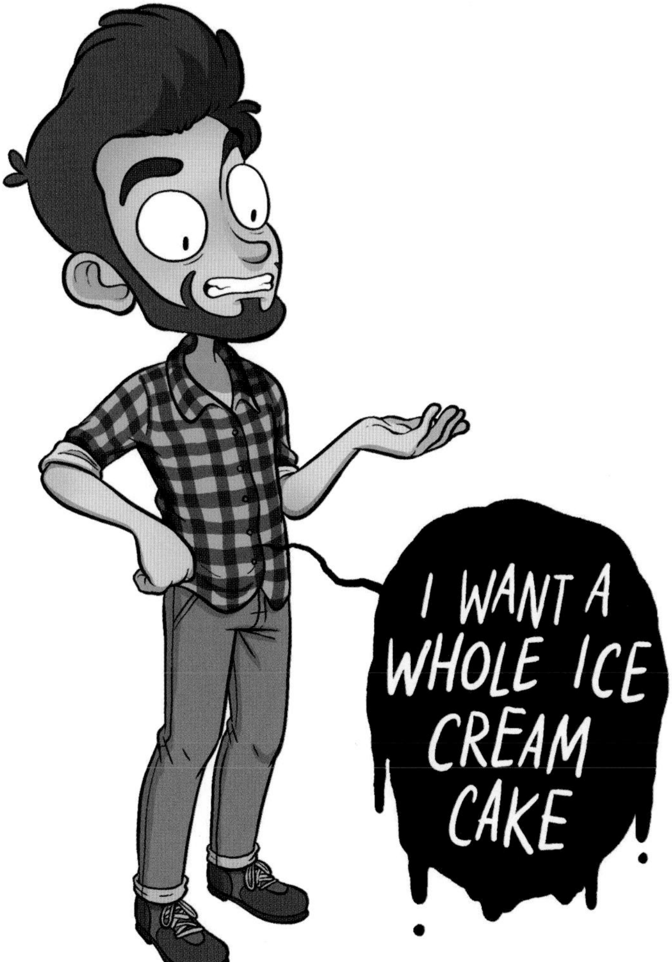
I WANT A WHOLE ICE CREAM CAKE

GREEN JUICE

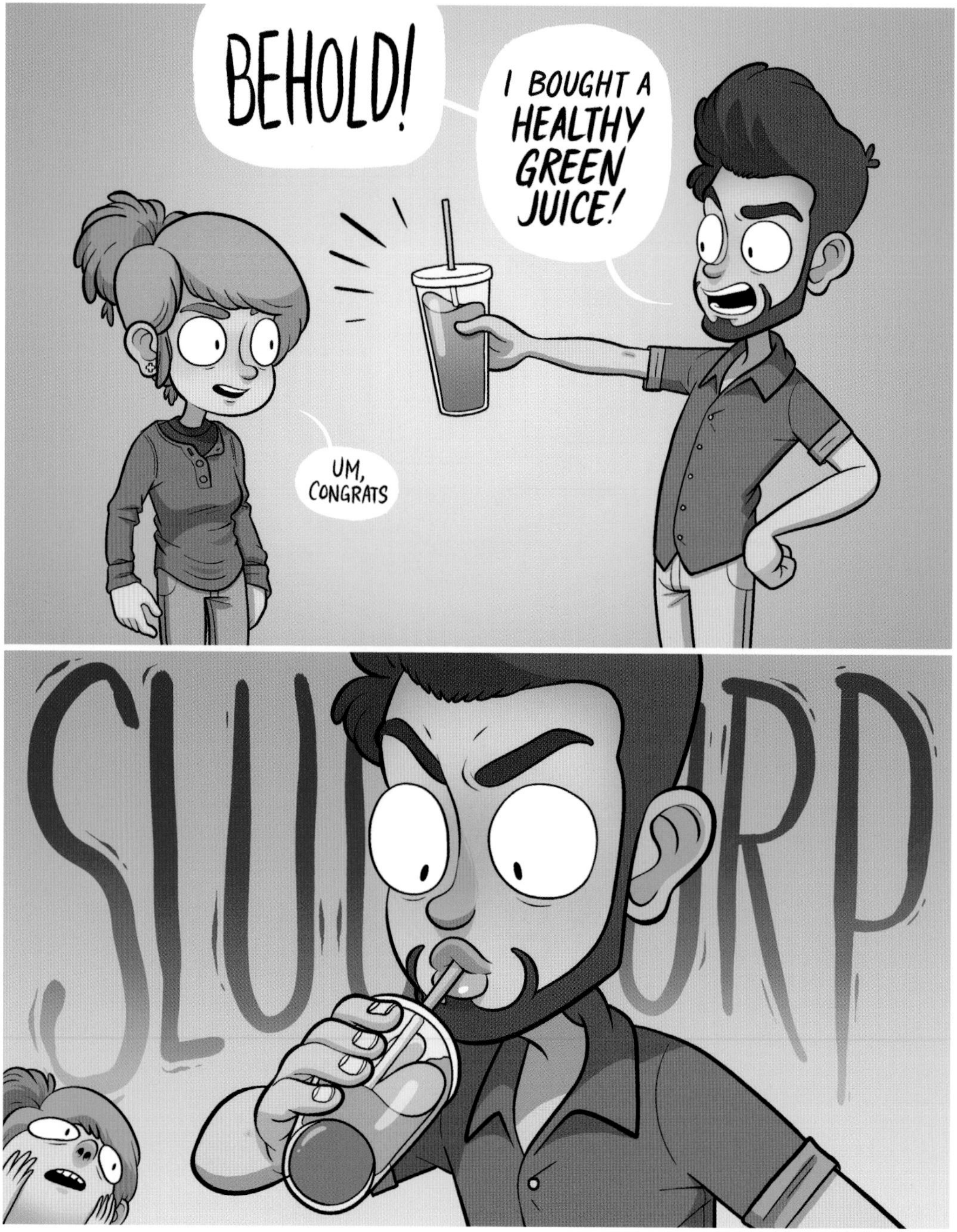
BEHOLD!
I BOUGHT A HEALTHY GREEN JUICE!
UM, CONGRATS
SLURP

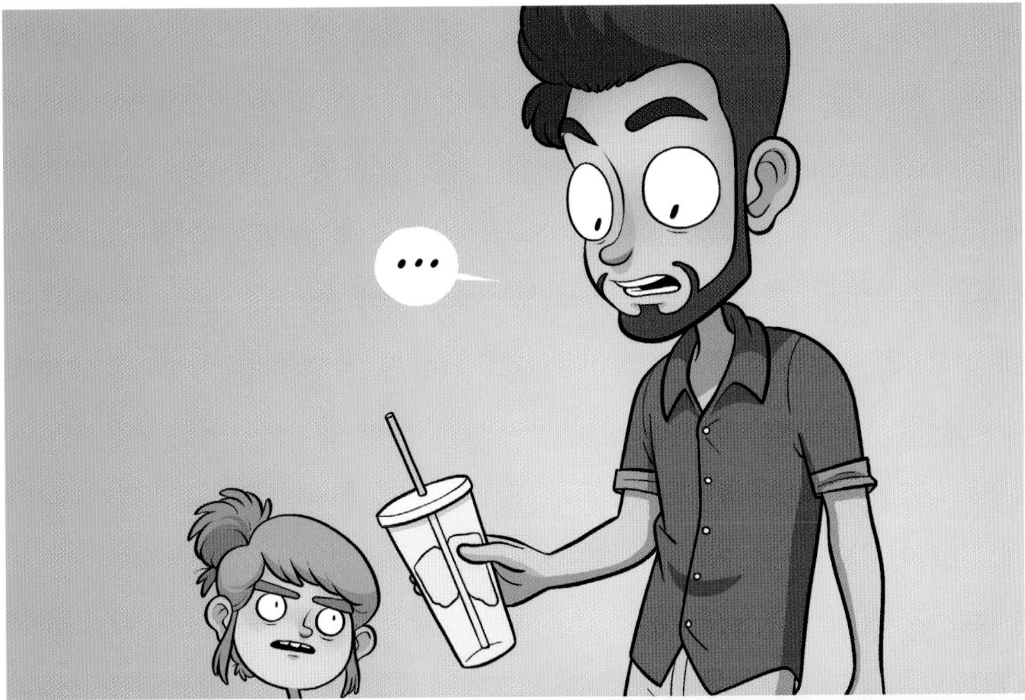
...
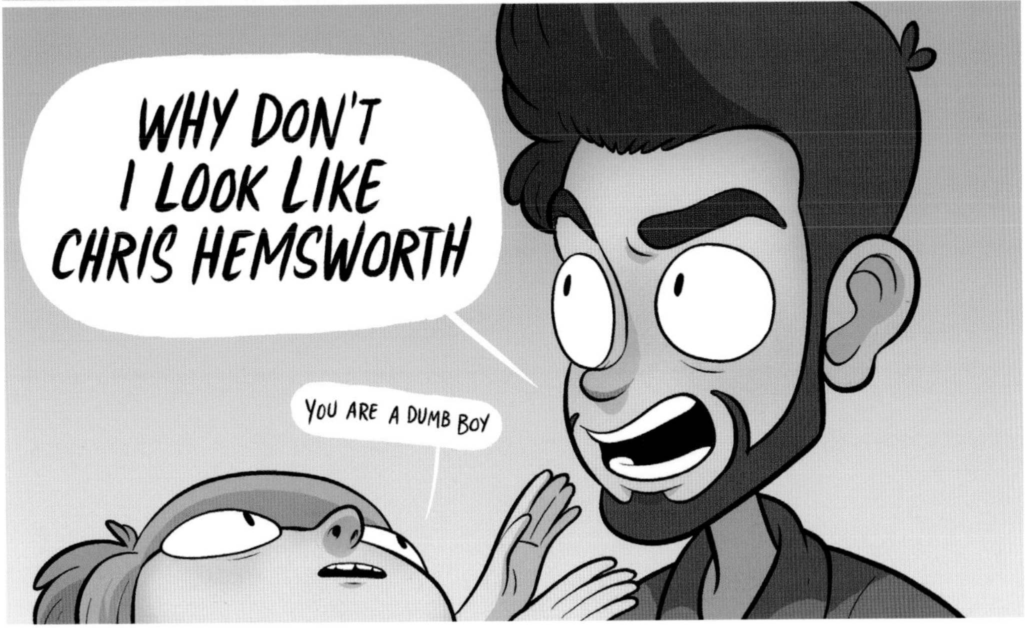
WHY DON'T I LOOK LIKE CHRIS HEMSWORTH
YOU ARE A DUMB BOY

PULL TAB

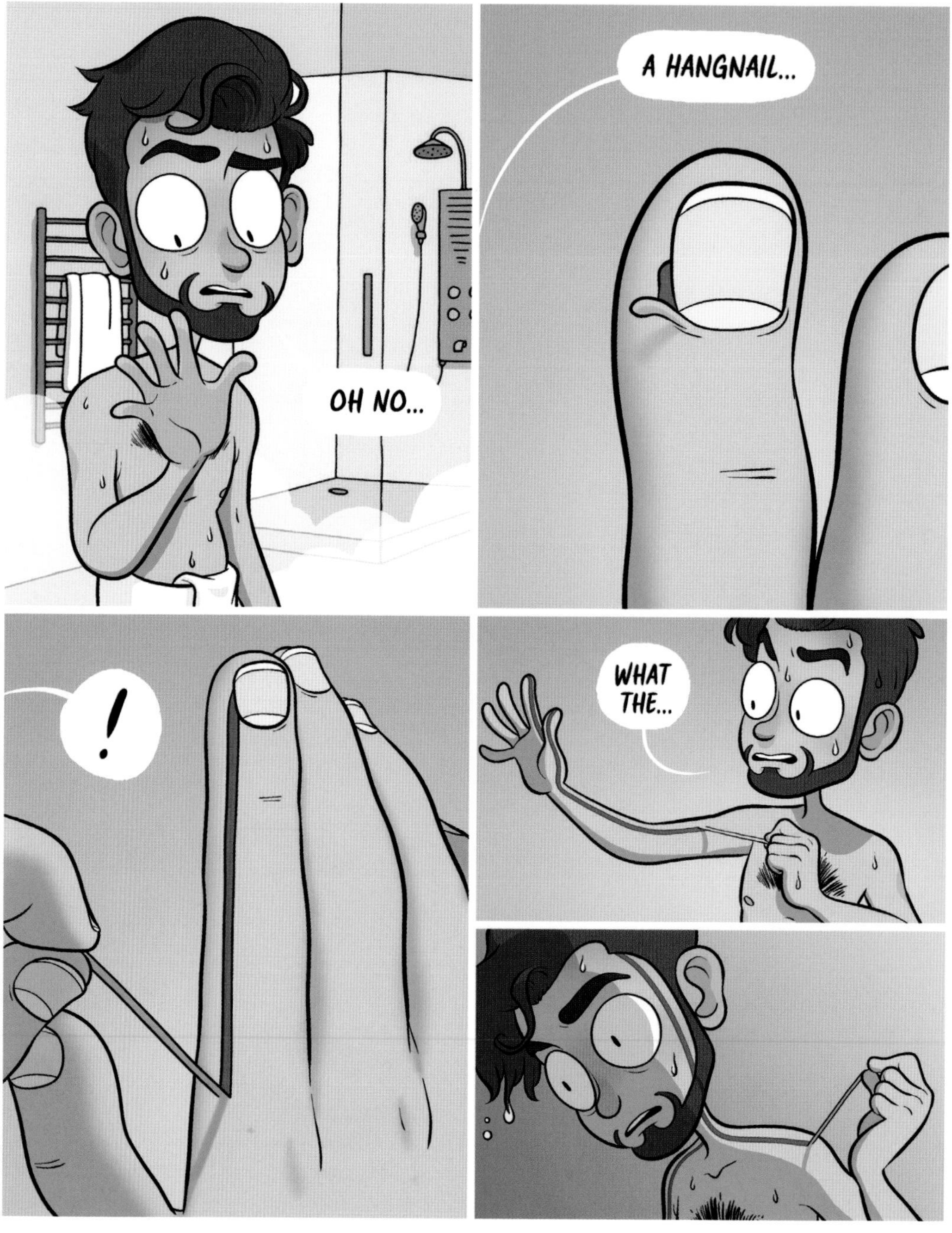

OH NO...
A HANGNAIL...
!
WHAT THE...

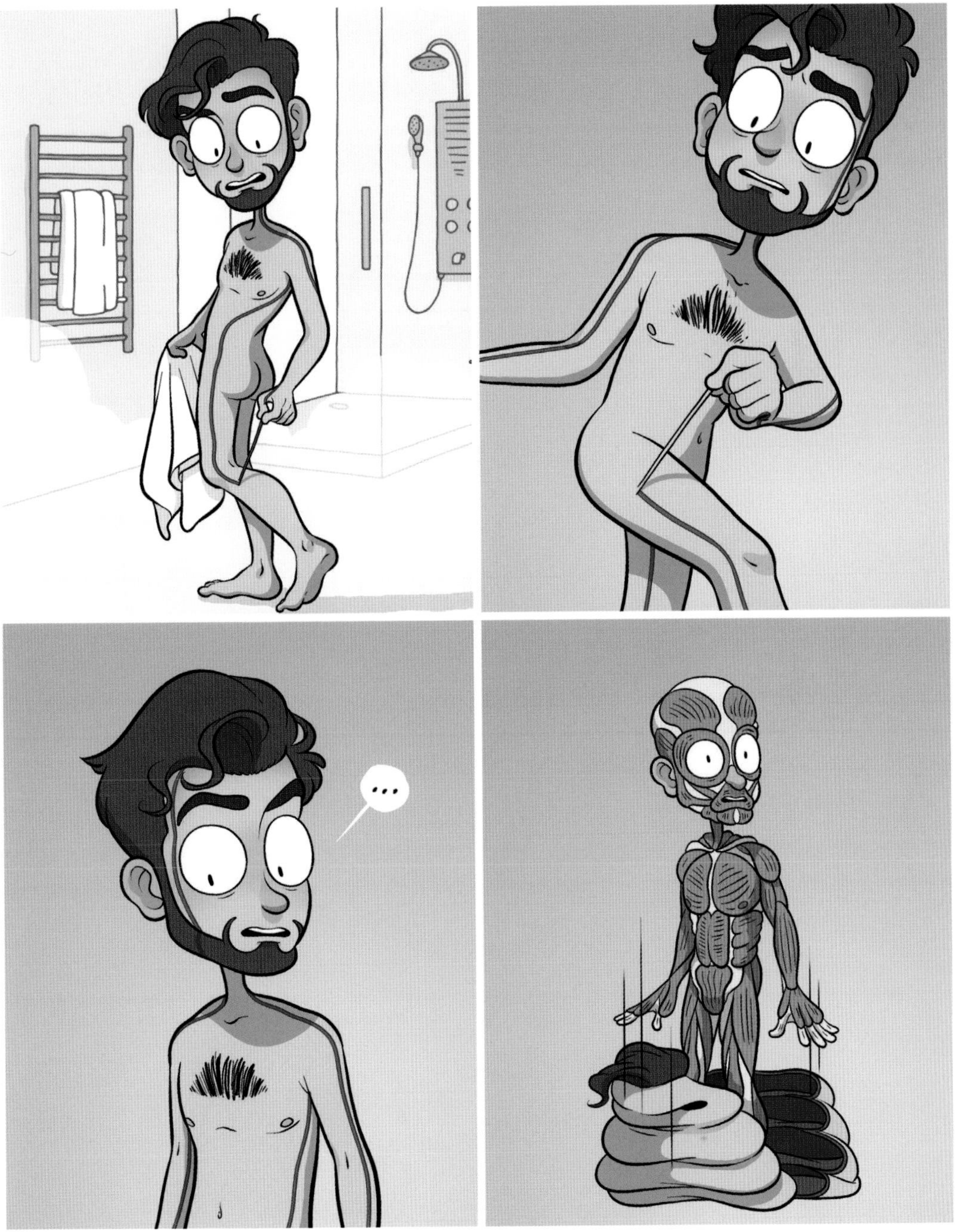
...

FIFTEEN POUNDS

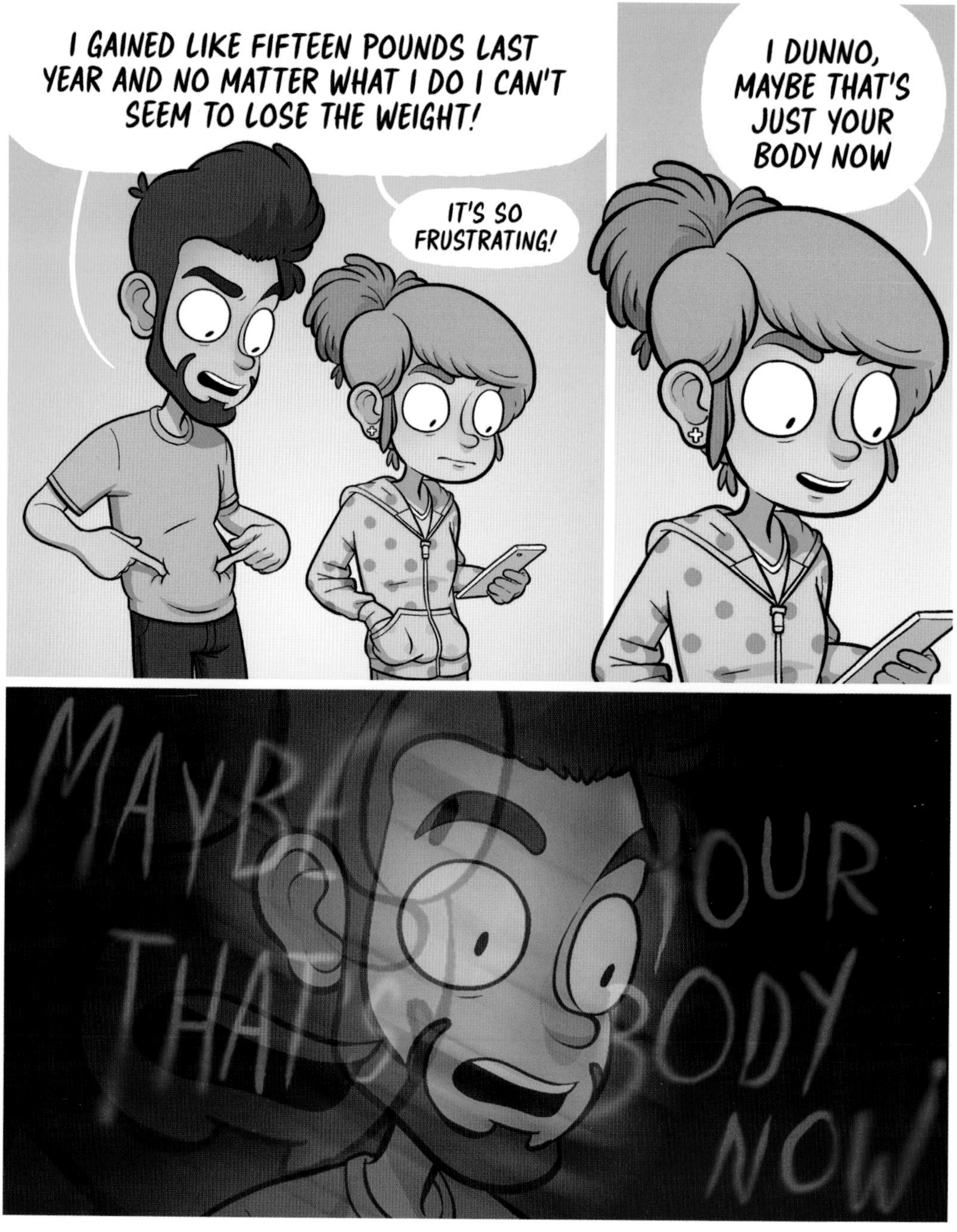
I GAINED LIKE FIFTEEN POUNDS LAST YEAR AND NO MATTER WHAT I DO I CAN'T SEEM TO LOSE THE WEIGHT!
IT'S SO FRUSTRATING!
I DUNNO, MAYBE THAT'S JUST YOUR BODY NOW
MAYBE THAT'S YOUR BODY NOW

TRANSLATION PART II

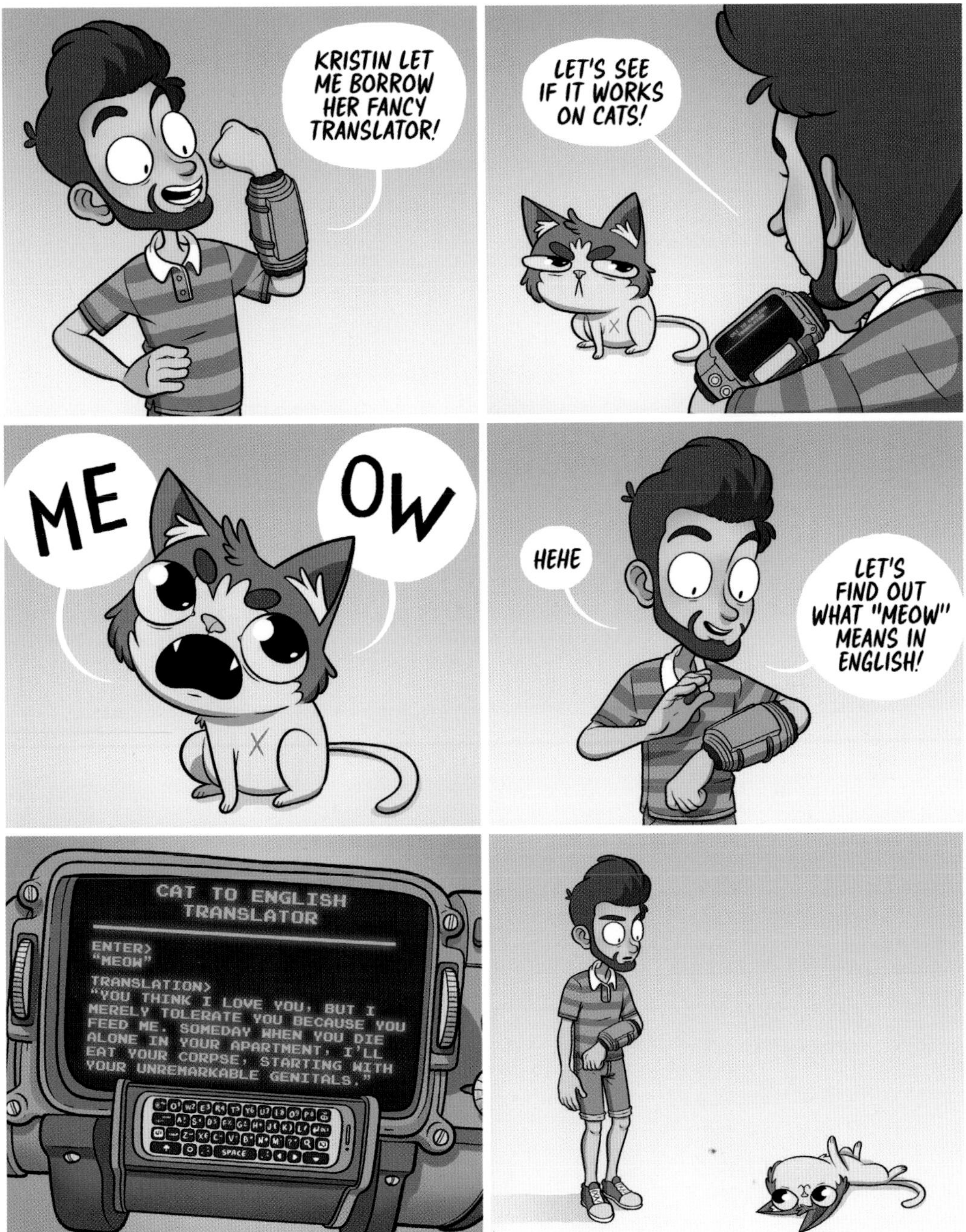
KRISTIN LET ME BORROW HER FANCY TRANSLATOR!
LET'S SEE IF IT WORKS ON CATS!
ME
OW
HEHE
LET'S FIND OUT WHAT "MEOW" MEANS IN ENGLISH!
CAT TO ENGLISH TRANSLATOR
ENTER>
"MEOW"
TRANSLATION>
"YOU THINK I LOVE YOU, BUT I MERELY TOLERATE YOU BECAUSE YOU FEED ME. SOMEDAY WHEN YOU DIE ALONE IN YOUR APARTMENT, I'LL EAT YOUR CORPSE, STARTING WITH YOUR UNREMARKABLE GENITALS."
SPACE

THIS WEEK ON TOP CHEF

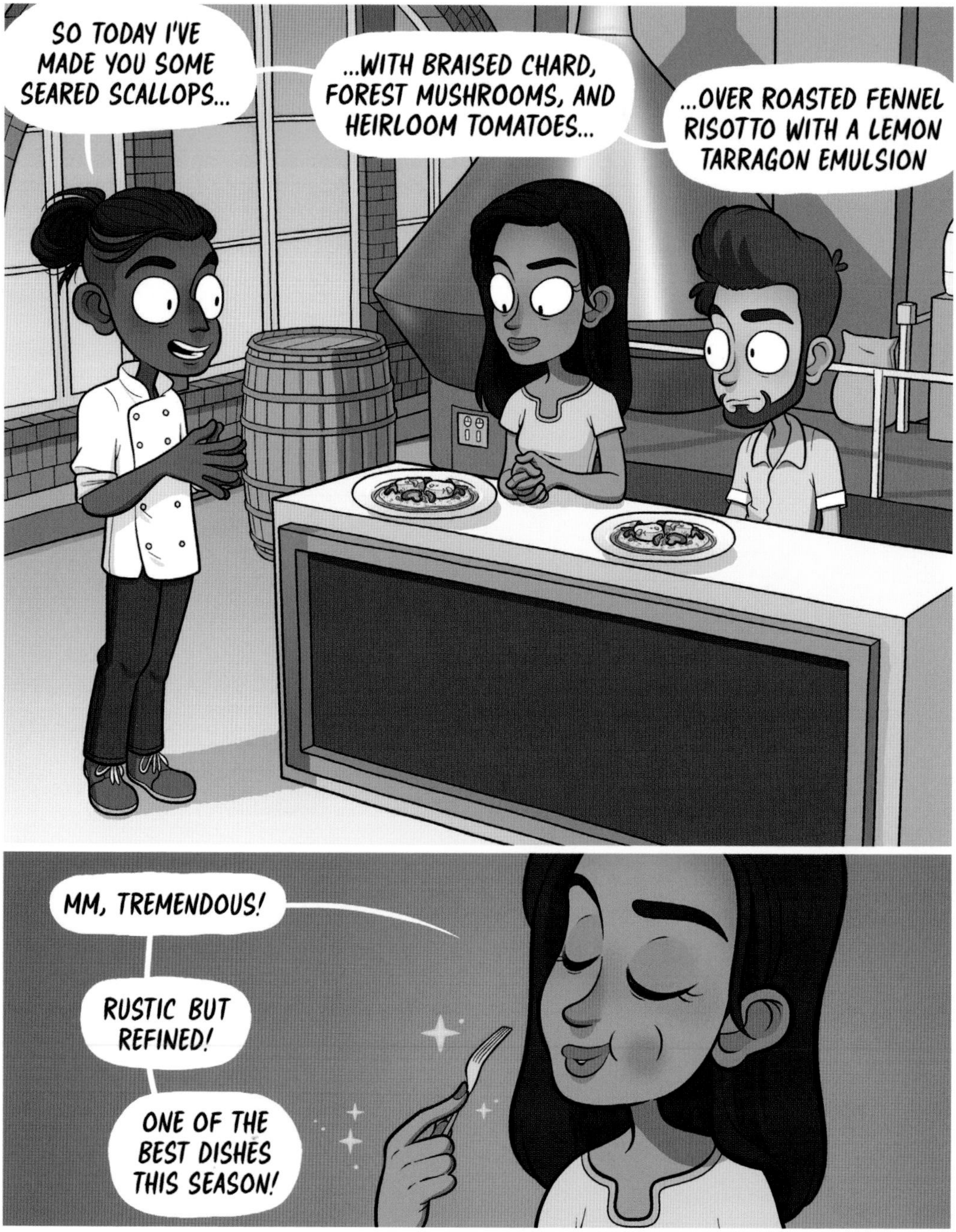
SO TODAY I'VE MADE YOU SOME SEARED SCALLOPS...
...WITH BRAISED CHARD, FOREST MUSHROOMS, AND HEIRLOOM TOMATOES...
...OVER ROASTED FENNEL RISOTTO WITH A LEMON TARRAGON EMULSION
MM, TREMENDOUS!
RUSTIC BUT REFINED!
ONE OF THE BEST DISHES THIS SEASON!

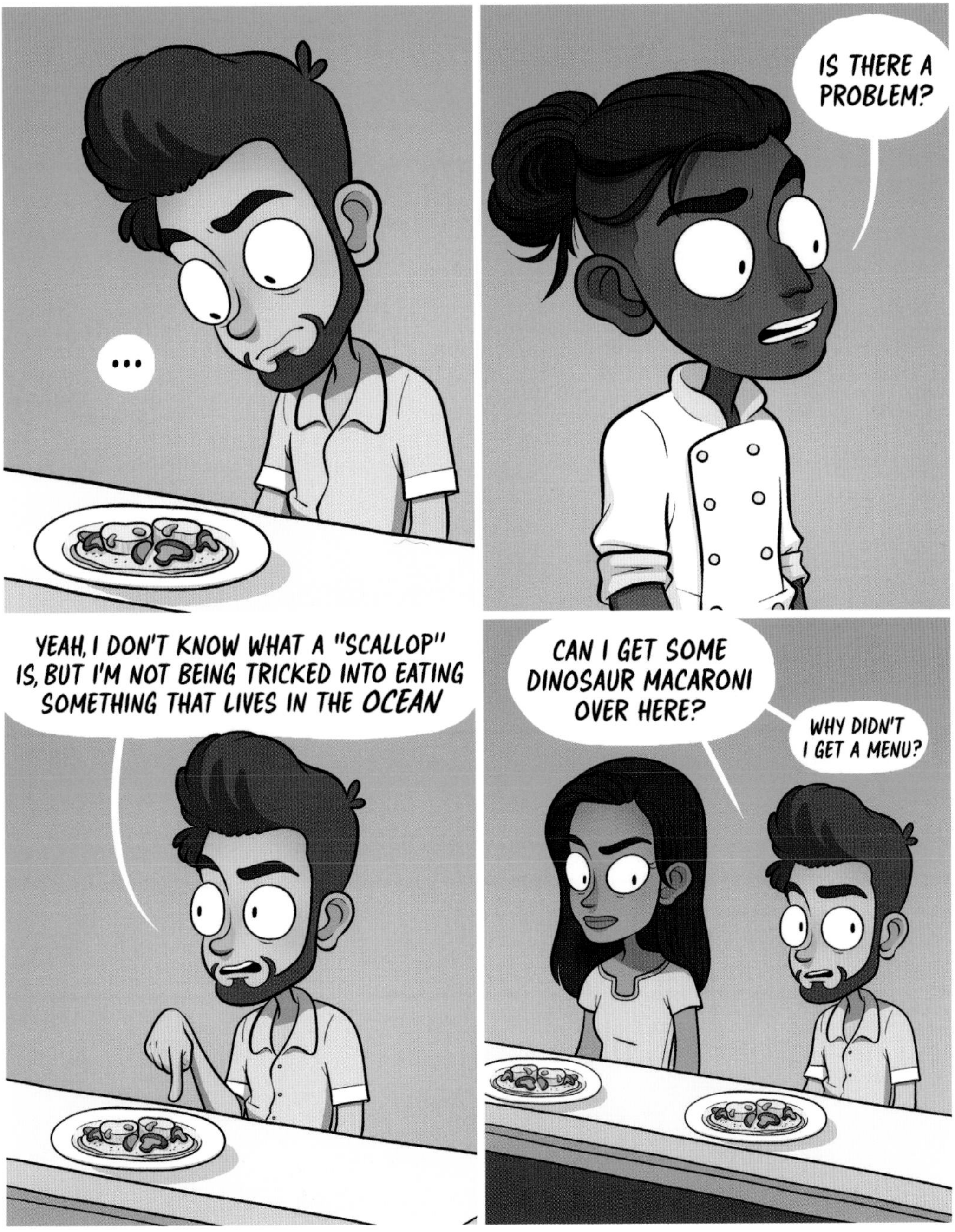
...
IS THERE A PROBLEM?
YEAH, I DON'T KNOW WHAT A "SCALLOP" IS, BUT I'M NOT BEING TRICKED INTO EATING SOMETHING THAT LIVES IN THE OCEAN
CAN I GET SOME DINOSAUR MACARONI OVER HERE?
WHY DIDN'T I GET A MENU?

FORGETFUL

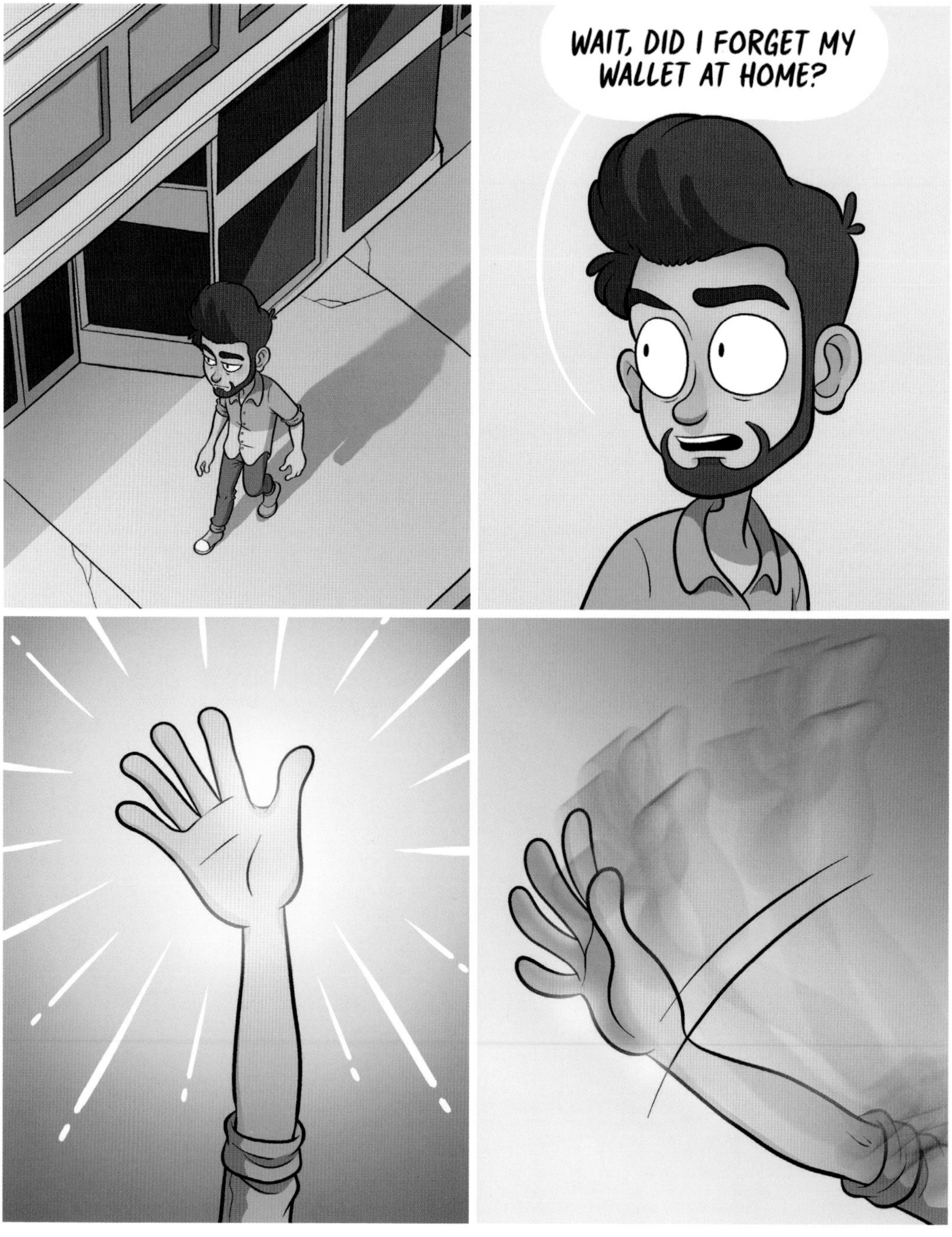

WAIT, DID I FORGET MY WALLET AT HOME?

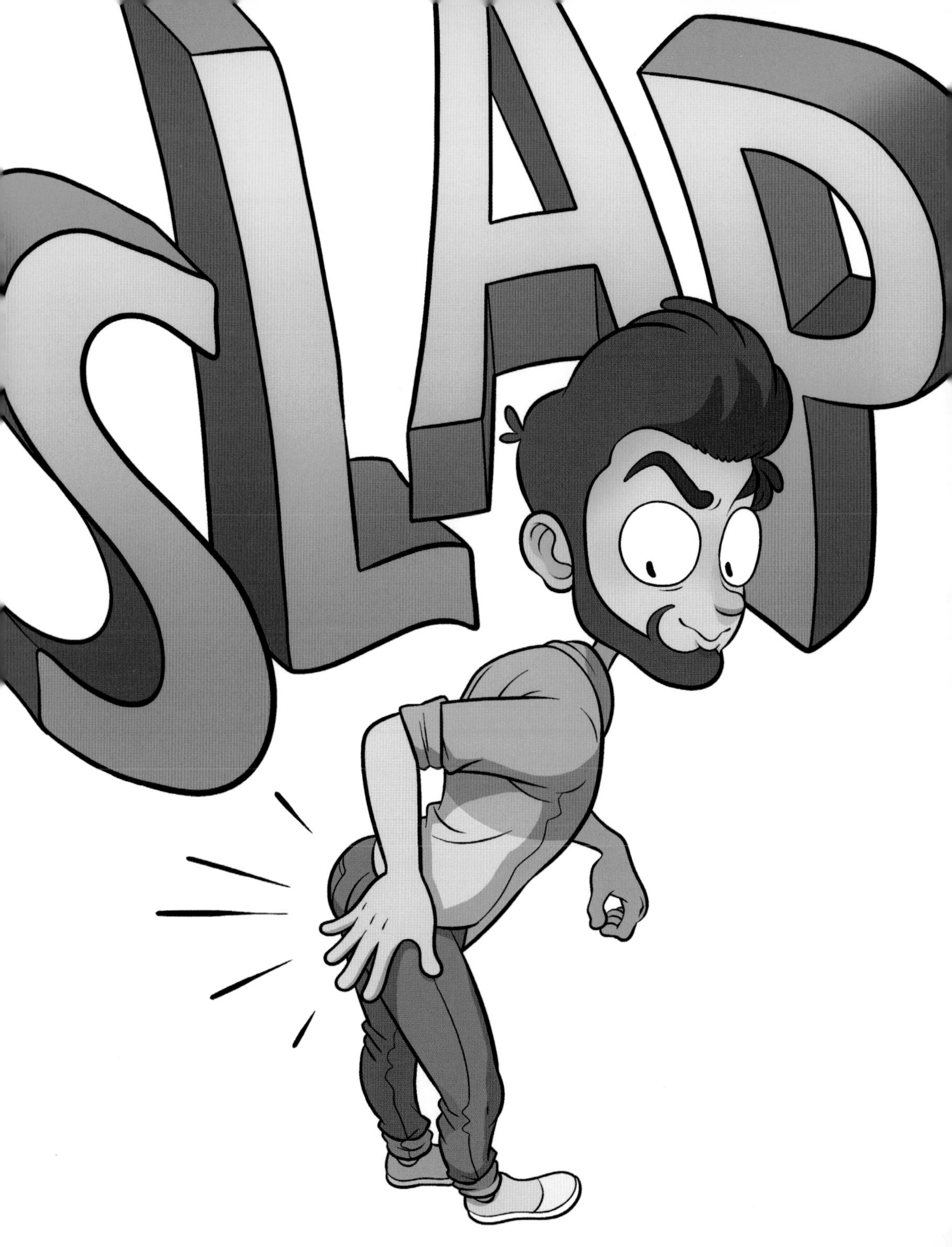
SLAP

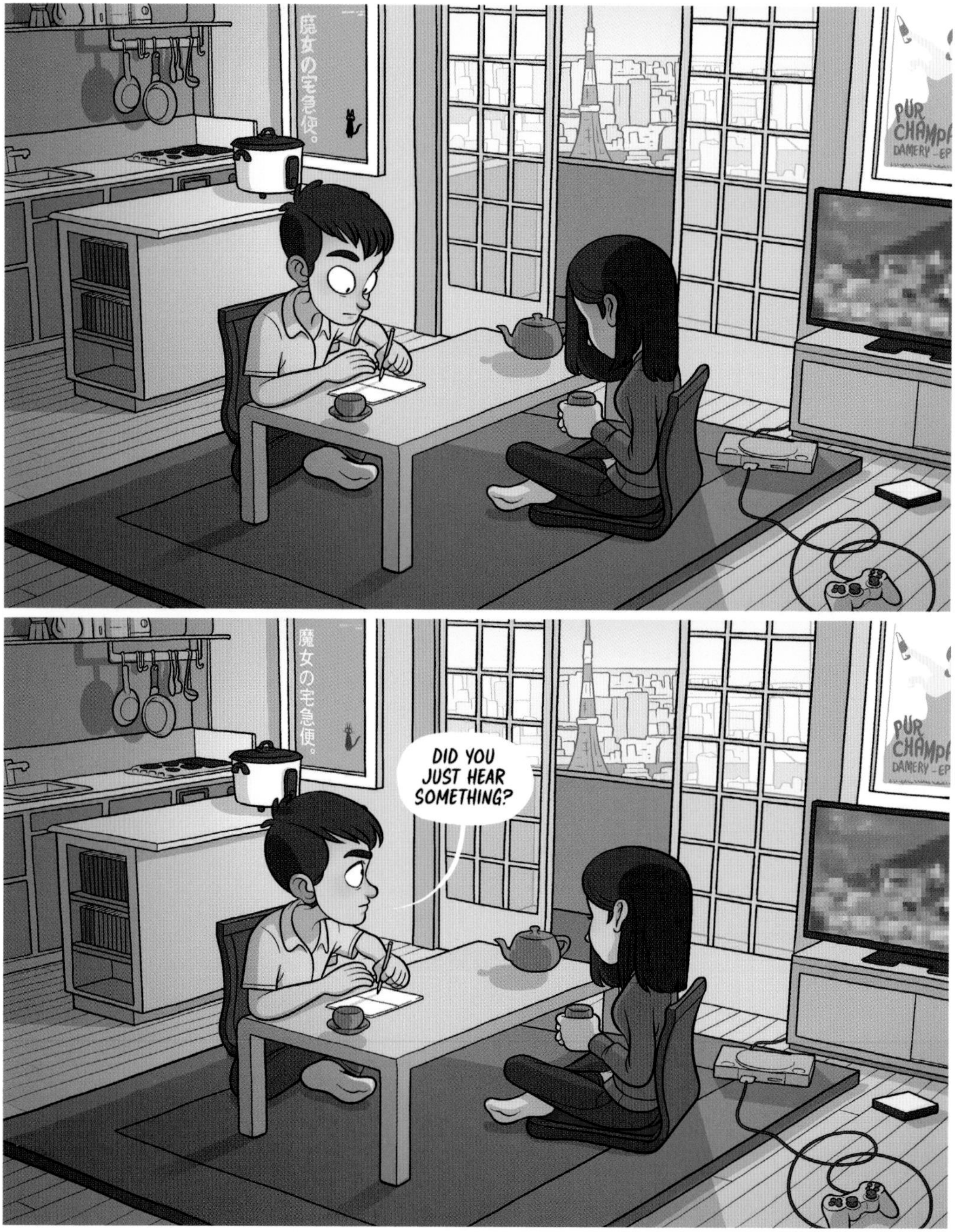
魔女の宅急便。
魔女の宅急便。
DID YOU JUST HEAR SOMETHING?

PEP TALK

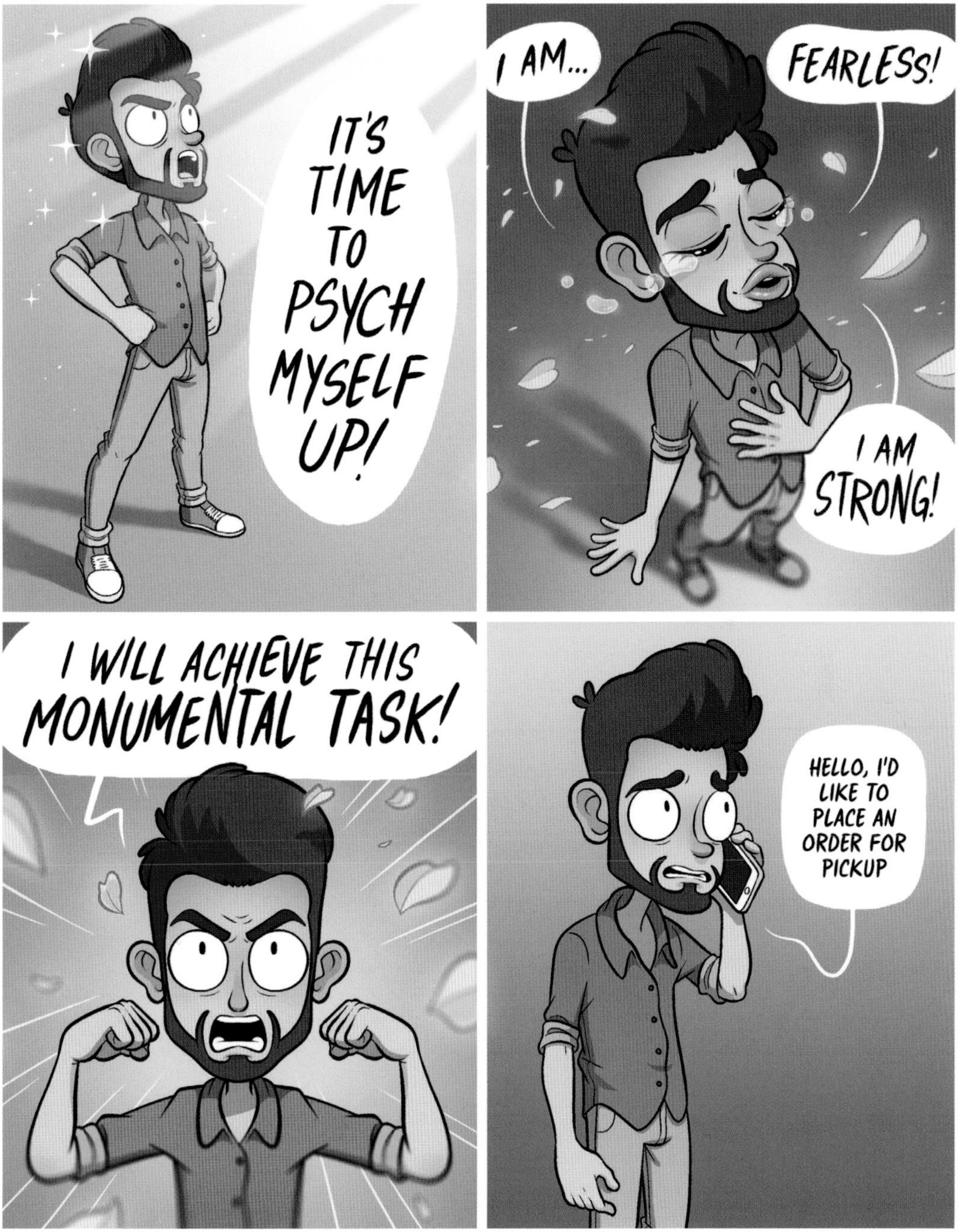
IT'S TIME TO PSYCH MYSELF UP!
I AM...
FEARLESS!
I AM STRONG!
I WILL ACHIEVE THIS MONUMENTAL TASK!
HELLO, I'D LIKE TO PLACE AN ORDER FOR PICKUP

ANTIQUES ROADSHOW

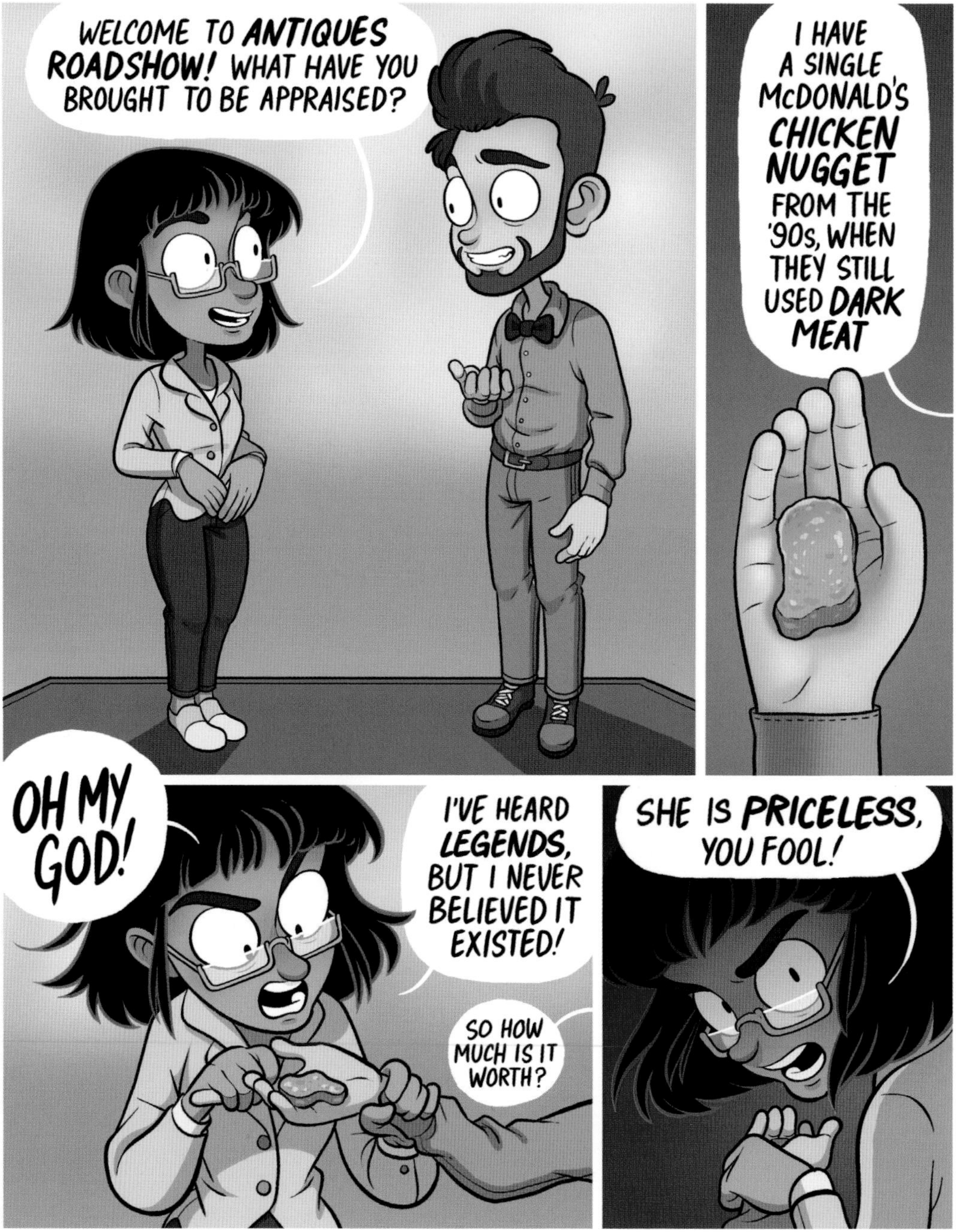

WELCOME TO **ANTIQUES ROADSHOW!** WHAT HAVE YOU BROUGHT TO BE APPRAISED?
I HAVE A SINGLE McDONALD'S **CHICKEN NUGGET** FROM THE '90s, WHEN THEY STILL USED **DARK MEAT**
OH MY GOD!
I'VE HEARD **LEGENDS**, BUT I NEVER BELIEVED IT EXISTED!
SO HOW MUCH IS IT WORTH?
SHE IS **PRICELESS**, YOU FOOL!

COCONUT OIL

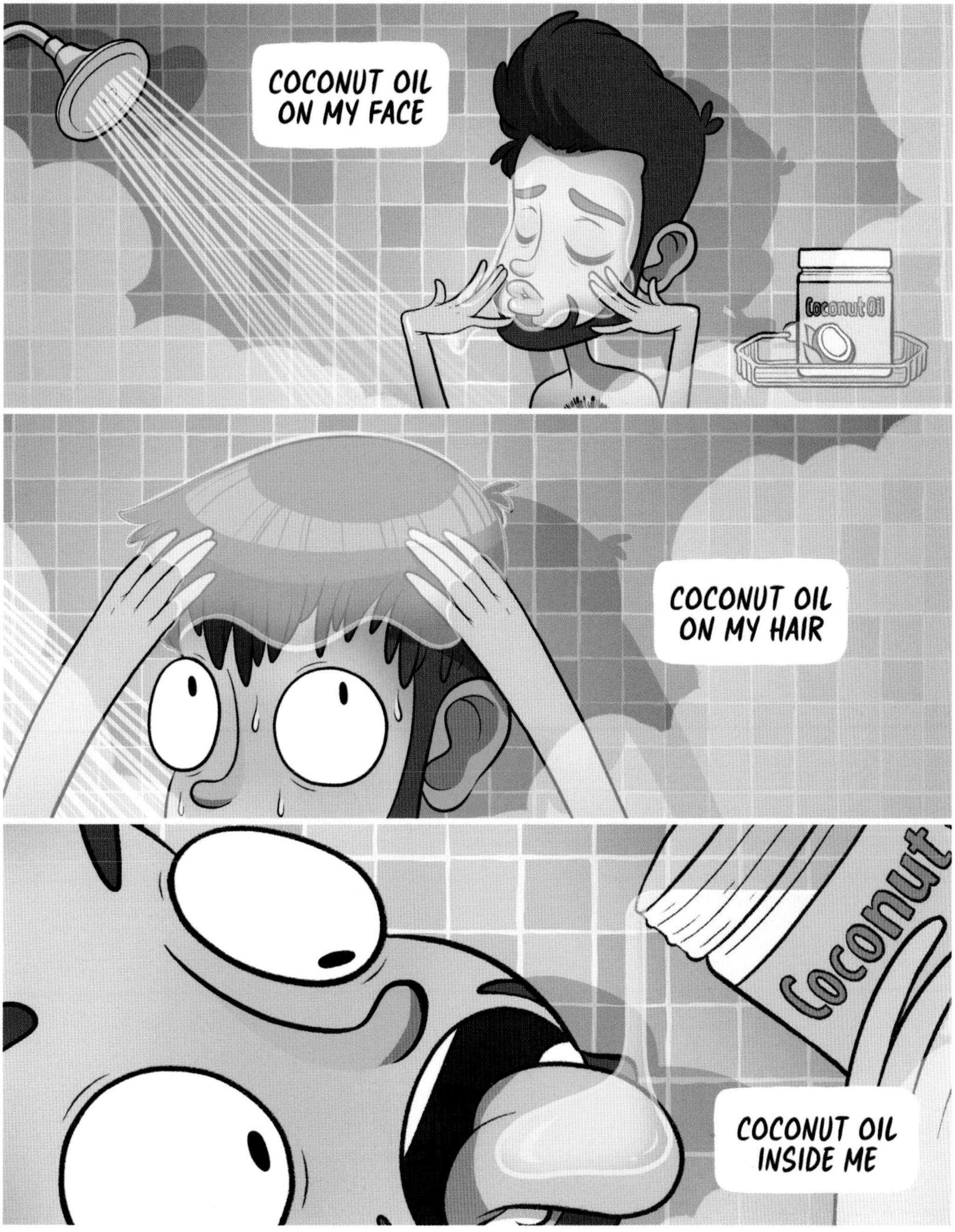
COCONUT OIL ON MY FACE
Coconut Oil
COCONUT OIL ON MY HAIR
Coconut
COCONUT OIL INSIDE ME

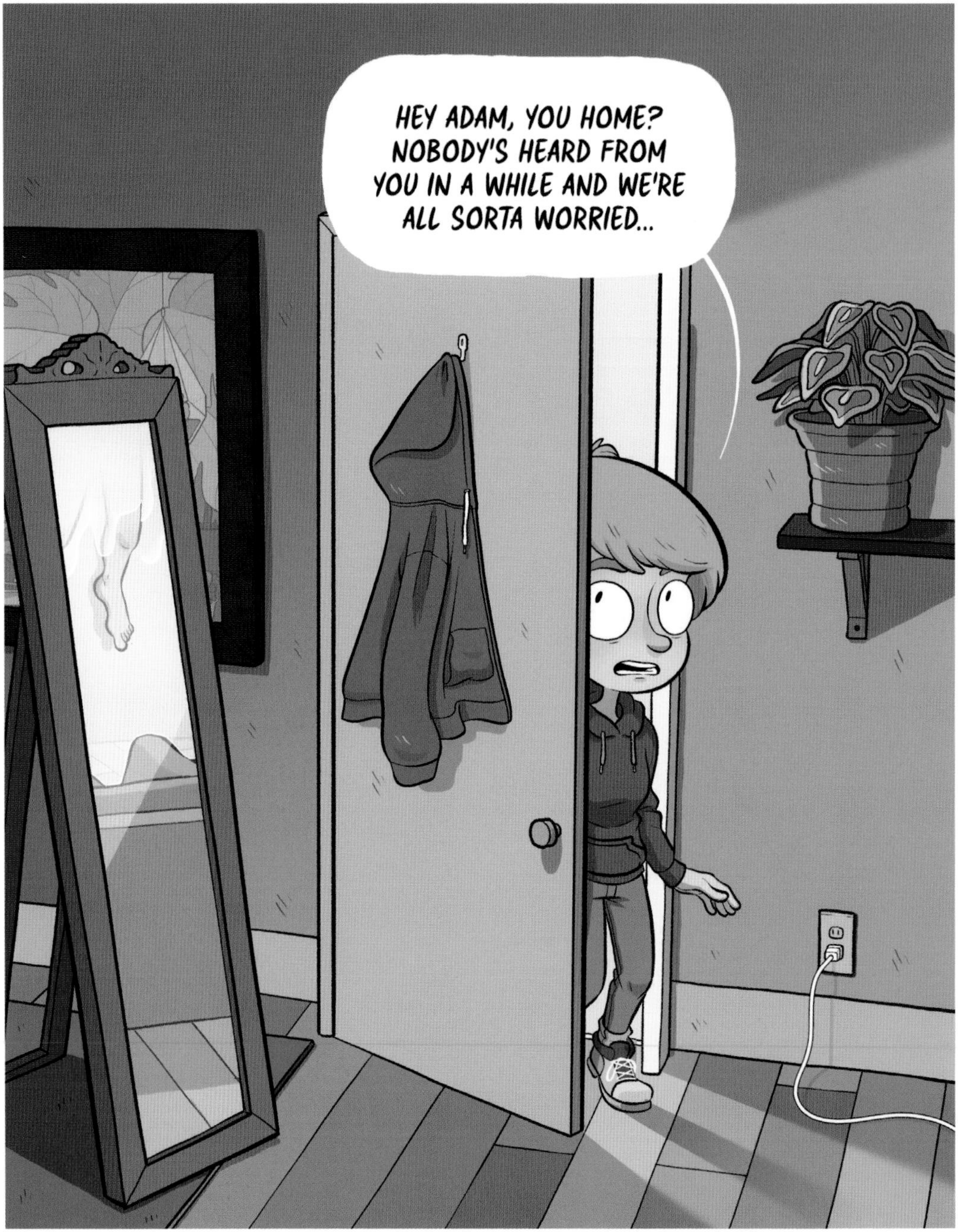
HEY ADAM, YOU HOME? NOBODY'S HEARD FROM YOU IN A WHILE AND WE'RE ALL SORTA WORRIED...

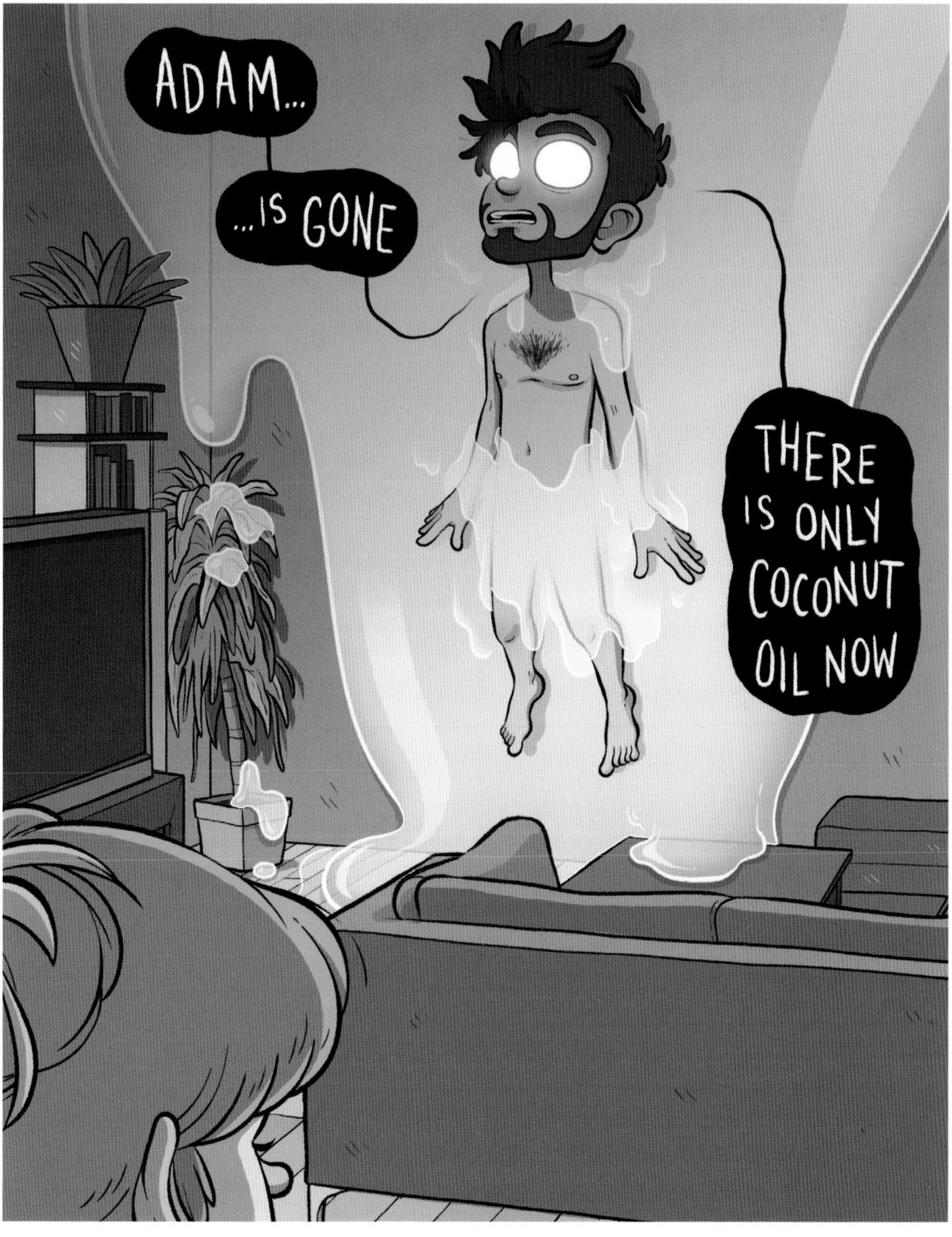
ADAM...
...IS GONE
THERE IS ONLY COCONUT OIL NOW

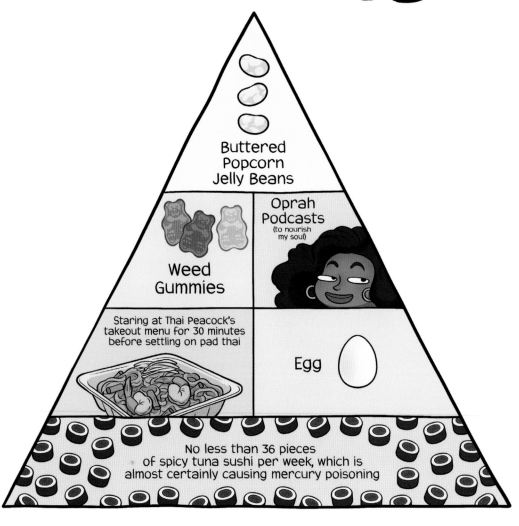

MY FOOD PYRAMID

Buttered
Popcorn
Jelly Beans

Oprah
Podcasts
(to nourish
my soul)

Weed
Gummies

Staring at Thai Peacock's
takeout menu for 30 minutes
before settling on pad thai

Egg

No less than 36 pieces
of spicy tuna sushi per week, which is
almost certainly causing mercury poisoning

TV DINNER

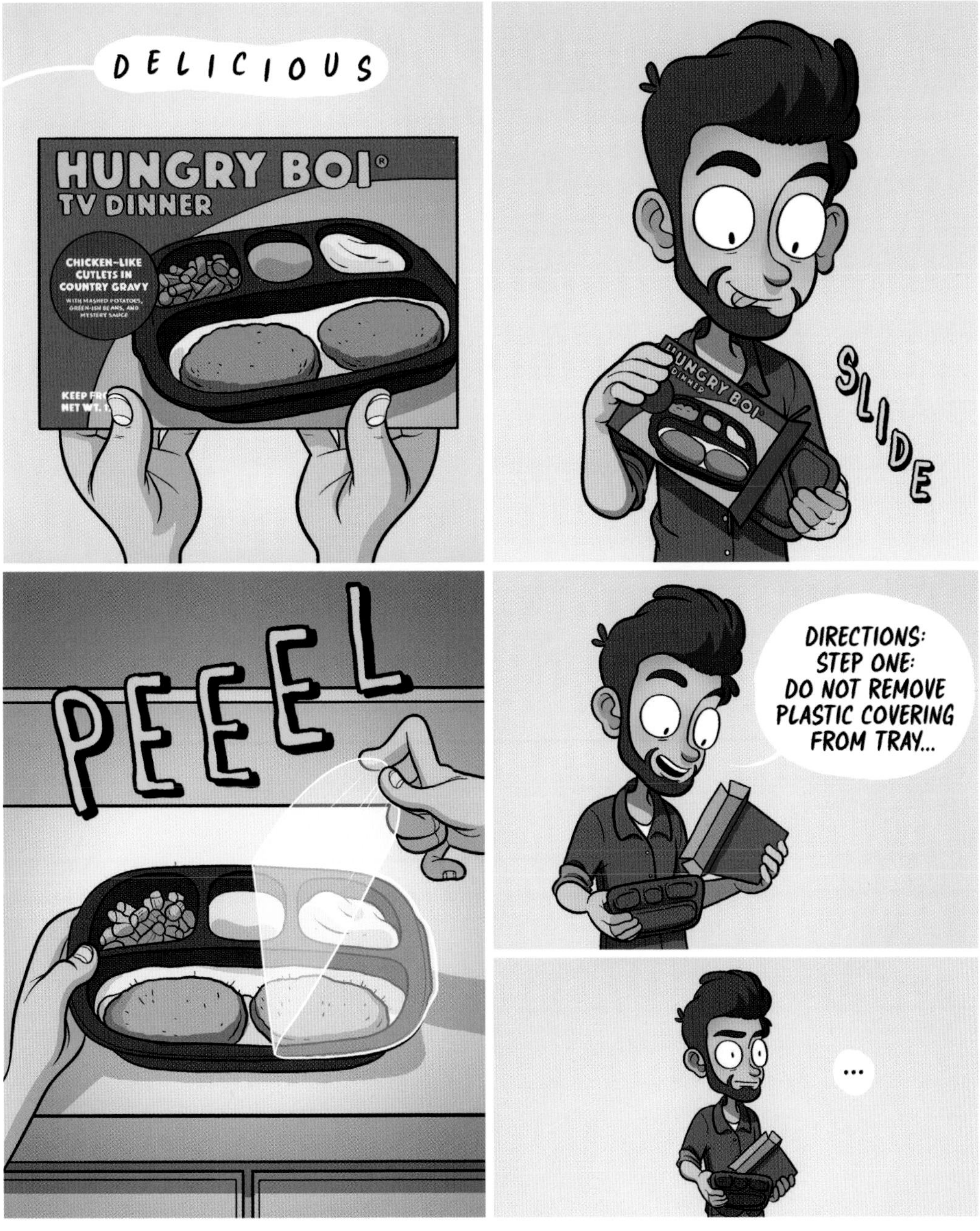
DELICIOUS
HUNGRY BOI®
TV DINNER
CHICKEN-LIKE CUTLETS IN COUNTRY GRAVY
SLIDE
PEEEL
DIRECTIONS: STEP ONE: DO NOT REMOVE PLASTIC COVERING FROM TRAY...
...

ONE WISH

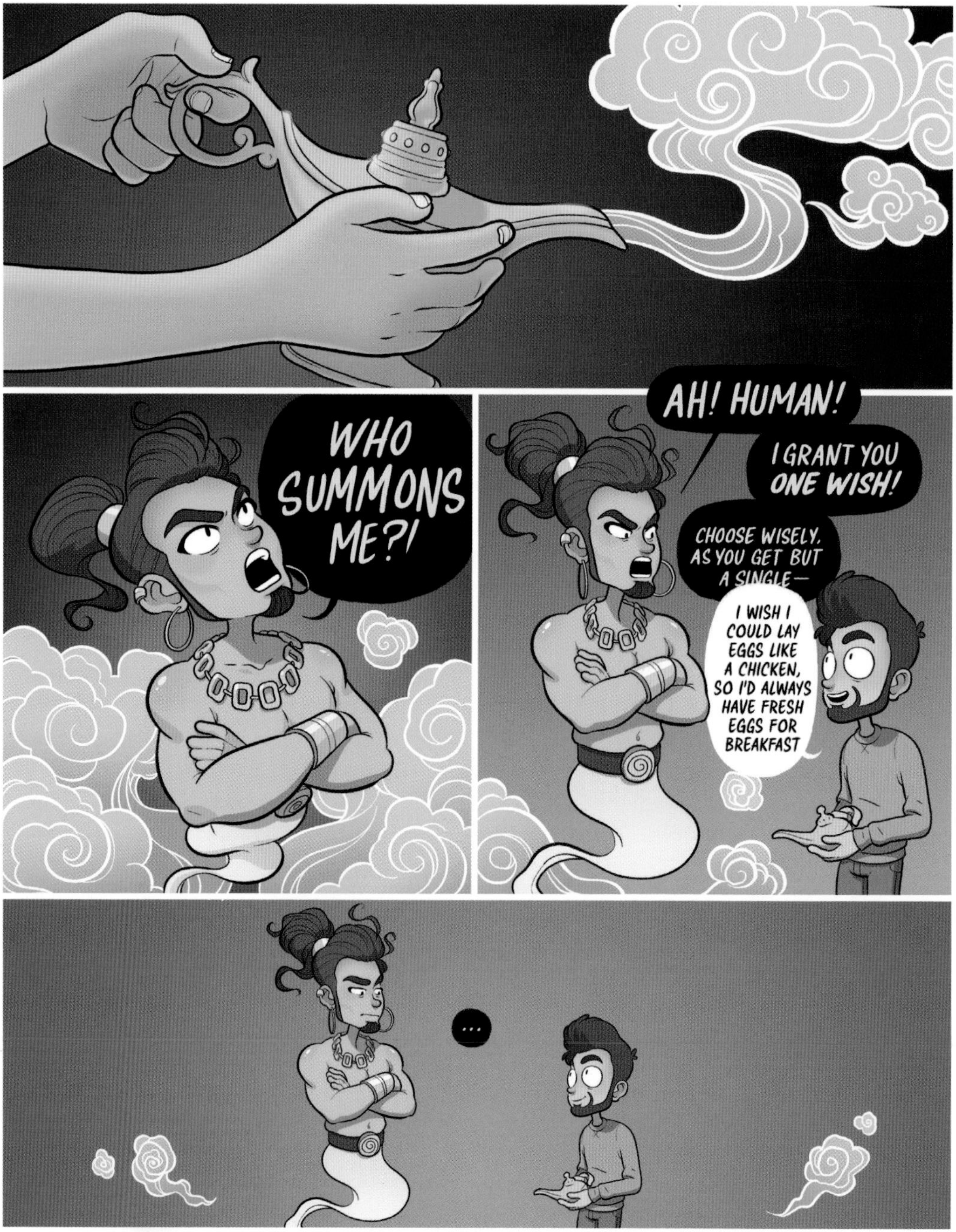
WHO SUMMONS ME?!
AH! HUMAN!
I GRANT YOU ONE WISH!
CHOOSE WISELY, AS YOU GET BUT A SINGLE—
I WISH I COULD LAY EGGS LIKE A CHICKEN, SO I'D ALWAYS HAVE FRESH EGGS FOR BREAKFAST
...

HOW DIET COLA WORKS IN THE BODY

A Lesson in Nutritional Science

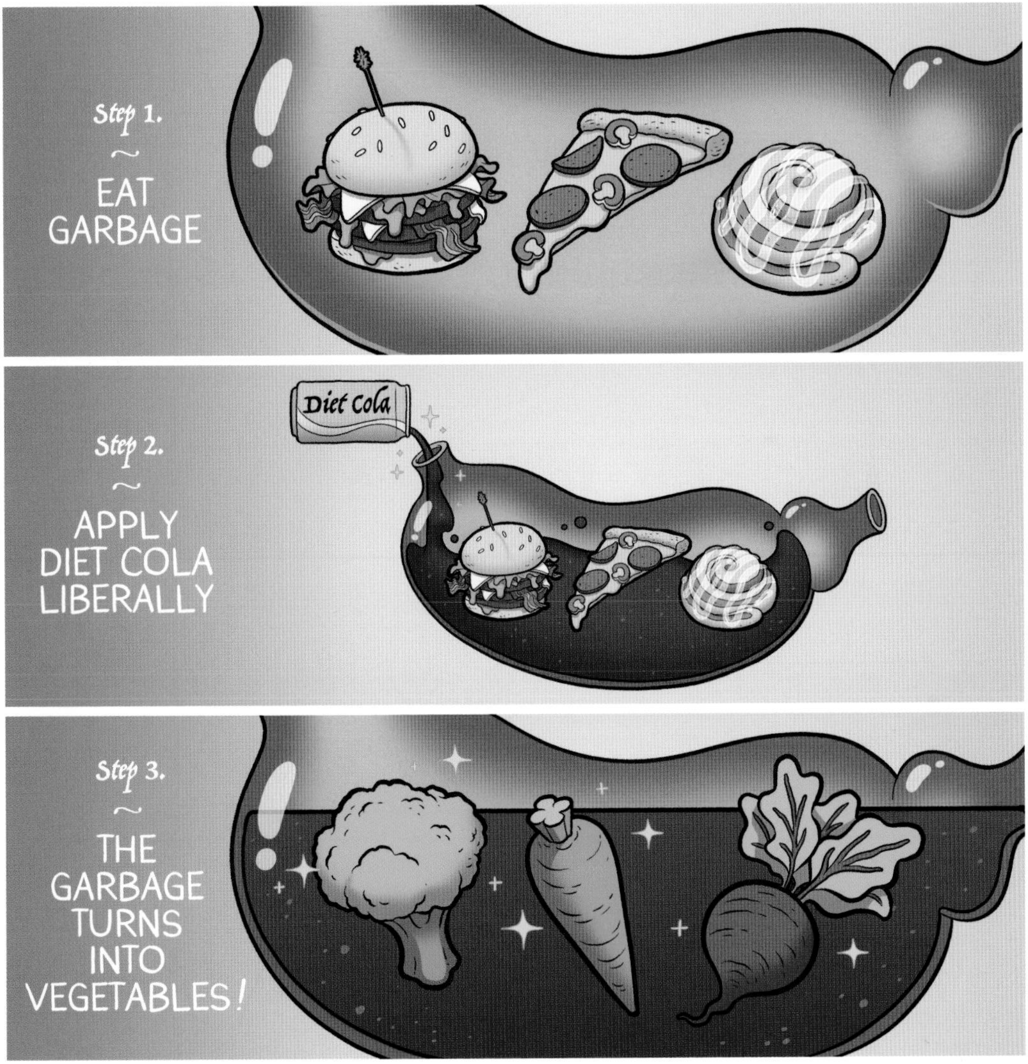

Step 1.
~
EAT GARBAGE
Step 2.
~
APPLY DIET COLA LIBERALLY
Diet Cola
Step 3.
~
THE GARBAGE TURNS INTO VEGETABLES!

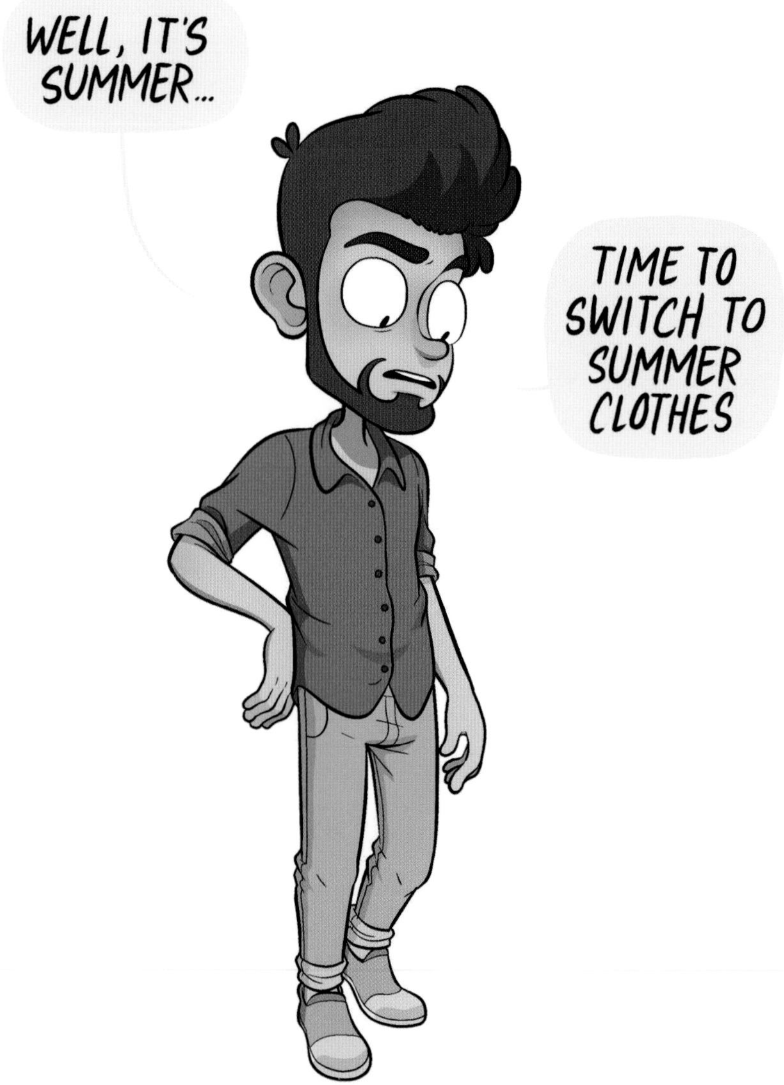
WELL, IT'S SUMMER...
TIME TO SWITCH TO SUMMER CLOTHES

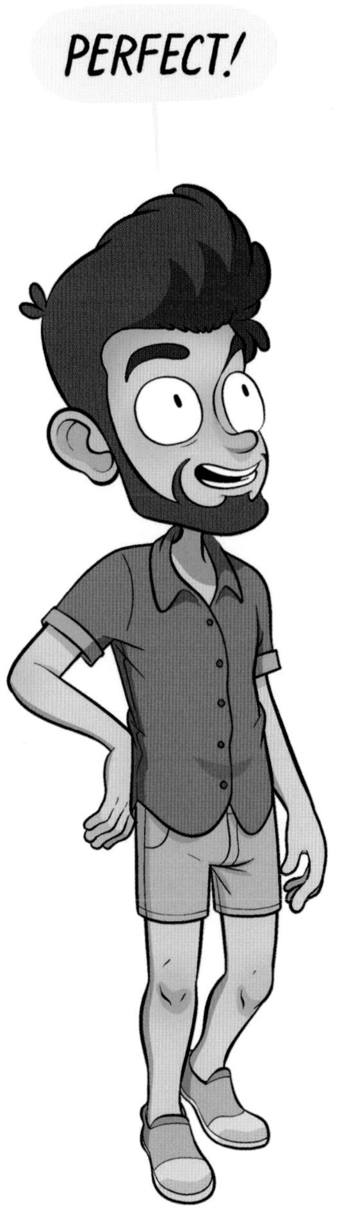
PERFECT!

VITAMIN D

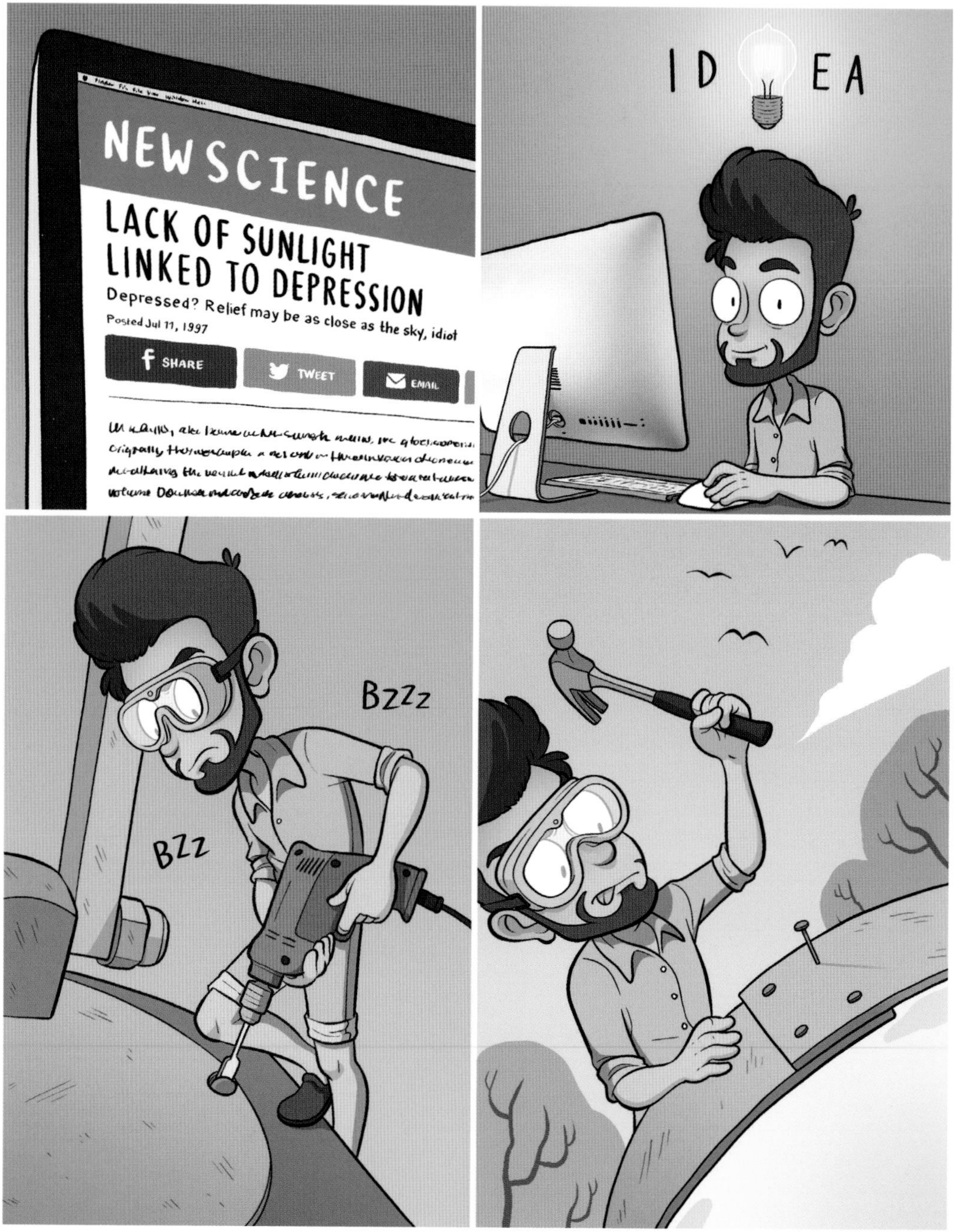
NEW SCIENCE
LACK OF SUNLIGHT LINKED TO DEPRESSION
Depressed? Relief may be as close as the sky, idiot
Posted Jul 11, 1997
SHARE
TWEET
EMAIL
IDEA
Bzzz
BZZ

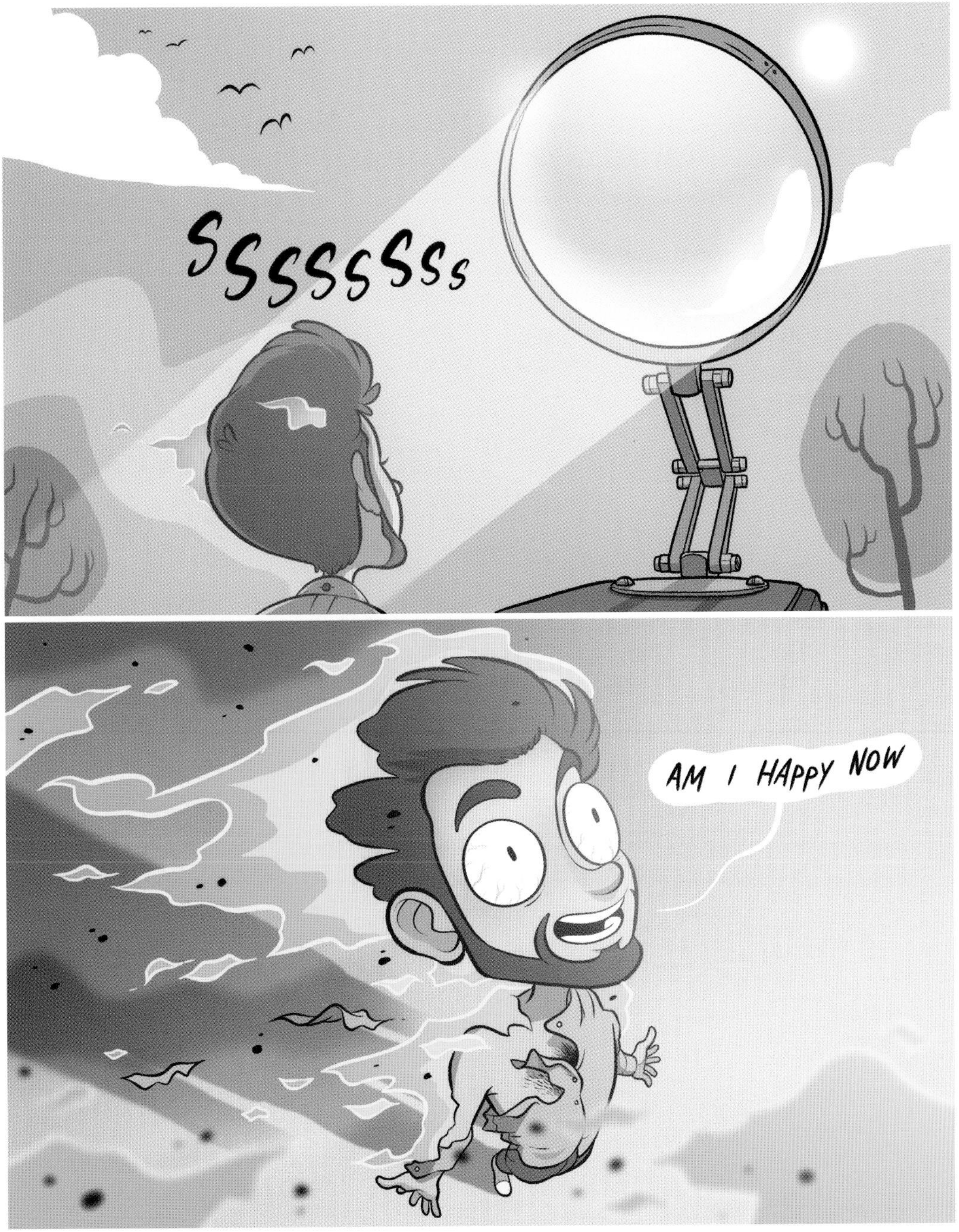
SSSSSSSSs
AM I HAPPY NOW

UNSTOPPABLE

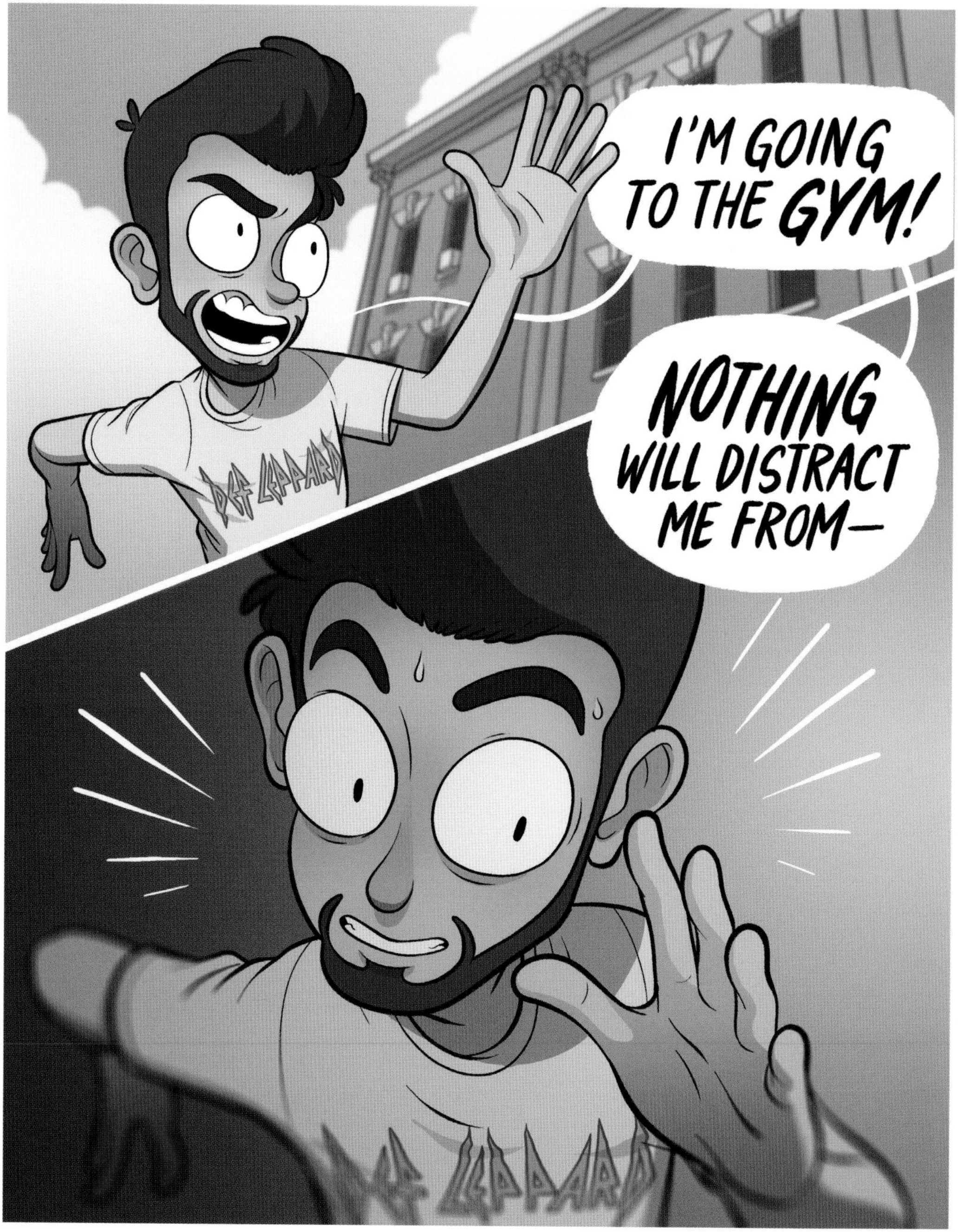
I'M GOING TO THE GYM!
NOTHING WILL DISTRACT ME FROM—
DEF LEPPARD

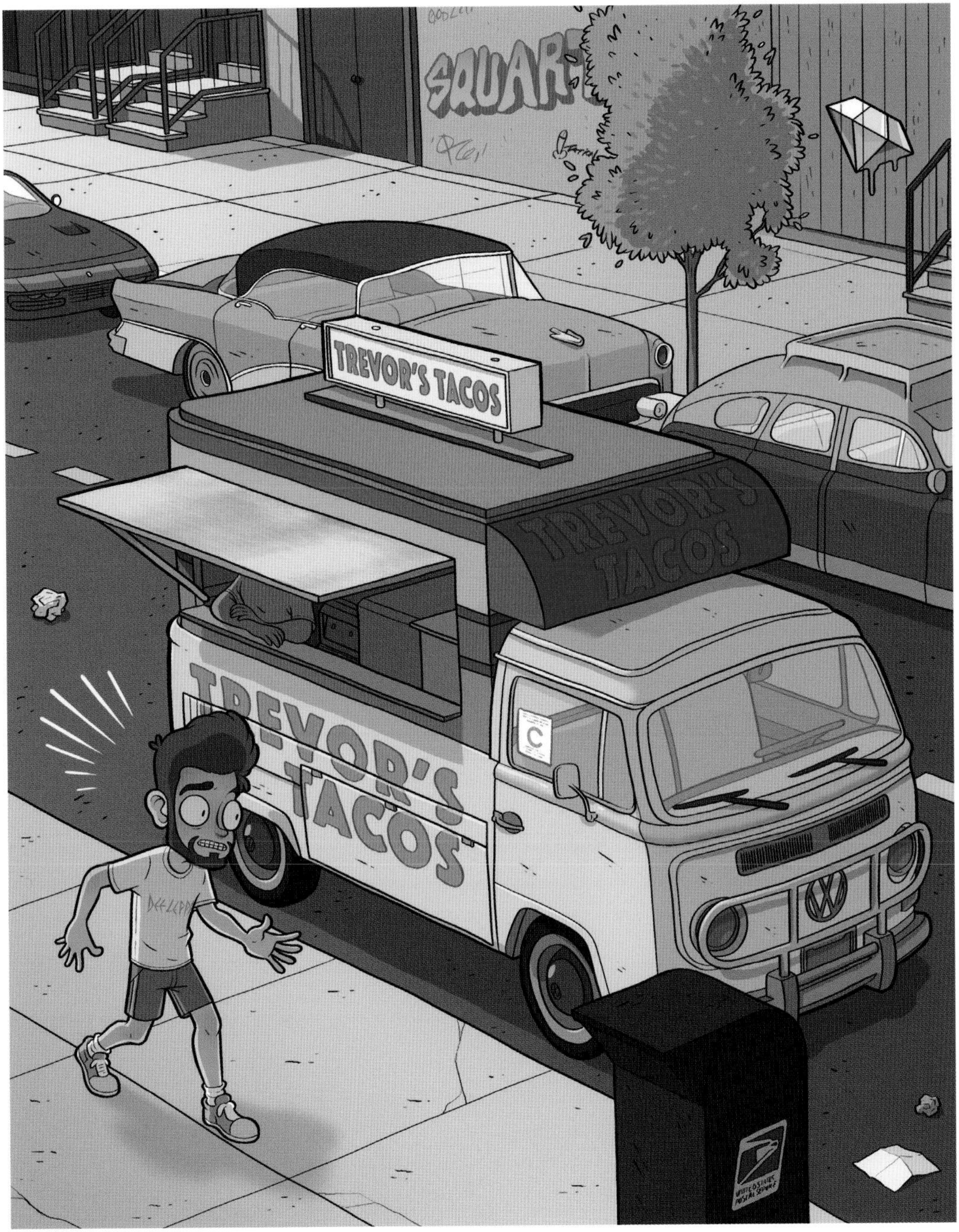
TREVOR'S TACOS
TREVOR'S TACOS
TREVOR'S TACOS

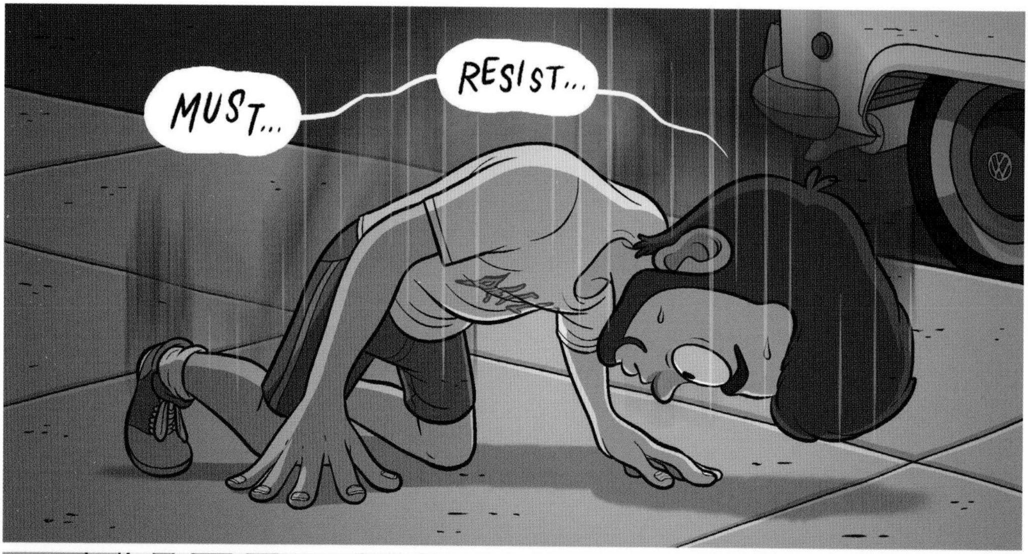
MUST...
RESIST...

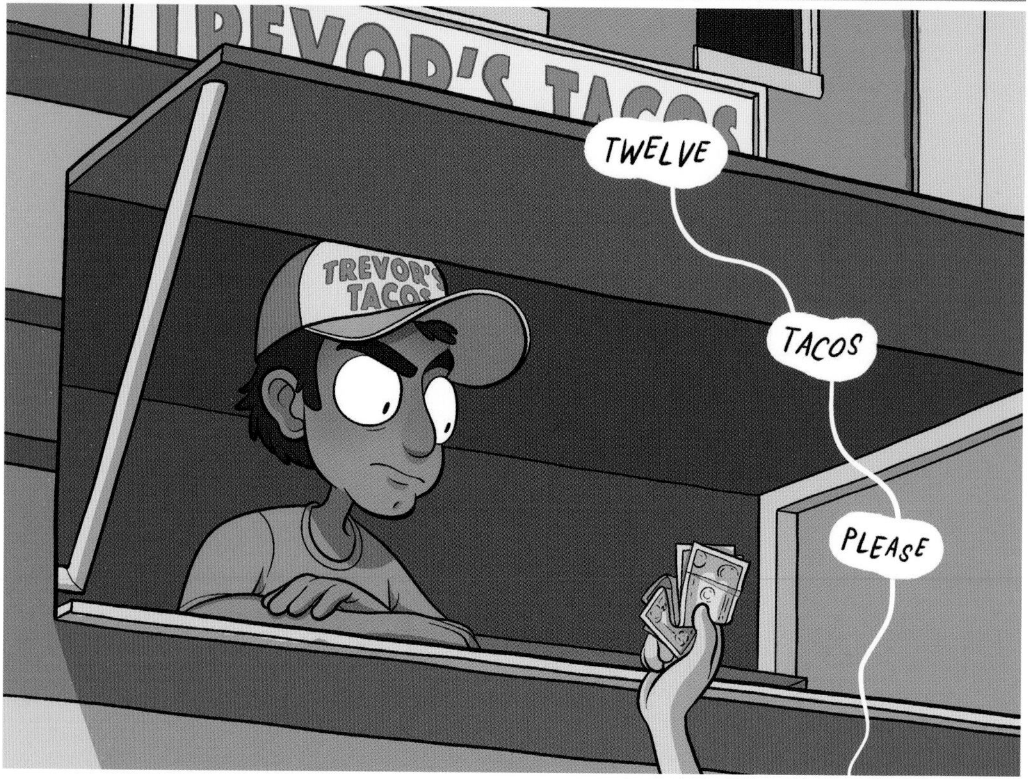
TREVOR'S TACOS
TREVOR'S TACOS
TWELVE
TACOS
PLEASE

JORTS

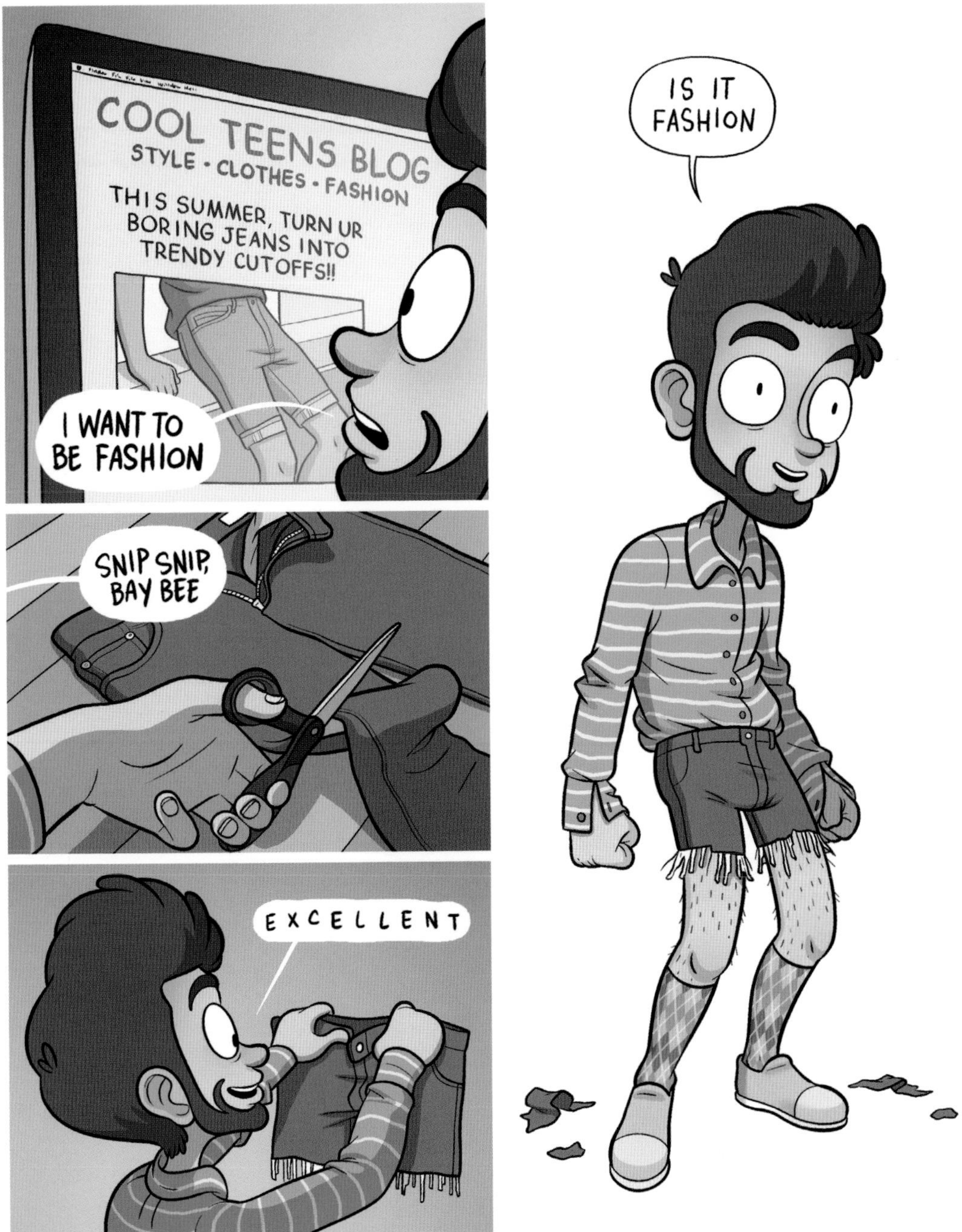
COOL TEENS BLOG
STYLE - CLOTHES - FASHION
THIS SUMMER, TURN UR BORING JEANS INTO TRENDY CUTOFFS!!
I WANT TO BE FASHION
SNIP SNIP, BAY BEE
EXCELLENT
IS IT FASHION

ZERO BALANCE

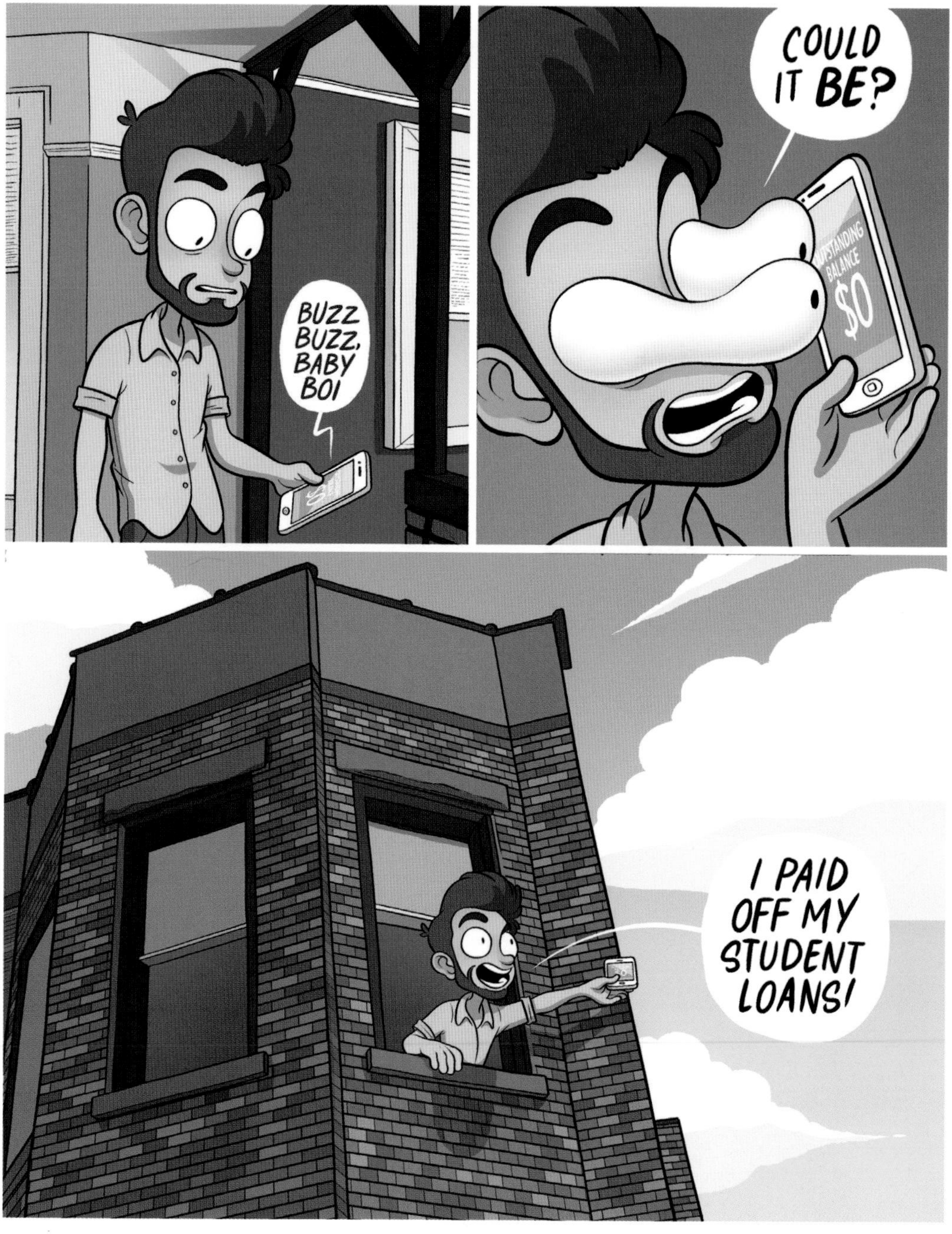
BUZZ BUZZ, BABY BOI
COULD IT BE?
OUTSTANDING BALANCE $0
I PAID OFF MY STUDENT LOANS!

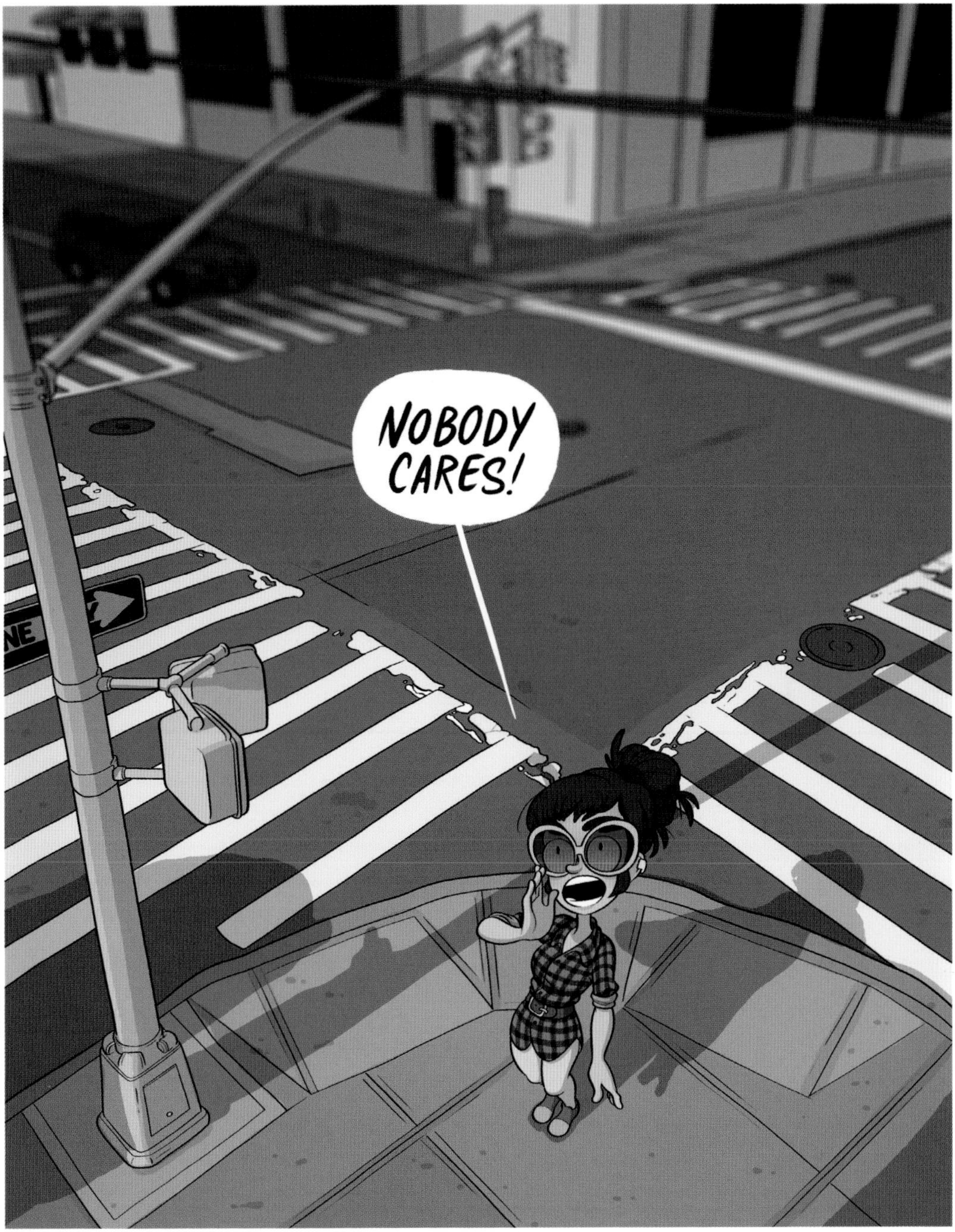
NOBODY CARES!
ONE

NEW SONG

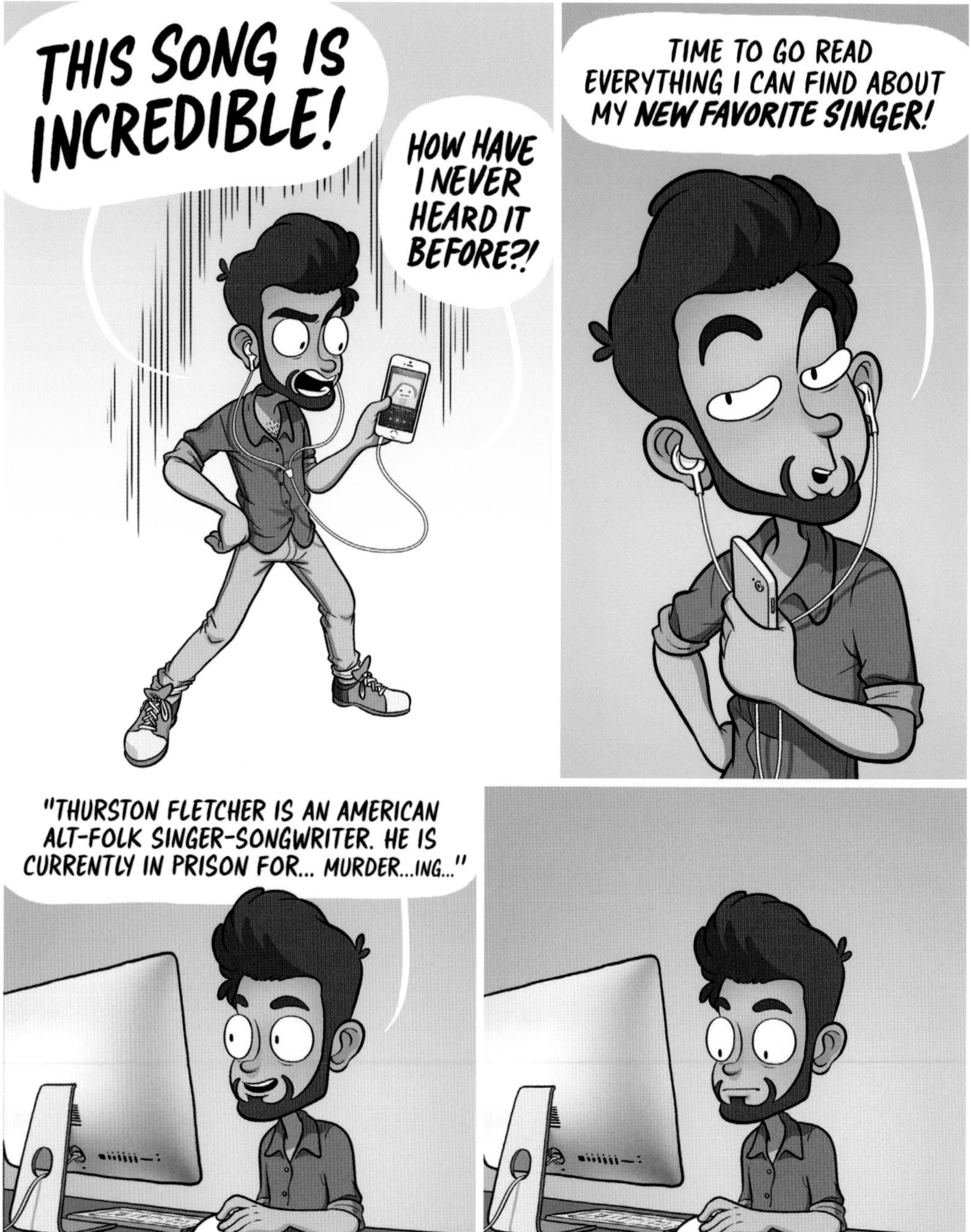
THIS SONG IS INCREDIBLE!
HOW HAVE I NEVER HEARD IT BEFORE?!
TIME TO GO READ EVERYTHING I CAN FIND ABOUT MY NEW FAVORITE SINGER!
"THURSTON FLETCHER IS AN AMERICAN ALT-FOLK SINGER-SONGWRITER. HE IS CURRENTLY IN PRISON FOR... MURDER...ING..."

ITINERARY

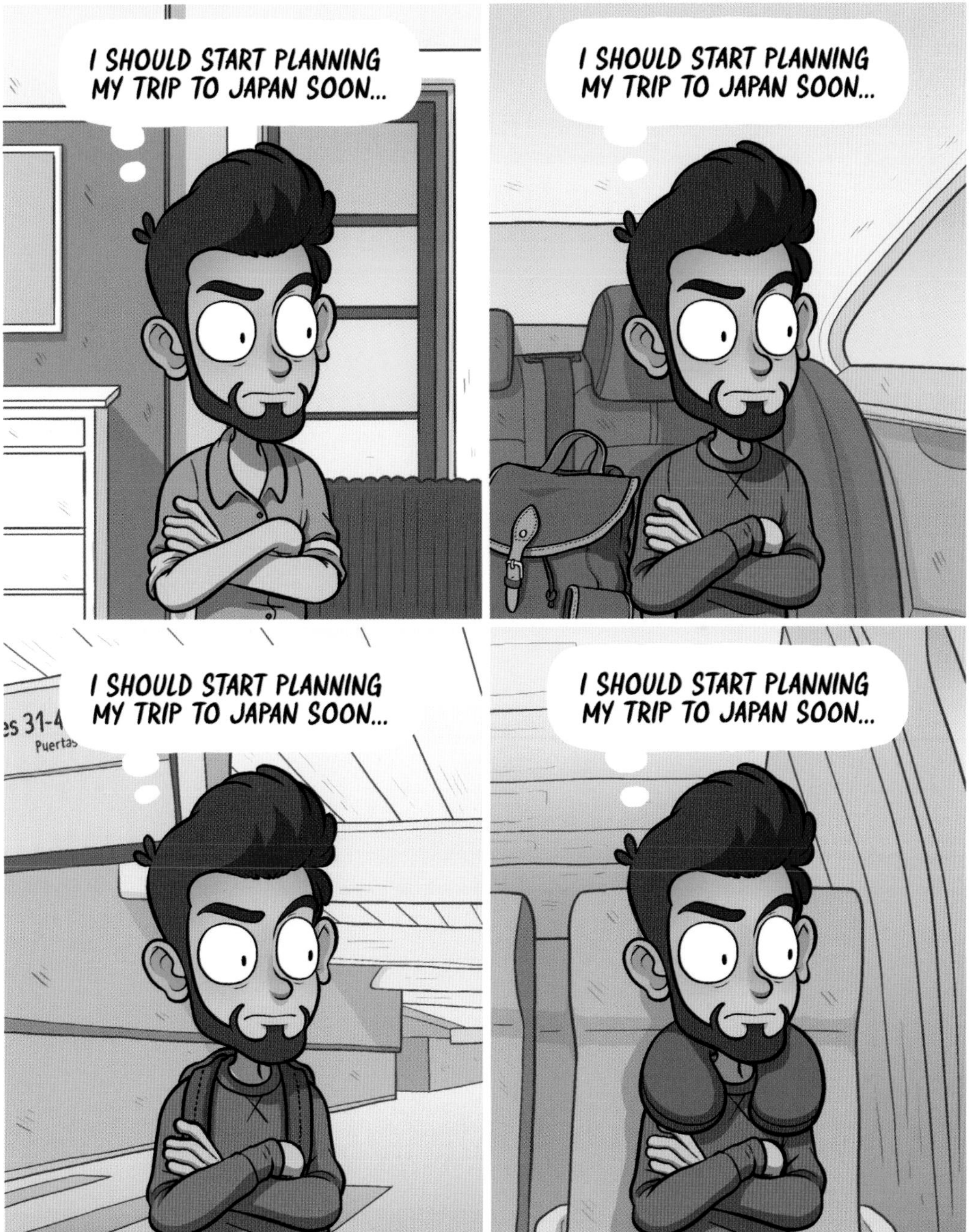
I SHOULD START PLANNING MY TRIP TO JAPAN SOON...
I SHOULD START PLANNING MY TRIP TO JAPAN SOON...
I SHOULD START PLANNING MY TRIP TO JAPAN SOON...
I SHOULD START PLANNING MY TRIP TO JAPAN SOON...

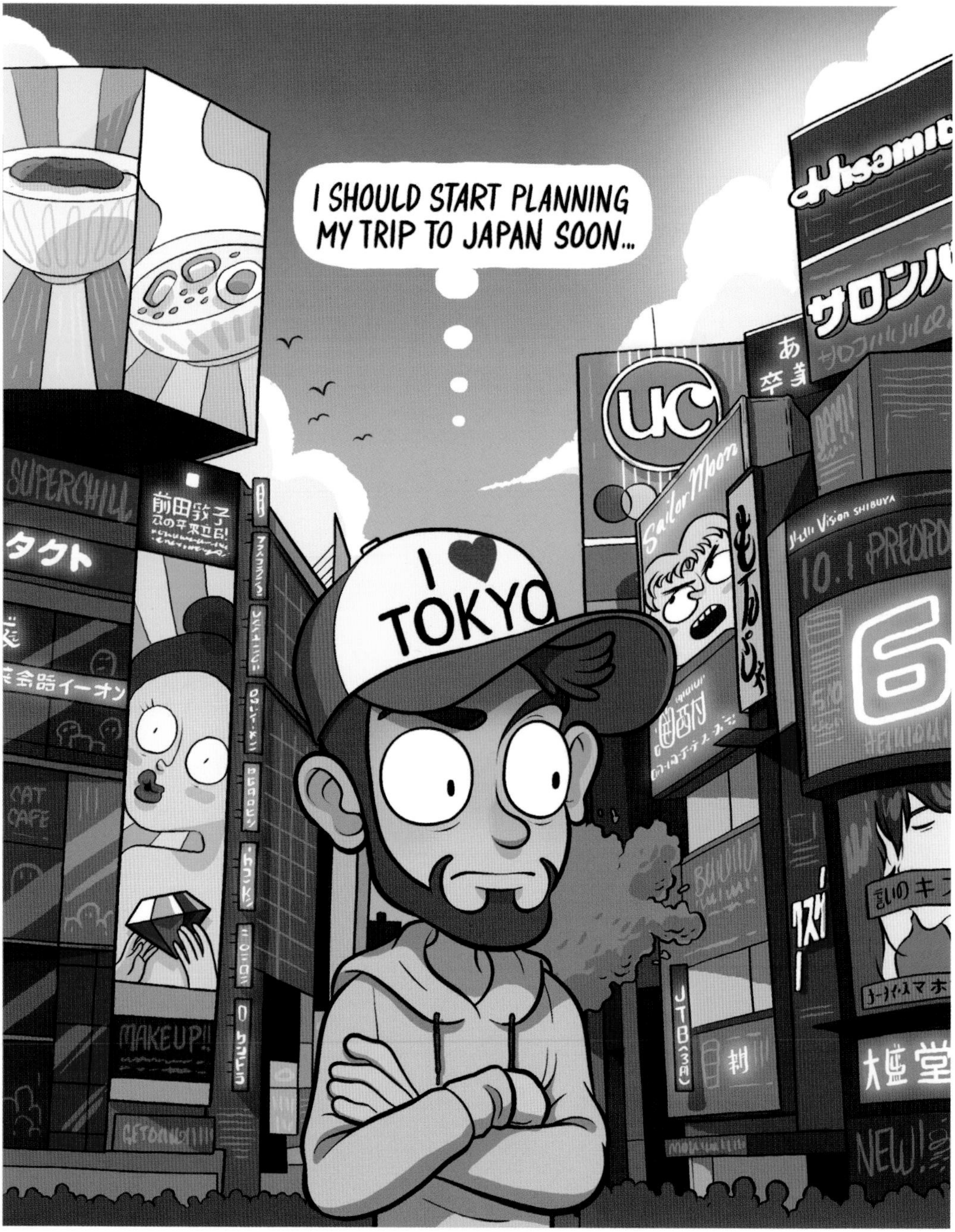
I SHOULD START PLANNING MY TRIP TO JAPAN SOON...
I ♥ TOKYO

LAZY BOY

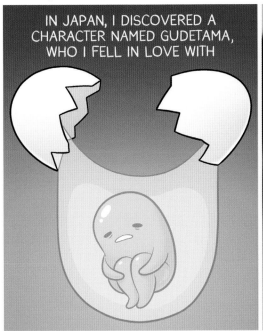

IN JAPAN, I DISCOVERED A CHARACTER NAMED GUDETAMA, WHO I FELL IN LOVE WITH

HE'S A LITTLE EGG WHO LACKS MOTIVATION TO DO ANYTHING

ALL HE WANTS TO DO IS SLEEP, AND HE COMPLAINS WHEN ANYTHING IS ASKED OF HIM

I HAVE NO IDEA WHY I RELATE TO HIM SO MUCH

VENDING MACHINE

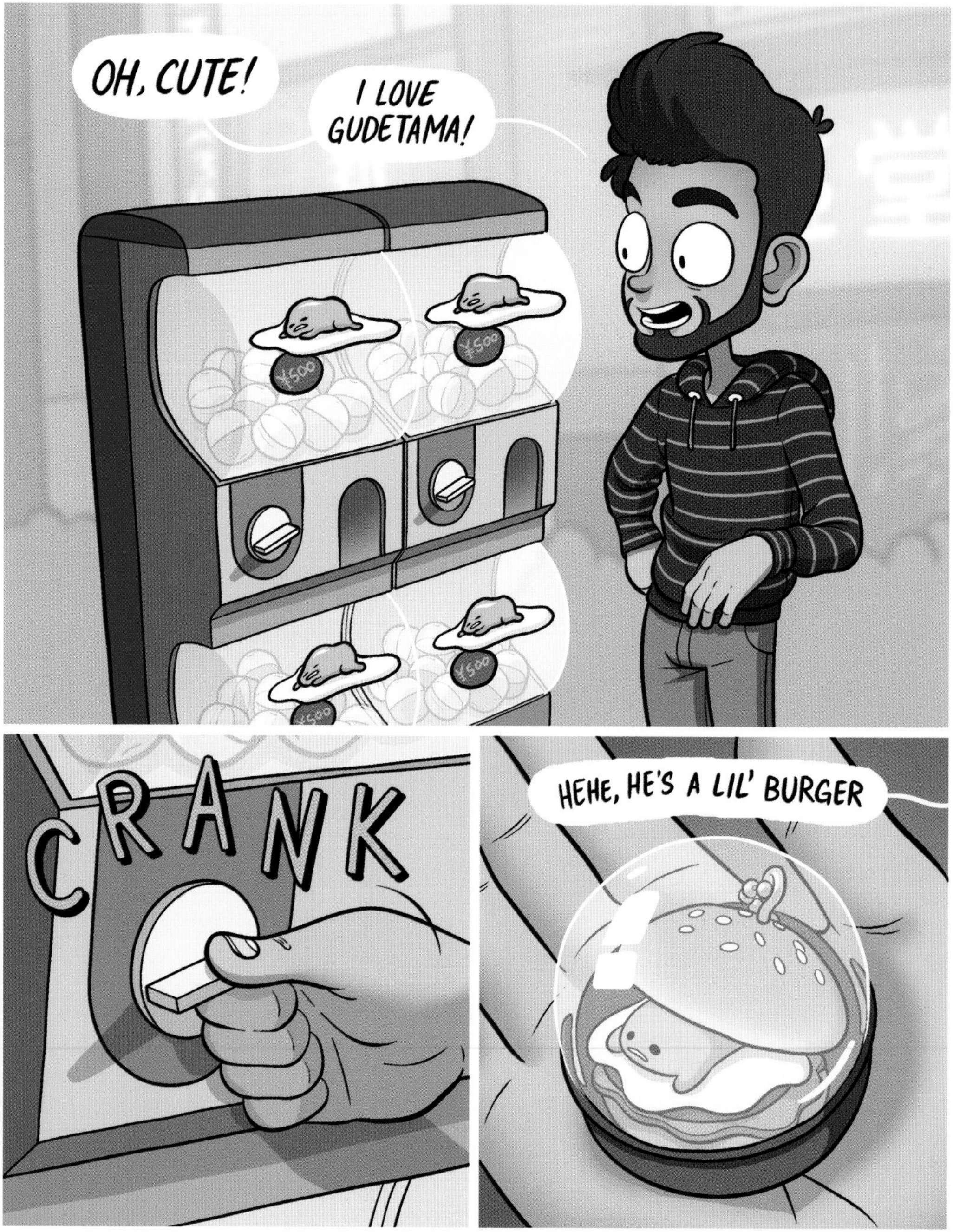
OH, CUTE!
I LOVE GUDETAMA!
¥500
¥500
¥500
¥500
CRANK
HEHE, HE'S A LIL' BURGER

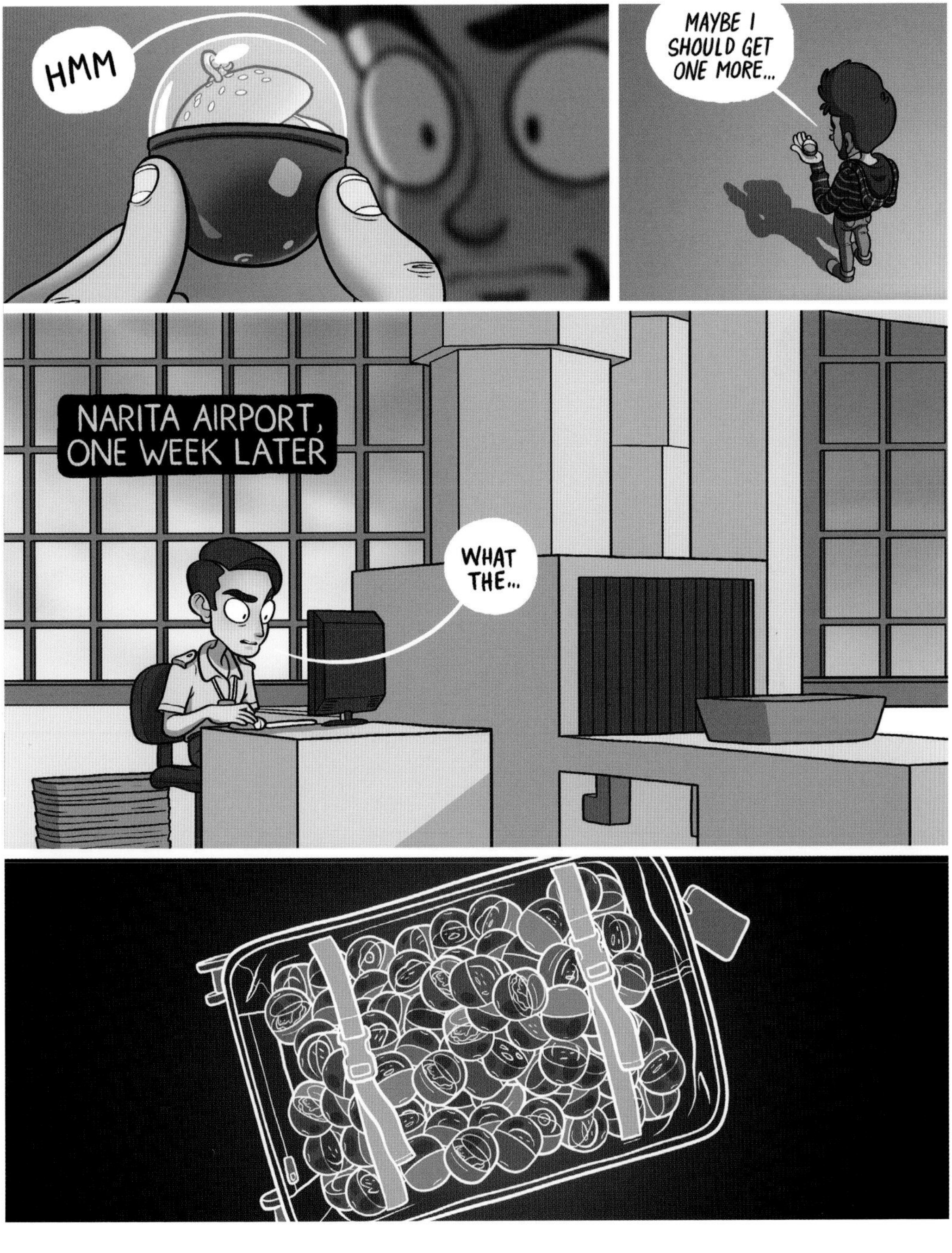
HMM
MAYBE I SHOULD GET ONE MORE...
NARITA AIRPORT, ONE WEEK LATER
WHAT THE...

FOOD I THOUGHT I'D BE EXCITED TO EAT IN JAPAN

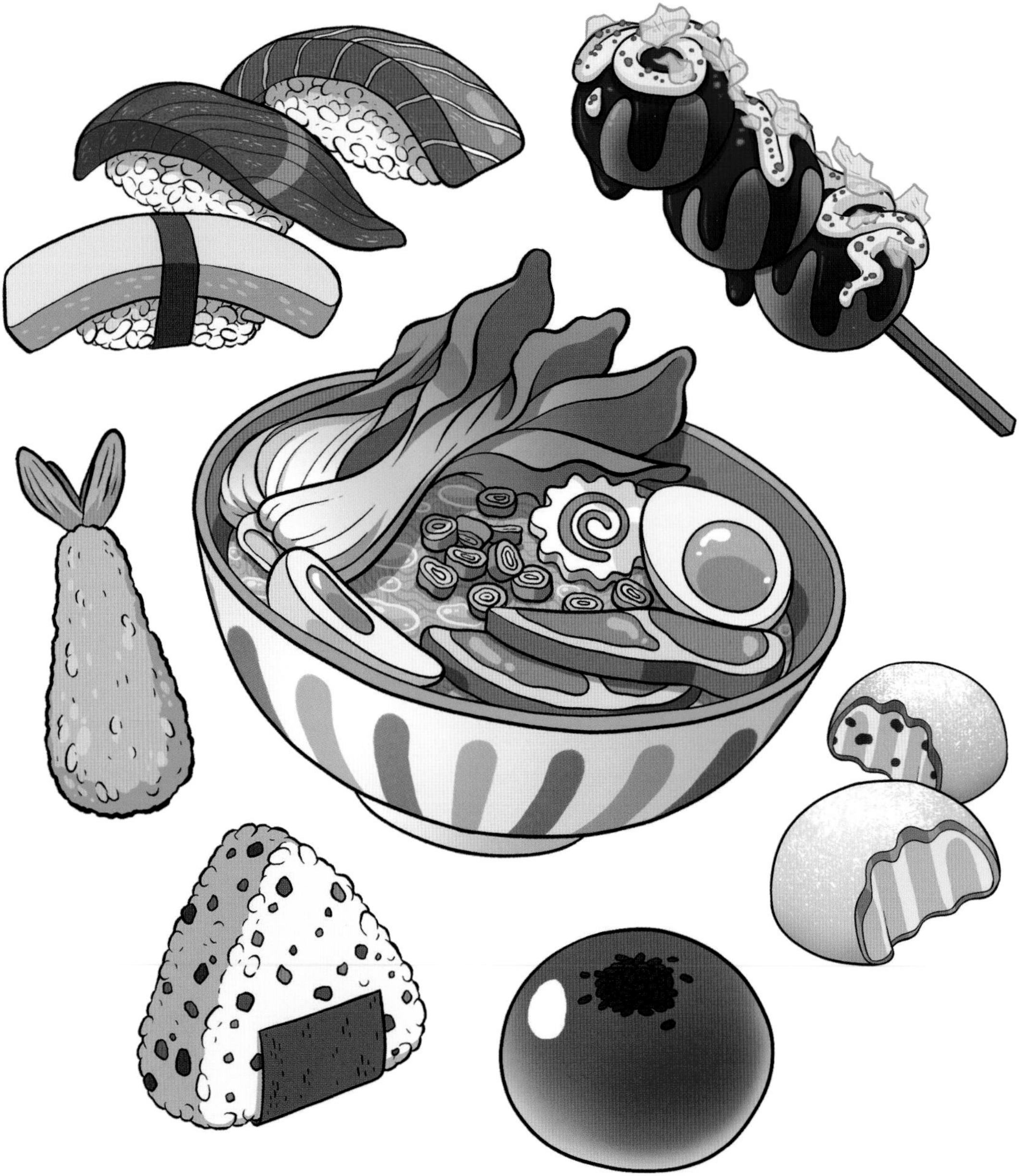

FOOD I WAS ACTUALLY EXCITED TO EAT IN JAPAN

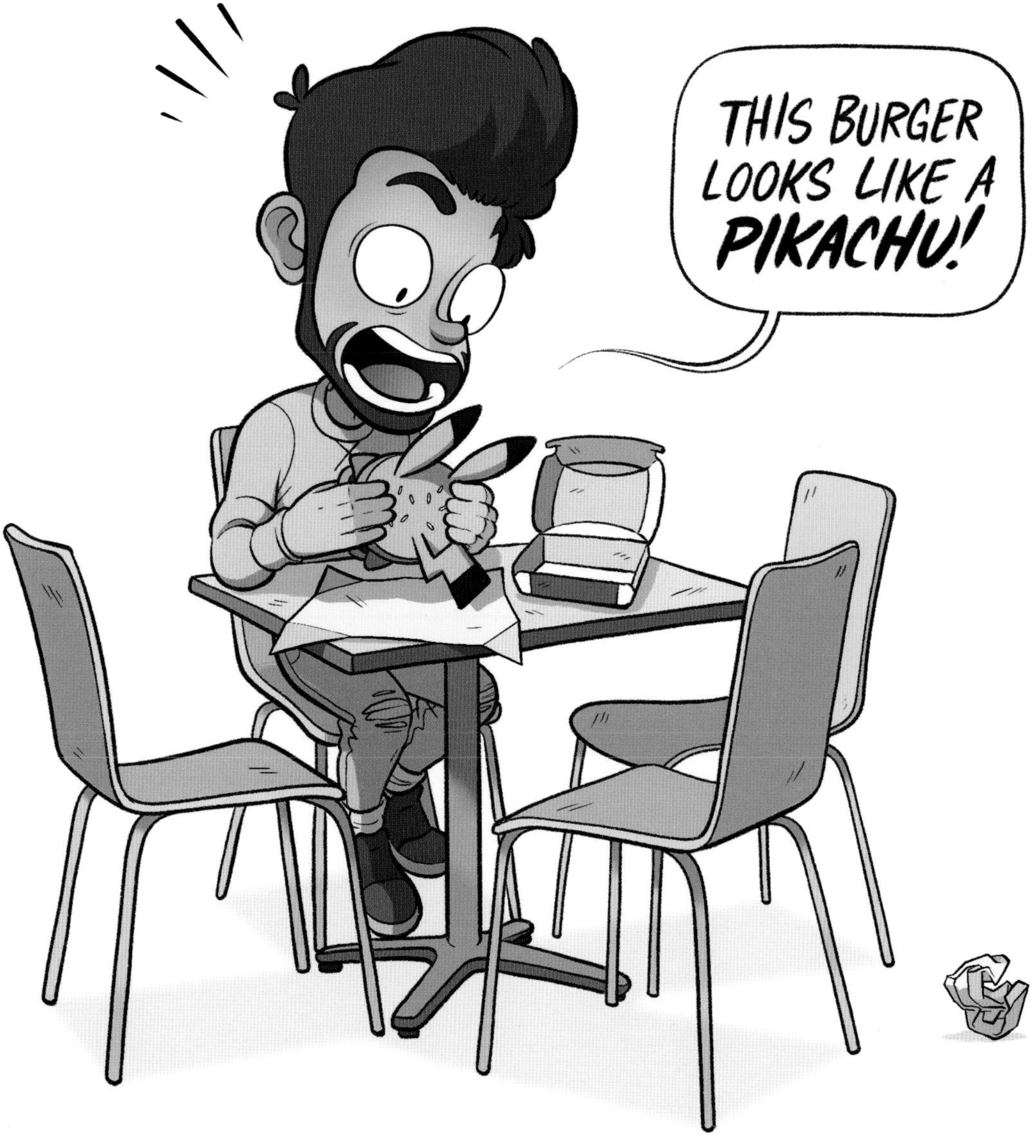
THIS BURGER LOOKS LIKE A PIKACHU!

JUST ONE

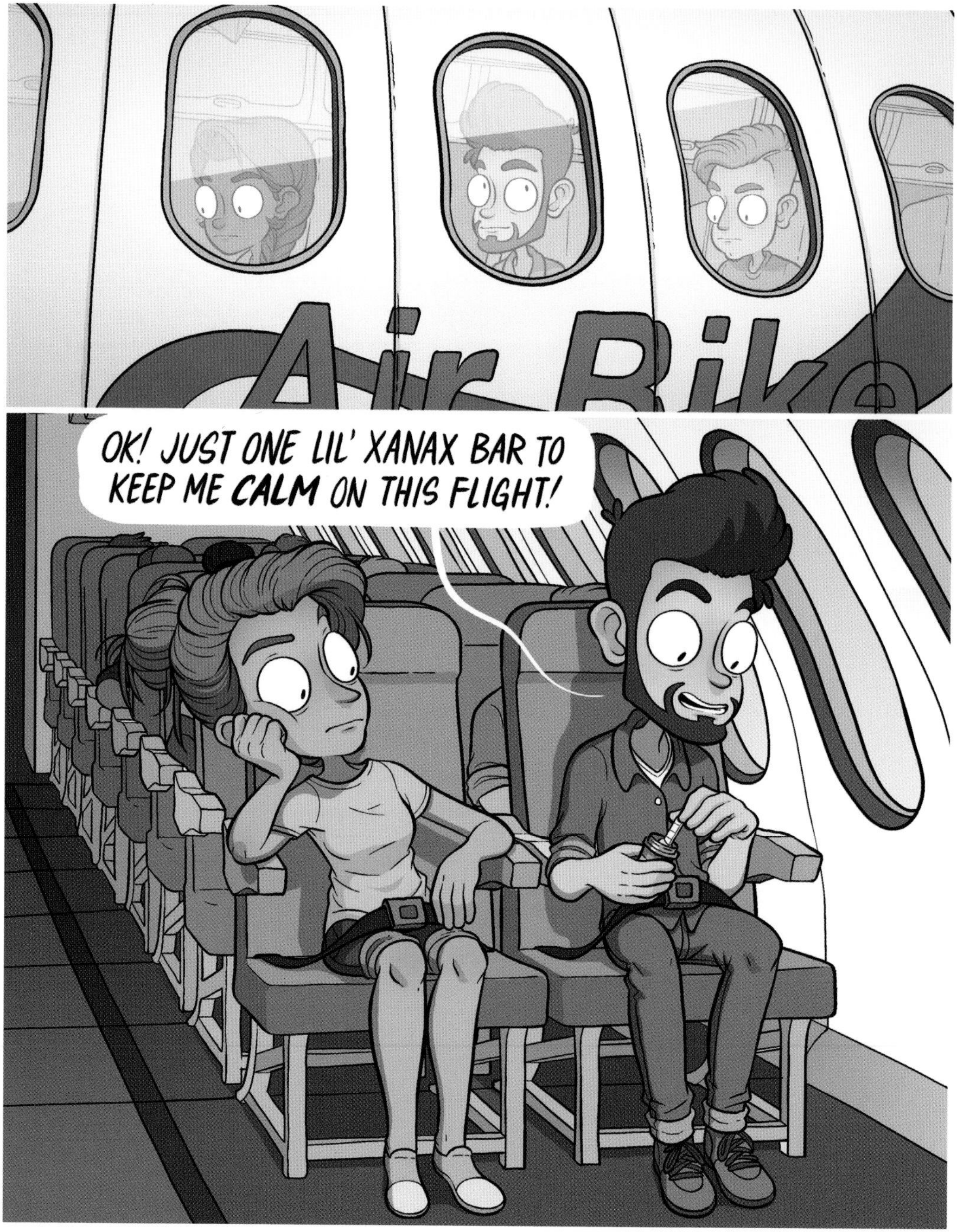

Air Bike
OK! JUST ONE LIL' XANAX BAR TO KEEP ME **CALM** ON THIS FLIGHT!

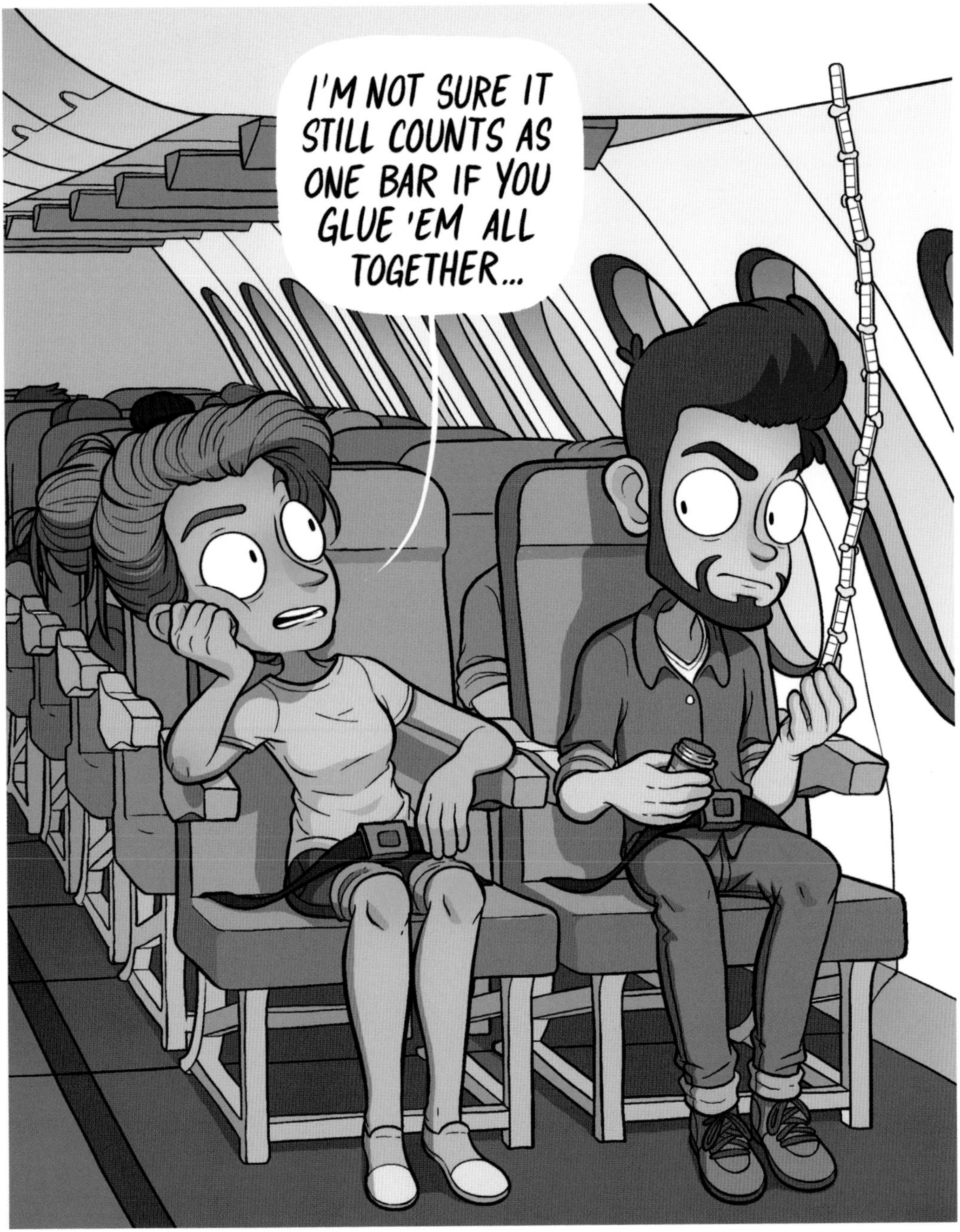
I'M NOT SURE IT STILL COUNTS AS ONE BAR IF YOU GLUE 'EM ALL TOGETHER...

DELICIOUS FOOD

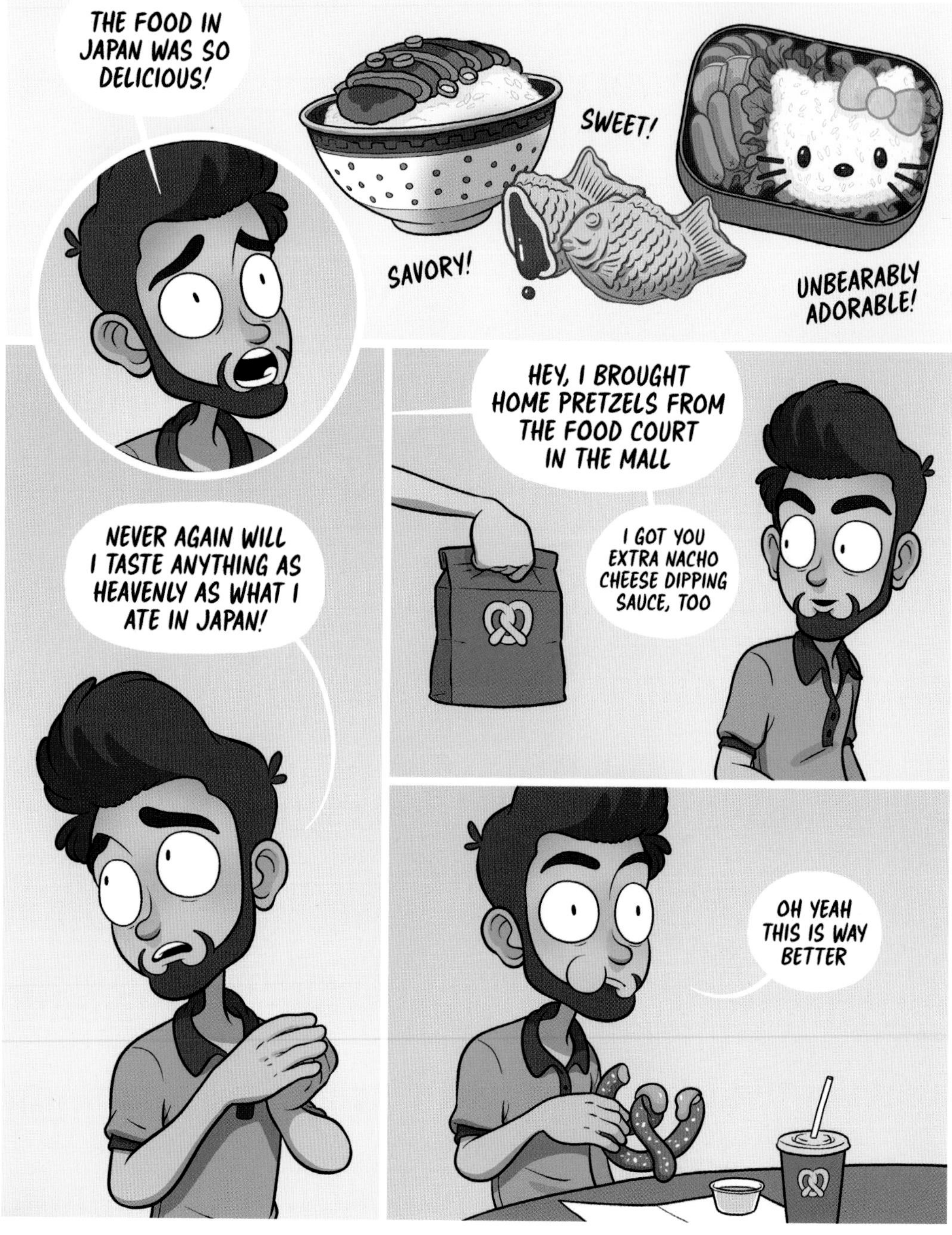
THE FOOD IN JAPAN WAS SO DELICIOUS!
SAVORY!
SWEET!
UNBEARABLY ADORABLE!
NEVER AGAIN WILL I TASTE ANYTHING AS HEAVENLY AS WHAT I ATE IN JAPAN!
HEY, I BROUGHT HOME PRETZELS FROM THE FOOD COURT IN THE MALL
I GOT YOU EXTRA NACHO CHEESE DIPPING SAUCE, TOO
OH YEAH THIS IS WAY BETTER

BEACH BODY

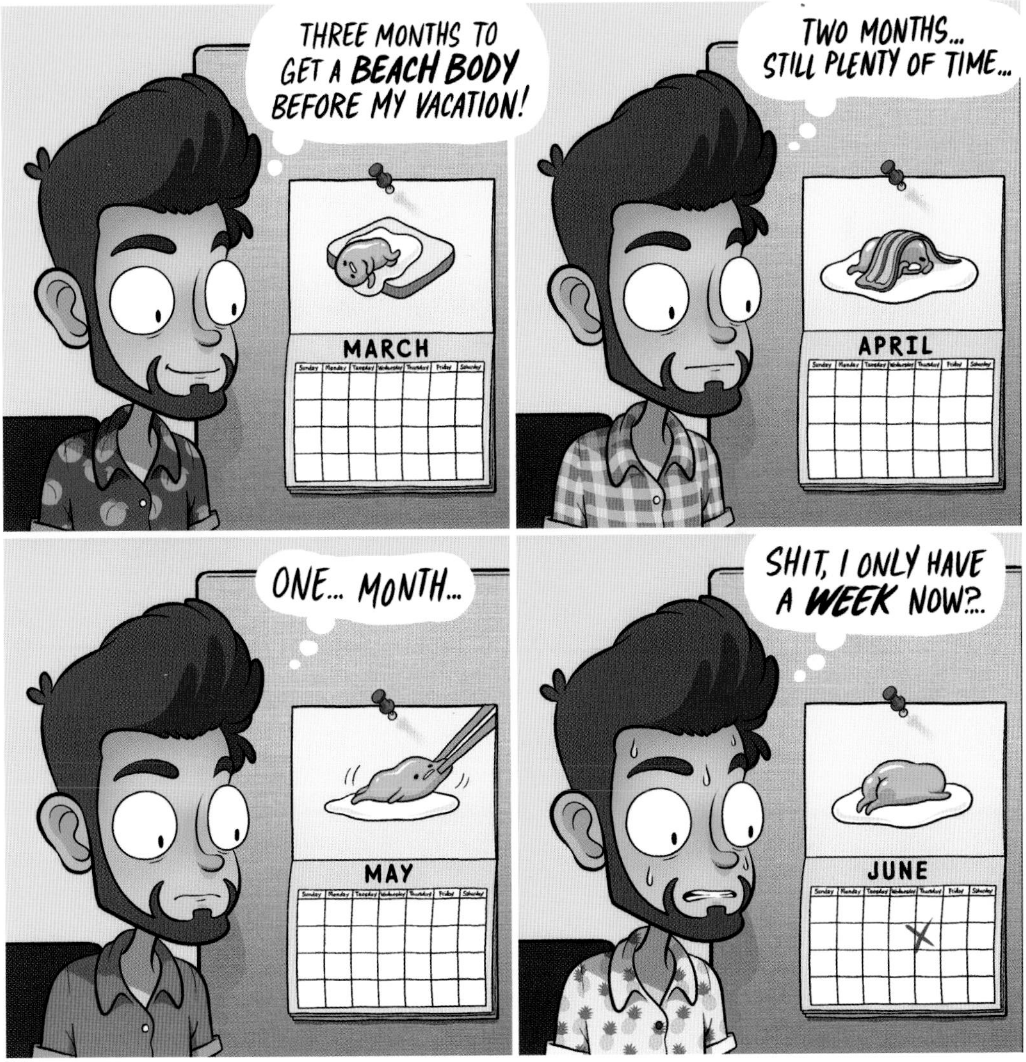
THREE MONTHS TO GET A BEACH BODY BEFORE MY VACATION!
MARCH
TWO MONTHS... STILL PLENTY OF TIME...
APRIL
ONE... MONTH...
MAY
SHIT, I ONLY HAVE A WEEK NOW?...
JUNE

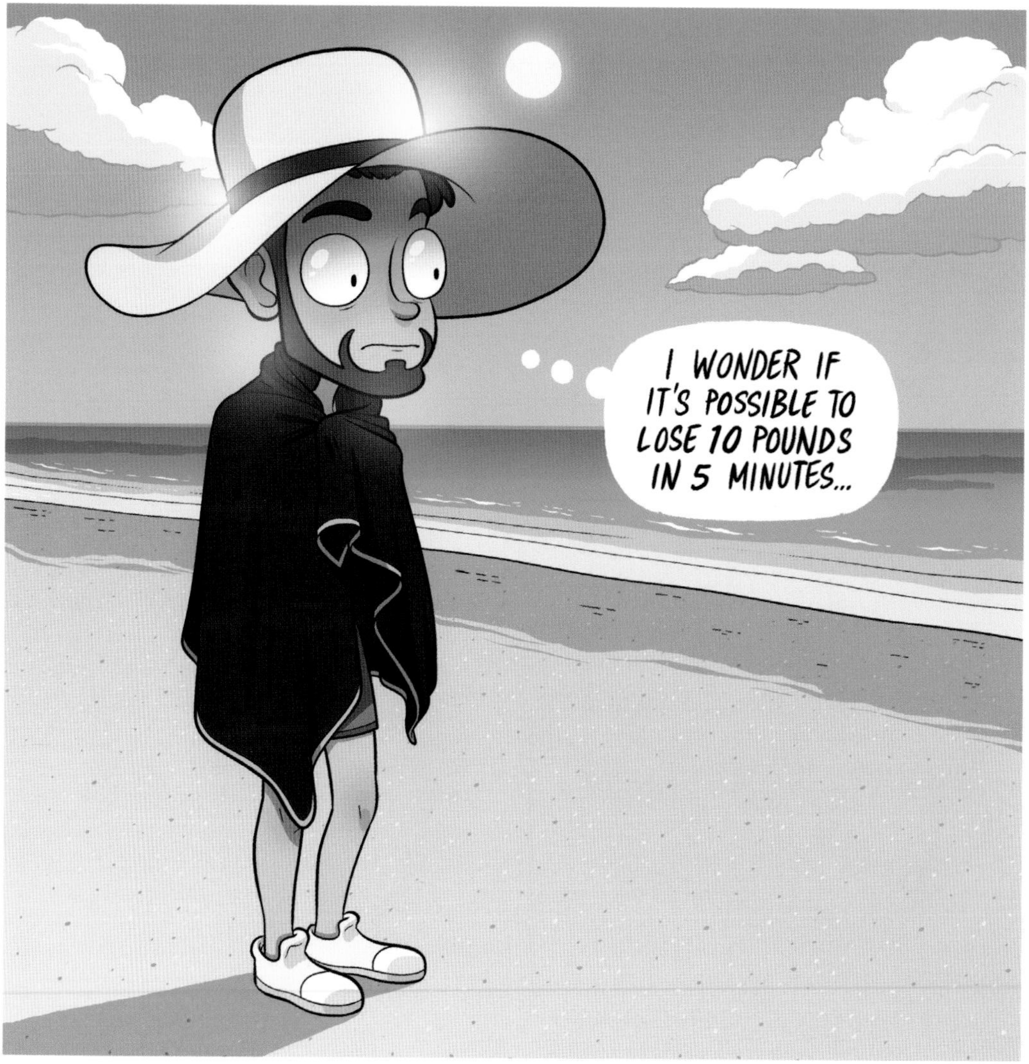
I WONDER IF IT'S POSSIBLE TO LOSE 10 POUNDS IN 5 MINUTES...

CLINGY

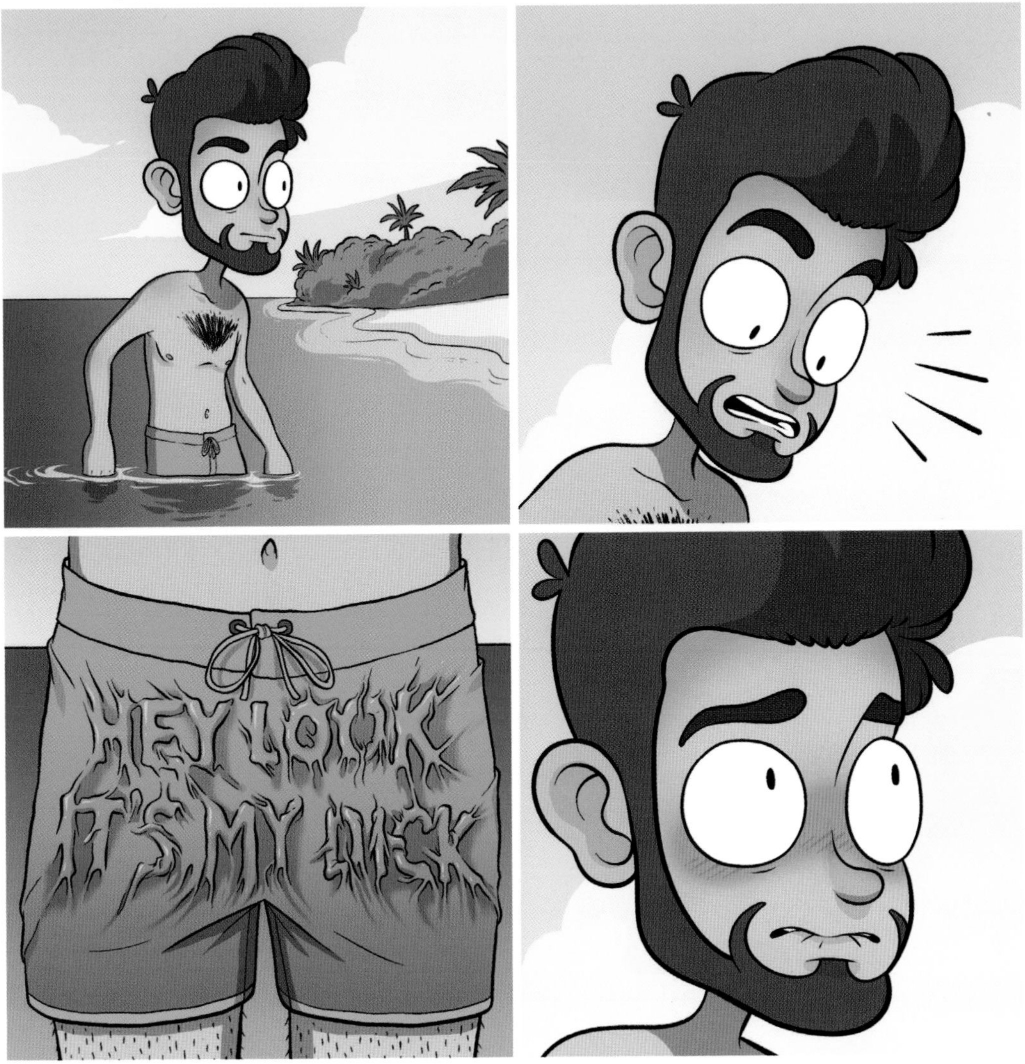
HEY LOOK
IT'S MY DICK

ALWAYS BE PREPARED

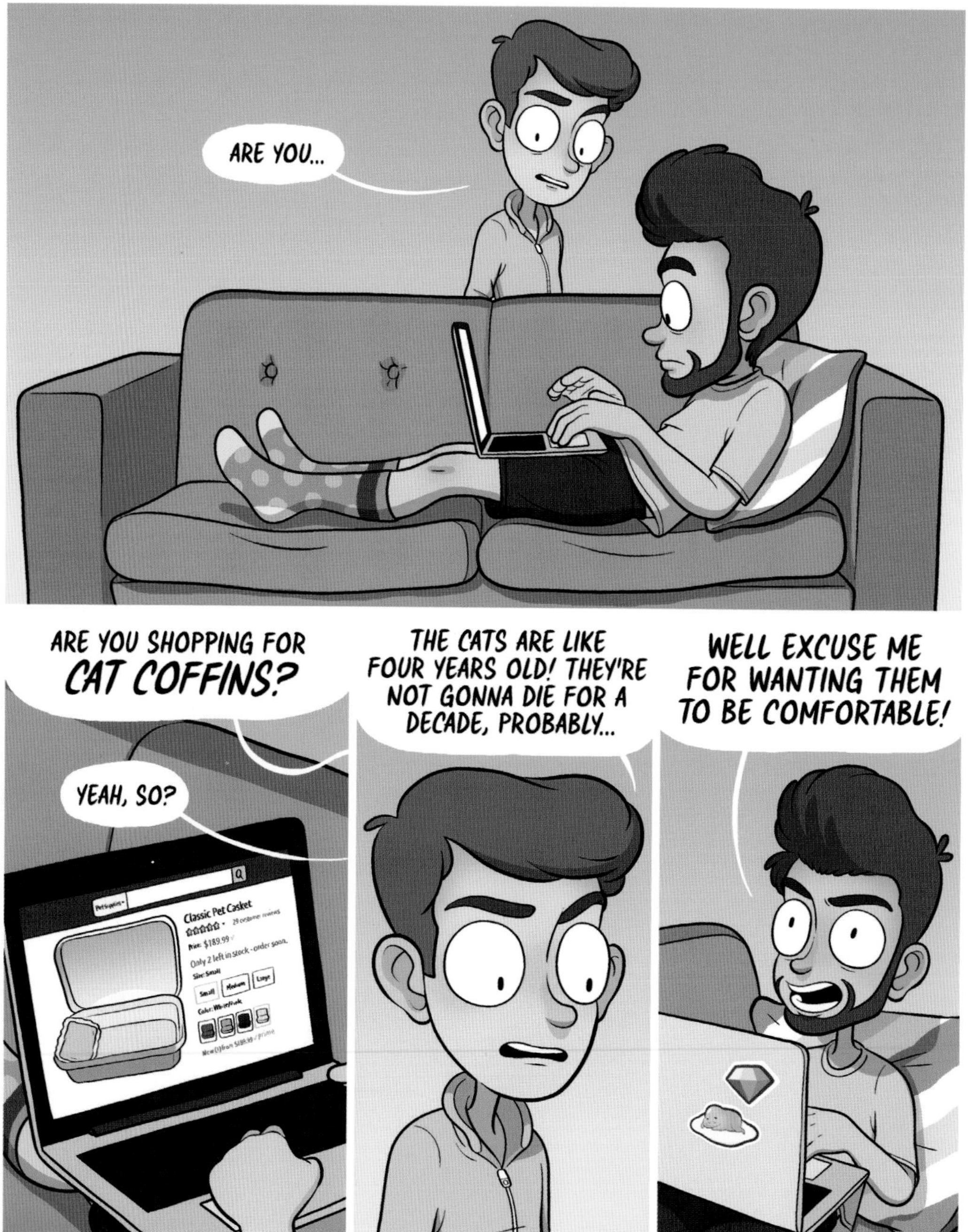

ARE YOU...
ARE YOU SHOPPING FOR CAT COFFINS?
YEAH, SO?
Classic Pet Casket
Price: $189.99
Only 2 left in stock - order soon.
THE CATS ARE LIKE FOUR YEARS OLD! THEY'RE NOT GONNA DIE FOR A DECADE, PROBABLY...
WELL EXCUSE ME FOR WANTING THEM TO BE COMFORTABLE!

WIZARD OF UGH

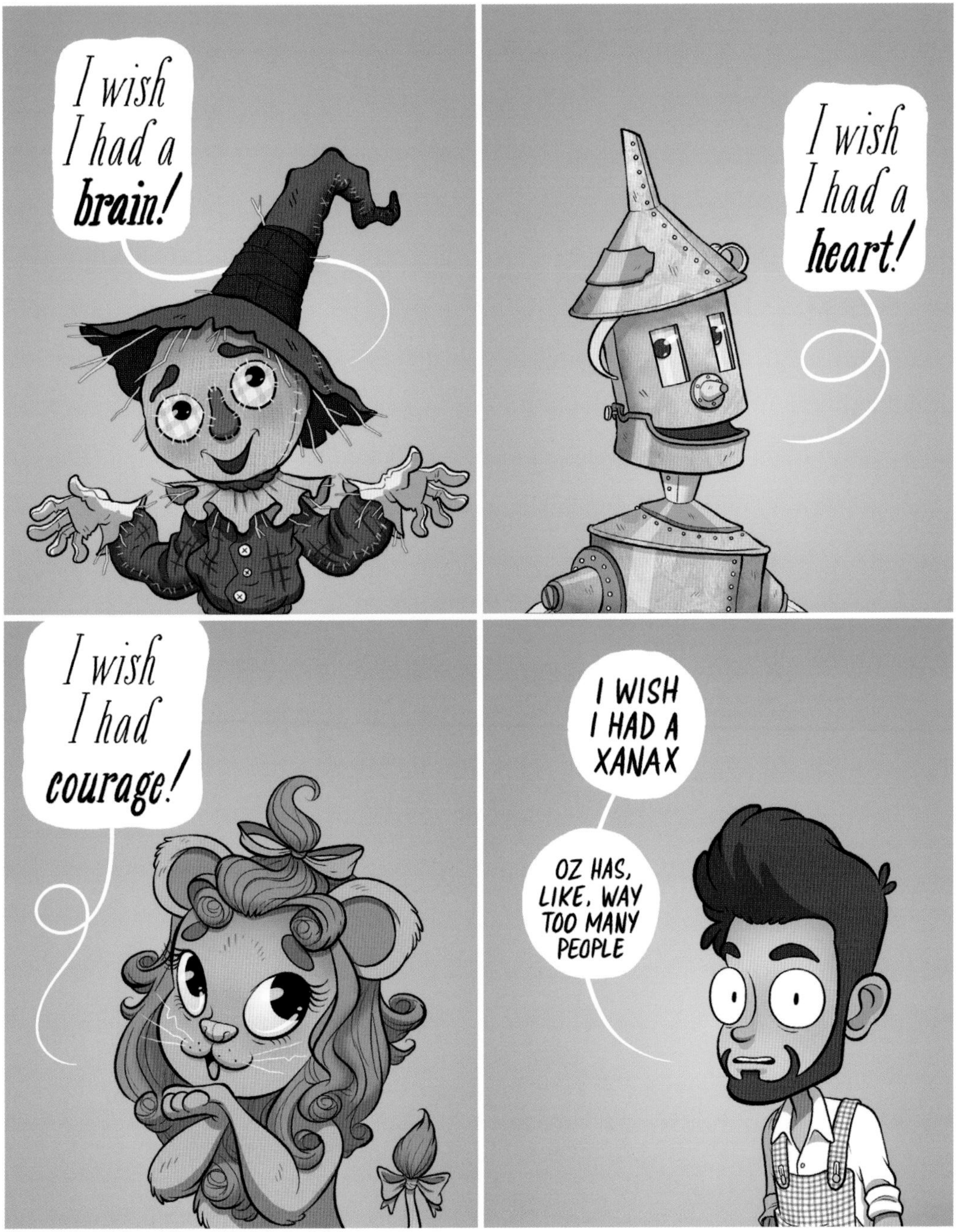

I wish I had a **brain!**
I wish I had a **heart!**
I wish I had **courage!**
I WISH I HAD A XANAX
OZ HAS, LIKE, WAY TOO MANY PEOPLE

PLANT KILLER

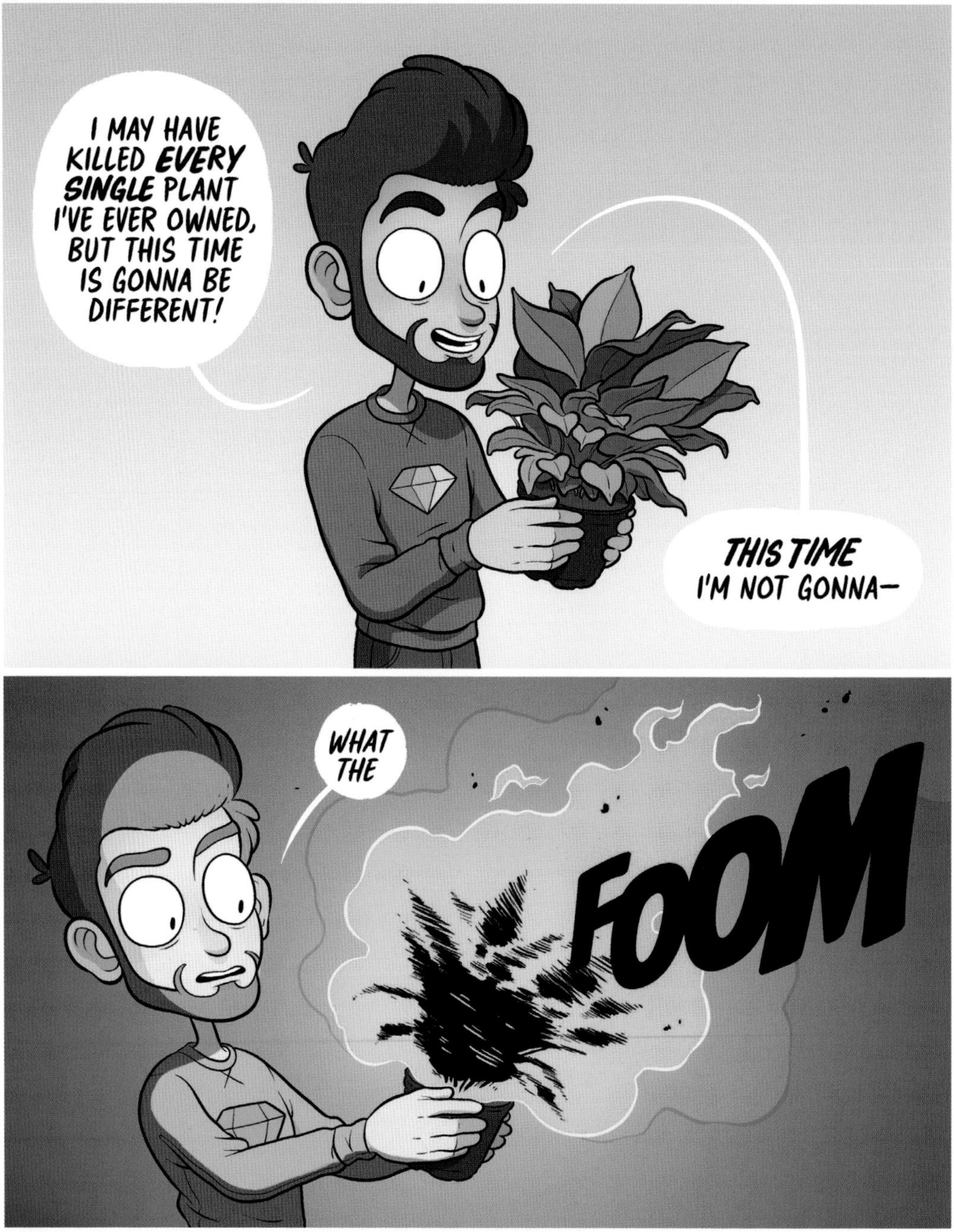
I MAY HAVE KILLED **EVERY SINGLE** PLANT I'VE EVER OWNED, BUT THIS TIME IS GONNA BE DIFFERENT!
THIS TIME I'M NOT GONNA—
WHAT THE
FOOM

CRYSTAL SHOPPE

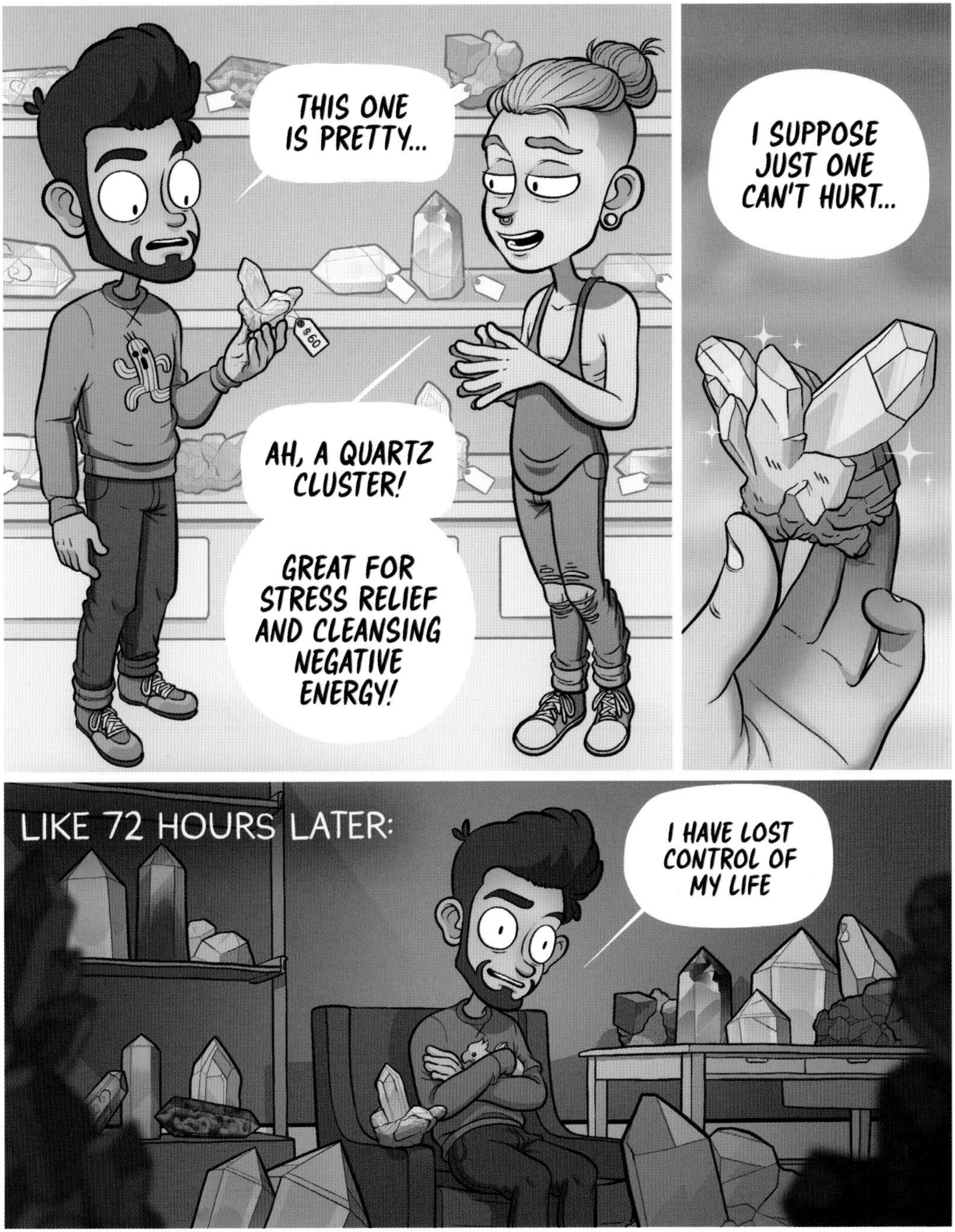
THIS ONE IS PRETTY...
$60
AH, A QUARTZ CLUSTER!
GREAT FOR STRESS RELIEF AND CLEANSING NEGATIVE ENERGY!
I SUPPOSE JUST ONE CAN'T HURT...
LIKE 72 HOURS LATER:
I HAVE LOST CONTROL OF MY LIFE

ADAM'S CRYSTAL

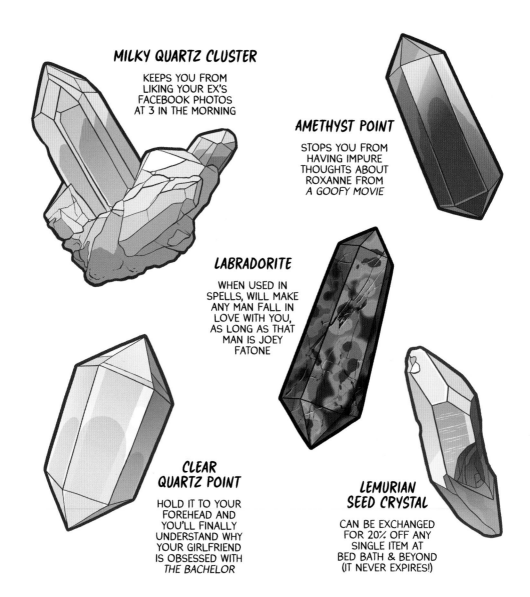

MILKY QUARTZ CLUSTER

KEEPS YOU FROM
LIKING YOUR EX'S
FACEBOOK PHOTOS
AT 3 IN THE MORNING

AMETHYST POINT

STOPS YOU FROM
HAVING IMPURE
THOUGHTS ABOUT
ROXANNE FROM
A GOOFY MOVIE

LABRADORITE

WHEN USED IN
SPELLS, WILL MAKE
ANY MAN FALL IN
LOVE WITH YOU,
AS LONG AS THAT
MAN IS JOEY
FATONE

**CLEAR
QUARTZ POINT**

HOLD IT TO YOUR
FOREHEAD AND
YOU'LL FINALLY
UNDERSTAND WHY
YOUR GIRLFRIEND
IS OBSESSED WITH
THE BACHELOR

**LEMURIAN
SEED CRYSTAL**

CAN BE EXCHANGED
FOR 20% OFF ANY
SINGLE ITEM AT
BED BATH & BEYOND
(IT NEVER EXPIRES!)

STARTER GUIDE

SMOKY QUARTZ CLUSTER

THIS CRYSTAL OPENS YOUR THIRD EYE! ALSO YOUR FOURTH, FIFTH, SIXTH, SEVENTH, AND EIGHTH EYES. YOU'RE A SPIDER NOW.

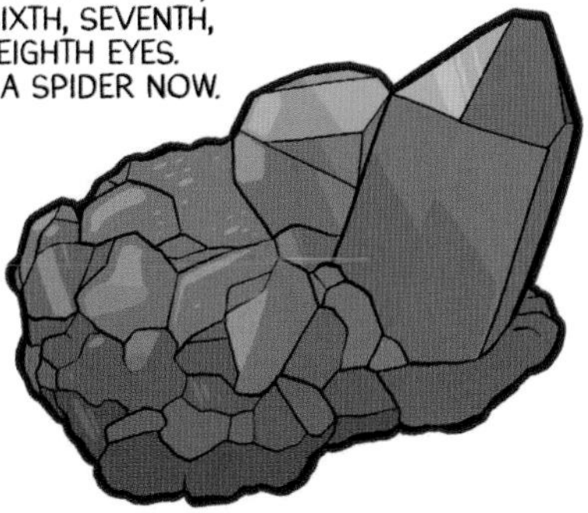

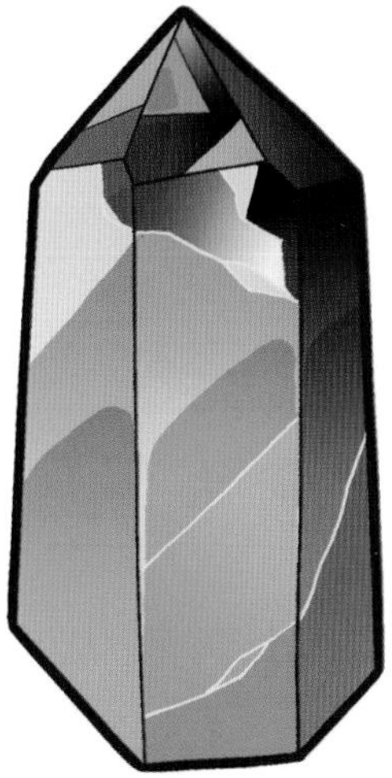

CITRINE TOWER

IF YOU HOLD THIS DURING KARAOKE, IT WON'T MAKE YOU SING BETTER, BUT IT WILL BE SOMETHING SHINY TO DISTRACT YOUR FRIENDS WITH

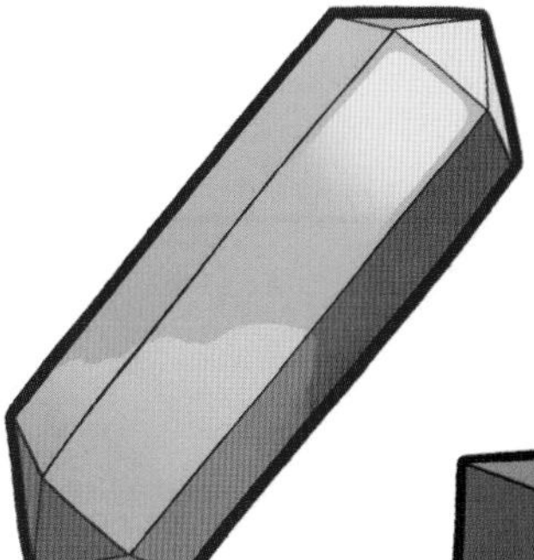

ROSE QUARTZ

THIS IS ACTUALLY JUST A PREGNANCY TEST! PEE ON IT!

PHANTOM QUARTZ

THIS CRYSTAL TRIPLES YOUR CHANCES OF BEING CHOSEN FROM THE AUDIENCE FOR *THE PRICE IS RIGHT* (AIRFARE AND ACCOMMODATIONS NOT INCLUDED)

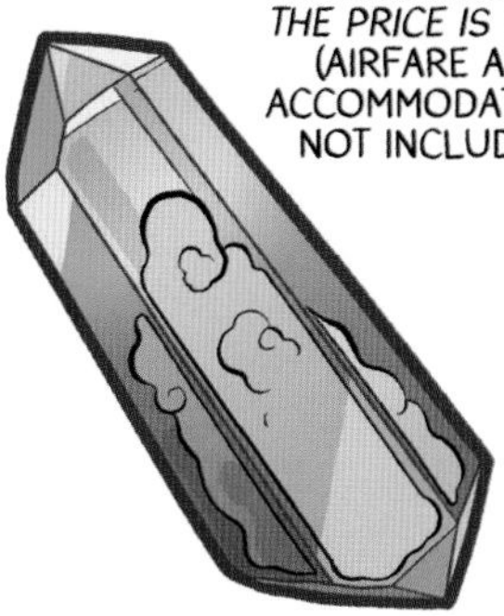

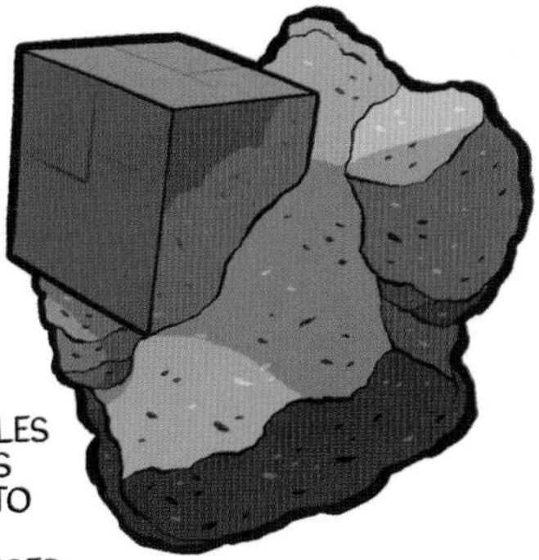

PYRITE CUBE

SUBMERGE THIS IN WATER AND ALL TURTLES IN A 6-MILE RADIUS WILL BE ATTRACTED TO YOU, SEXUALLY. THIS CANNOT BE REVERSED.

SELFIE

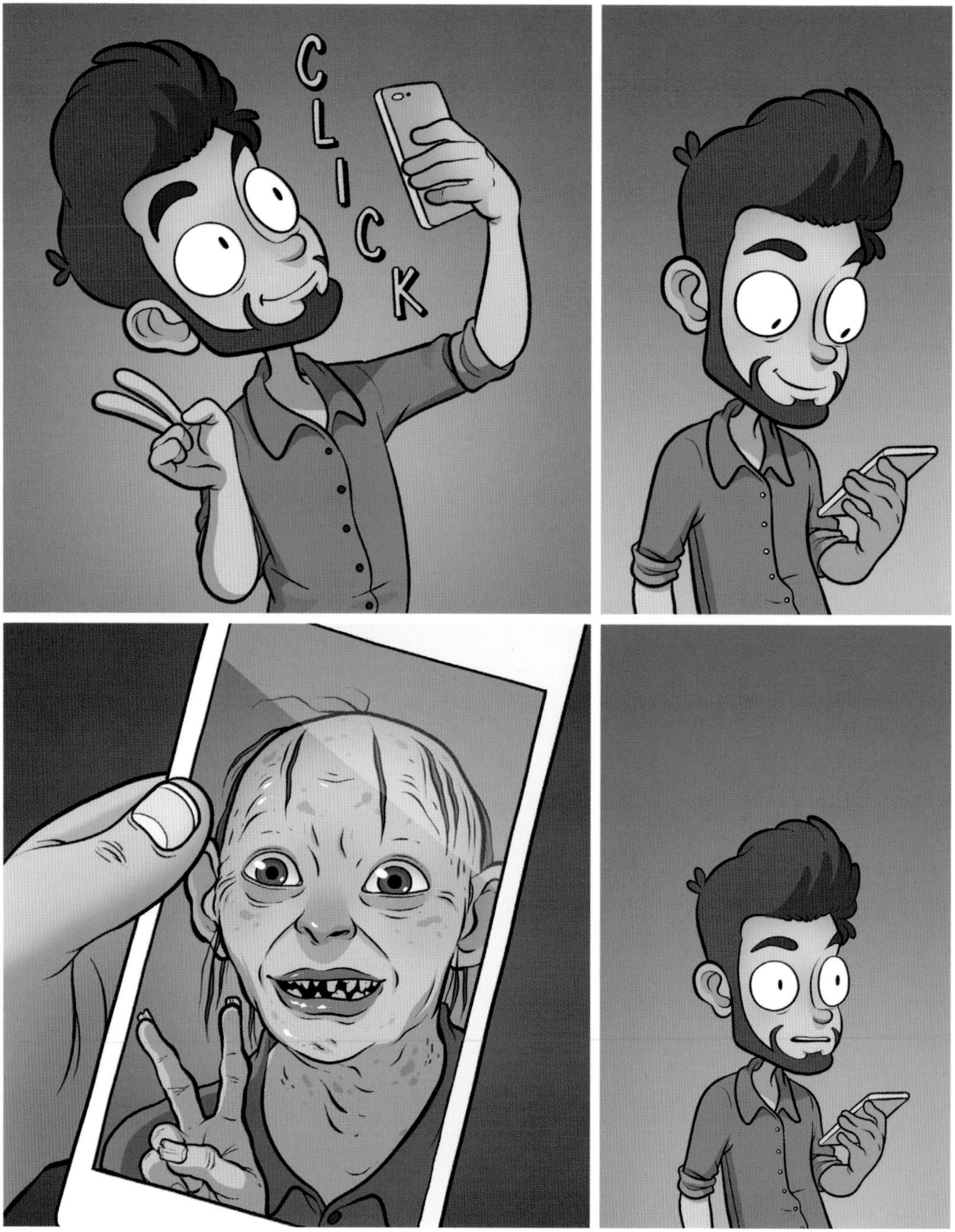
CLICK

QUICK NAP

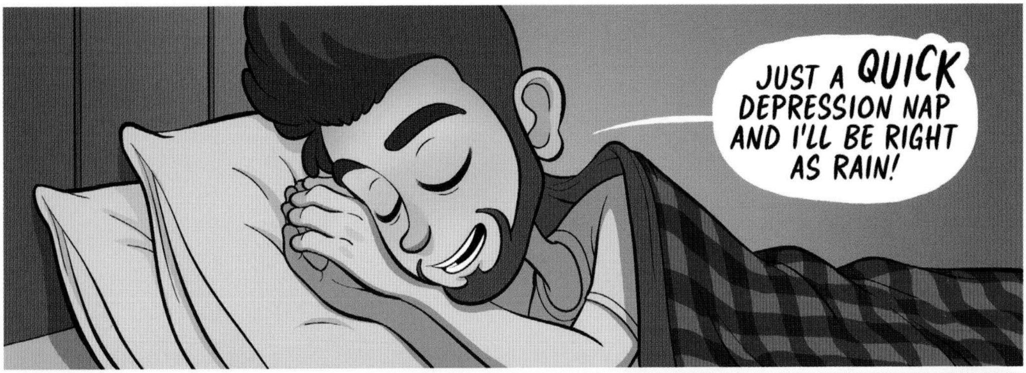
JUST A QUICK DEPRESSION NAP AND I'LL BE RIGHT AS RAIN!

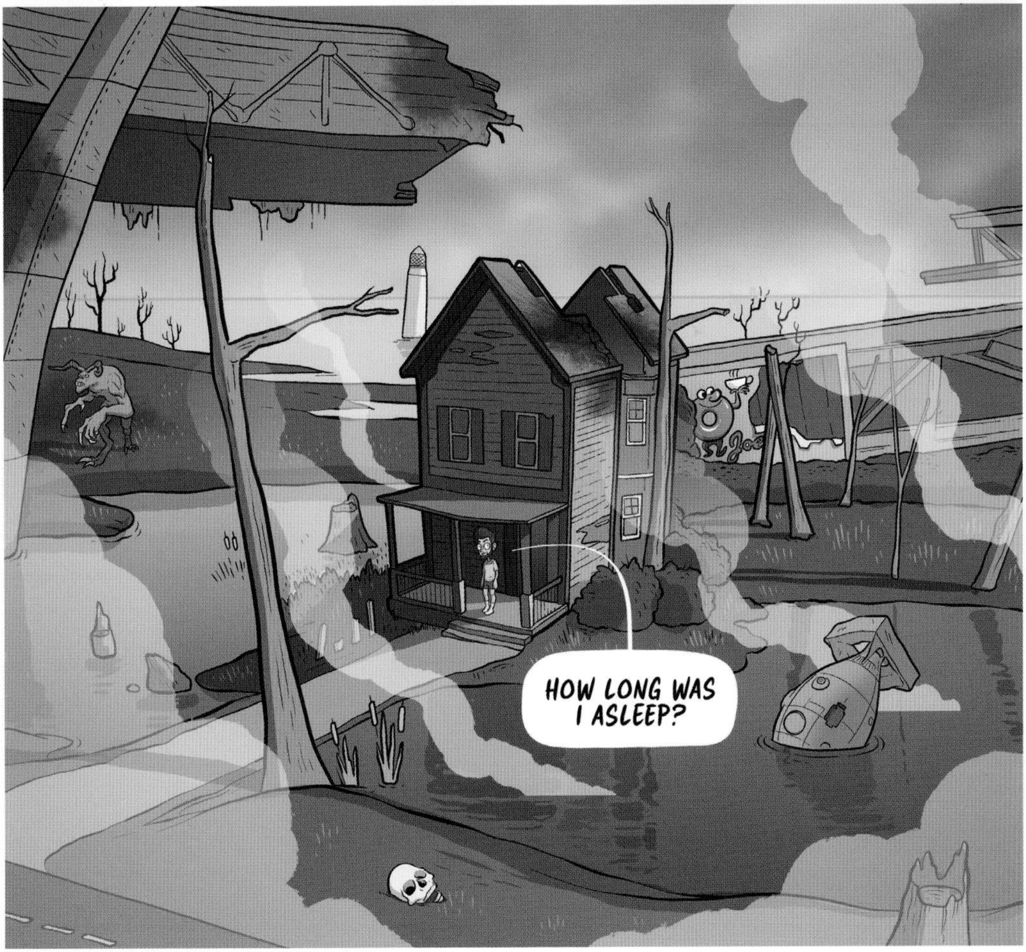
HOW LONG WAS I ASLEEP?

DEPRESSION

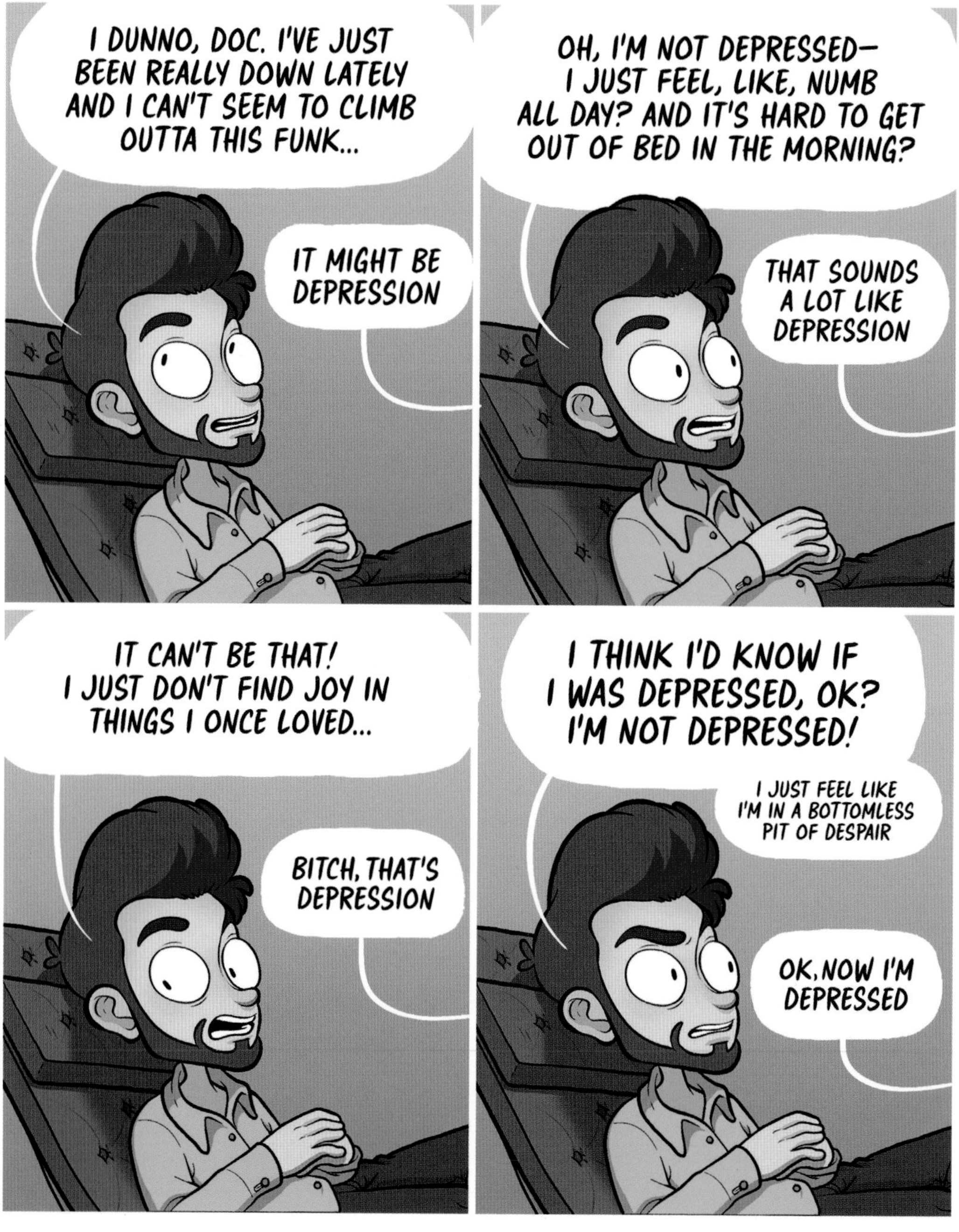
I DUNNO, DOC. I'VE JUST BEEN REALLY DOWN LATELY AND I CAN'T SEEM TO CLIMB OUTTA THIS FUNK...
IT MIGHT BE DEPRESSION
OH, I'M NOT DEPRESSED— I JUST FEEL, LIKE, NUMB ALL DAY? AND IT'S HARD TO GET OUT OF BED IN THE MORNING?
THAT SOUNDS A LOT LIKE DEPRESSION
IT CAN'T BE THAT! I JUST DON'T FIND JOY IN THINGS I ONCE LOVED...
BITCH, THAT'S DEPRESSION
I THINK I'D KNOW IF I WAS DEPRESSED, OK? I'M NOT DEPRESSED!
I JUST FEEL LIKE I'M IN A BOTTOMLESS PIT OF DESPAIR
OK, NOW I'M DEPRESSED

AMERICA'S NEXT TOP THERAPIST

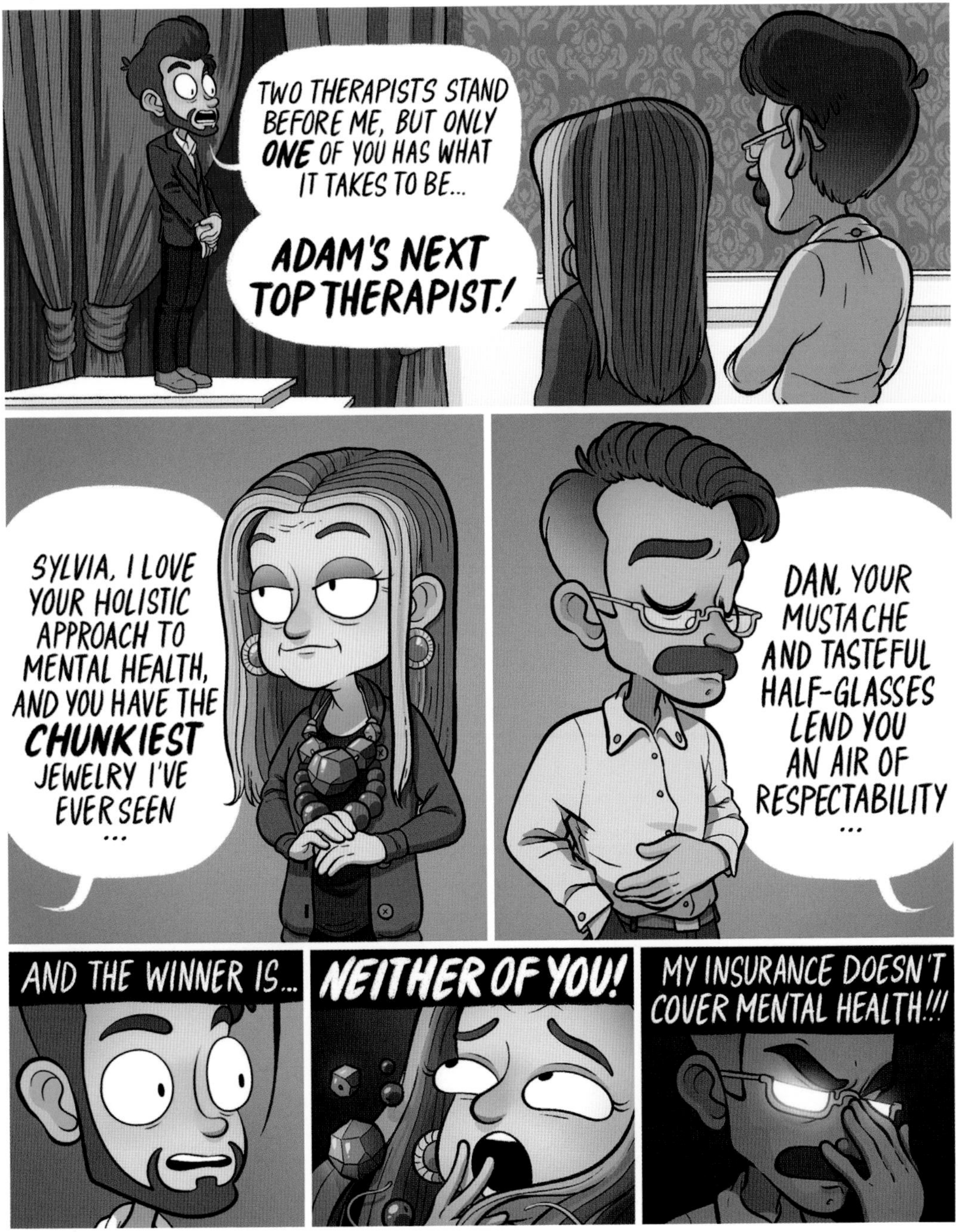
TWO THERAPISTS STAND BEFORE ME, BUT ONLY ONE OF YOU HAS WHAT IT TAKES TO BE...
ADAM'S NEXT TOP THERAPIST!
SYLVIA, I LOVE YOUR HOLISTIC APPROACH TO MENTAL HEALTH, AND YOU HAVE THE CHUNKIEST JEWELRY I'VE EVER SEEN ...
DAN, YOUR MUSTACHE AND TASTEFUL HALF-GLASSES LEND YOU AN AIR OF RESPECTABILITY ...
AND THE WINNER IS...
NEITHER OF YOU!
MY INSURANCE DOESN'T COVER MENTAL HEALTH!!!

HUSH, BABY

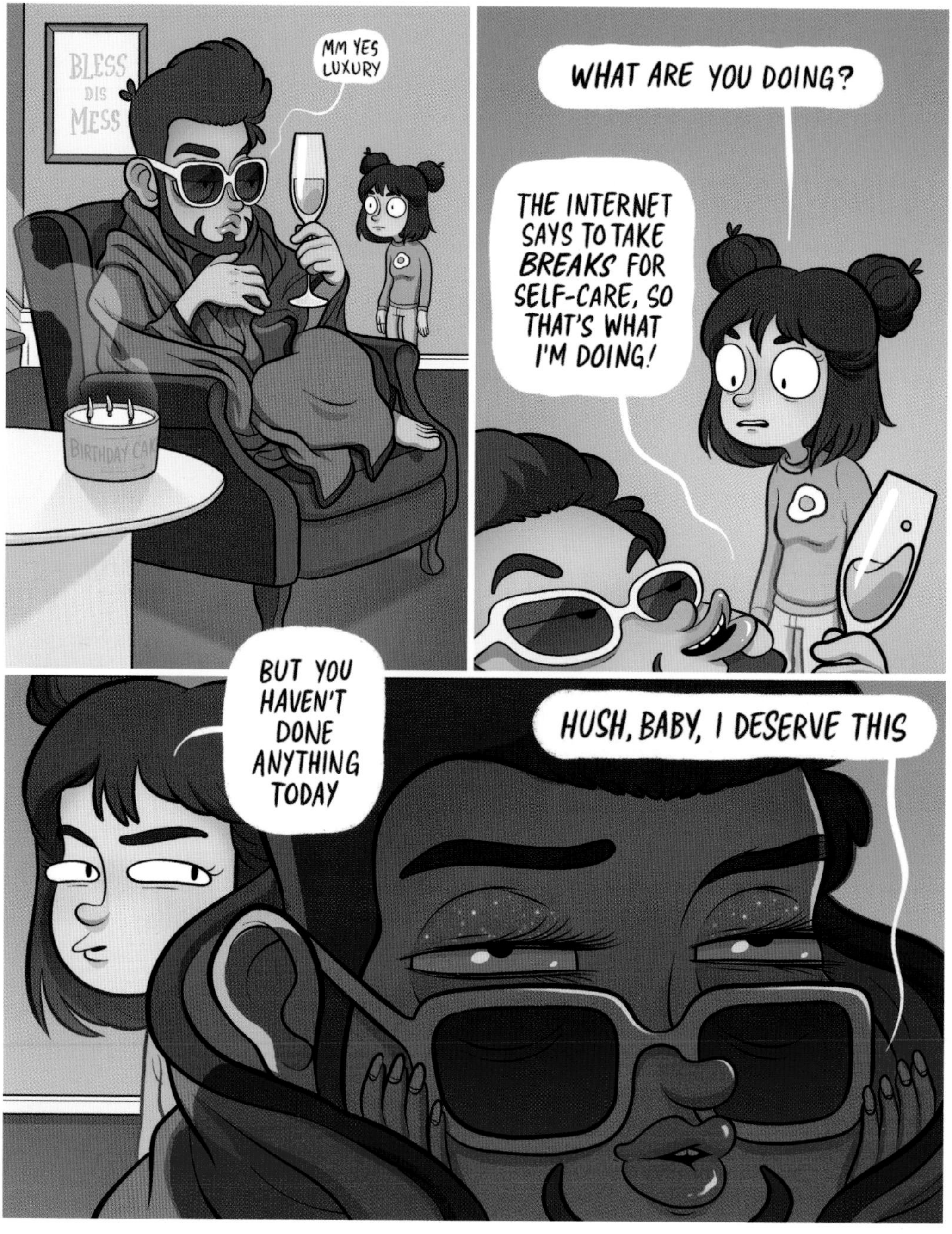
BLESS DIS MESS
MM YES LUXURY
BIRTHDAY CAK
WHAT ARE YOU DOING?
THE INTERNET SAYS TO TAKE *BREAKS* FOR SELF-CARE, SO THAT'S WHAT I'M DOING!
BUT YOU HAVEN'T DONE ANYTHING TODAY
HUSH, BABY, I DESERVE THIS

LIFE HACK

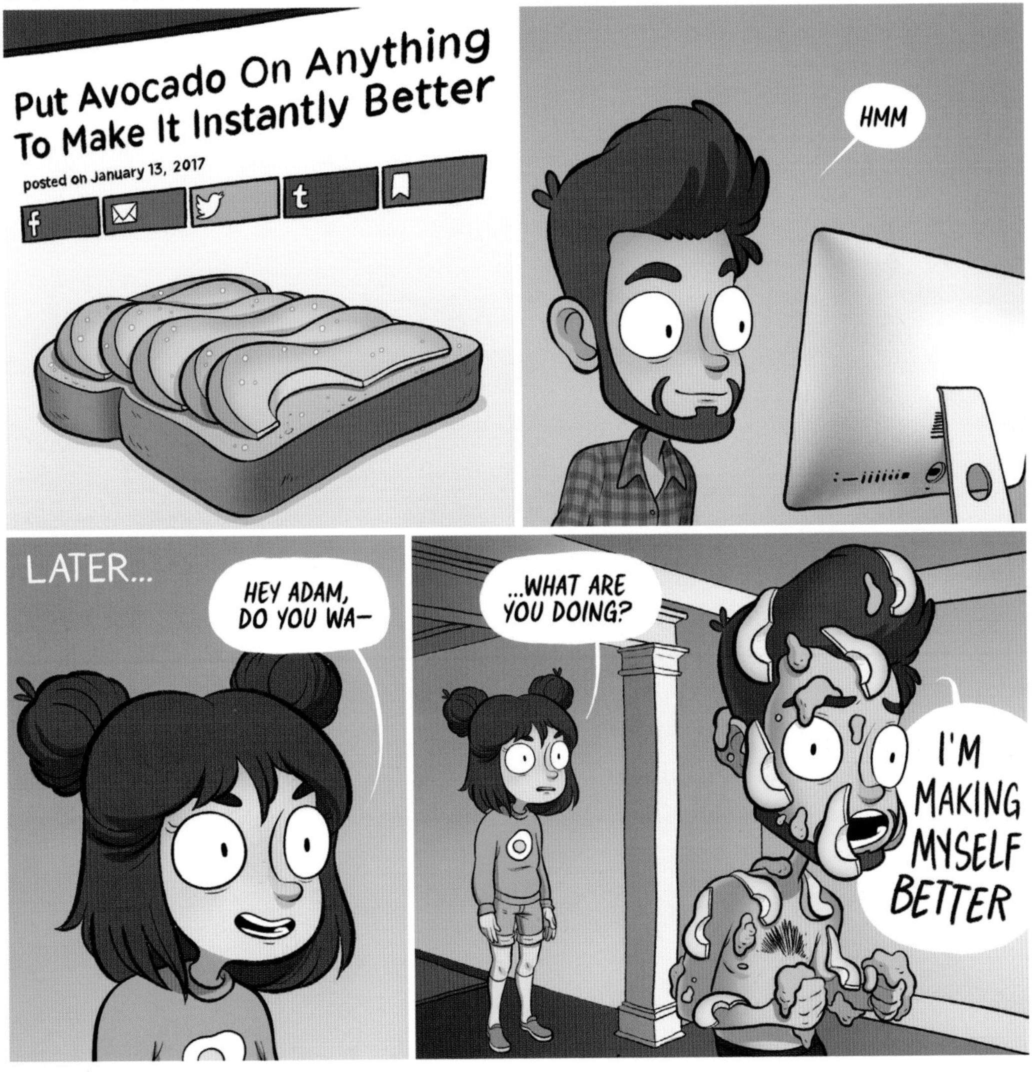

Put Avocado On Anything To Make It Instantly Better
posted on January 13, 2017
HMM
LATER...
HEY ADAM, DO YOU WA-
...WHAT ARE YOU DOING?
I'M MAKING MYSELF BETTER

PERFECT FIT

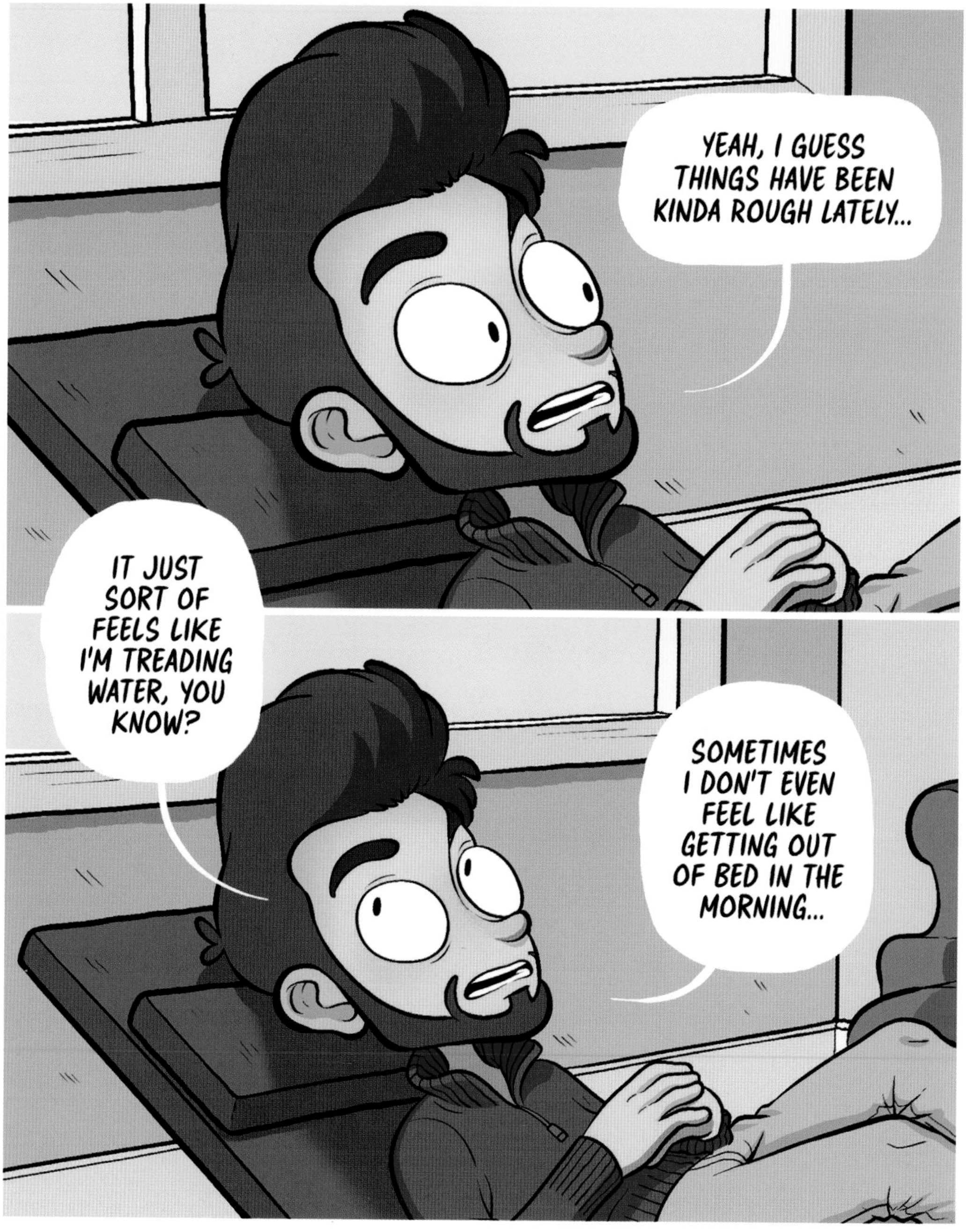

YEAH, I GUESS THINGS HAVE BEEN KINDA ROUGH LATELY...
IT JUST SORT OF FEELS LIKE I'M TREADING WATER, YOU KNOW?
SOMETIMES I DON'T EVEN FEEL LIKE GETTING OUT OF BED IN THE MORNING...

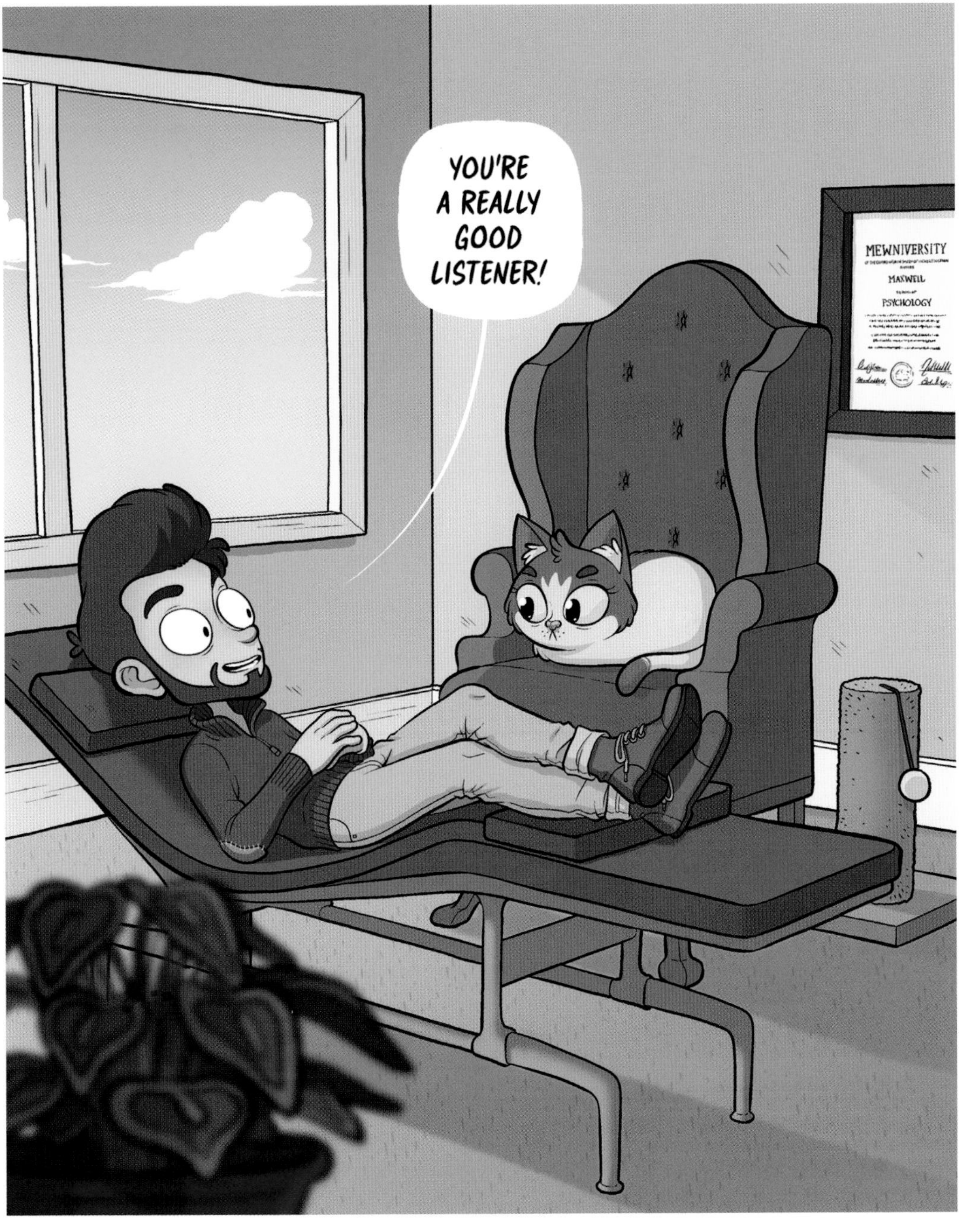
YOU'RE A REALLY GOOD LISTENER!
MEWNIVERSITY
MAXWELL
PSYCHOLOGY

PERSONALITY QUIZ

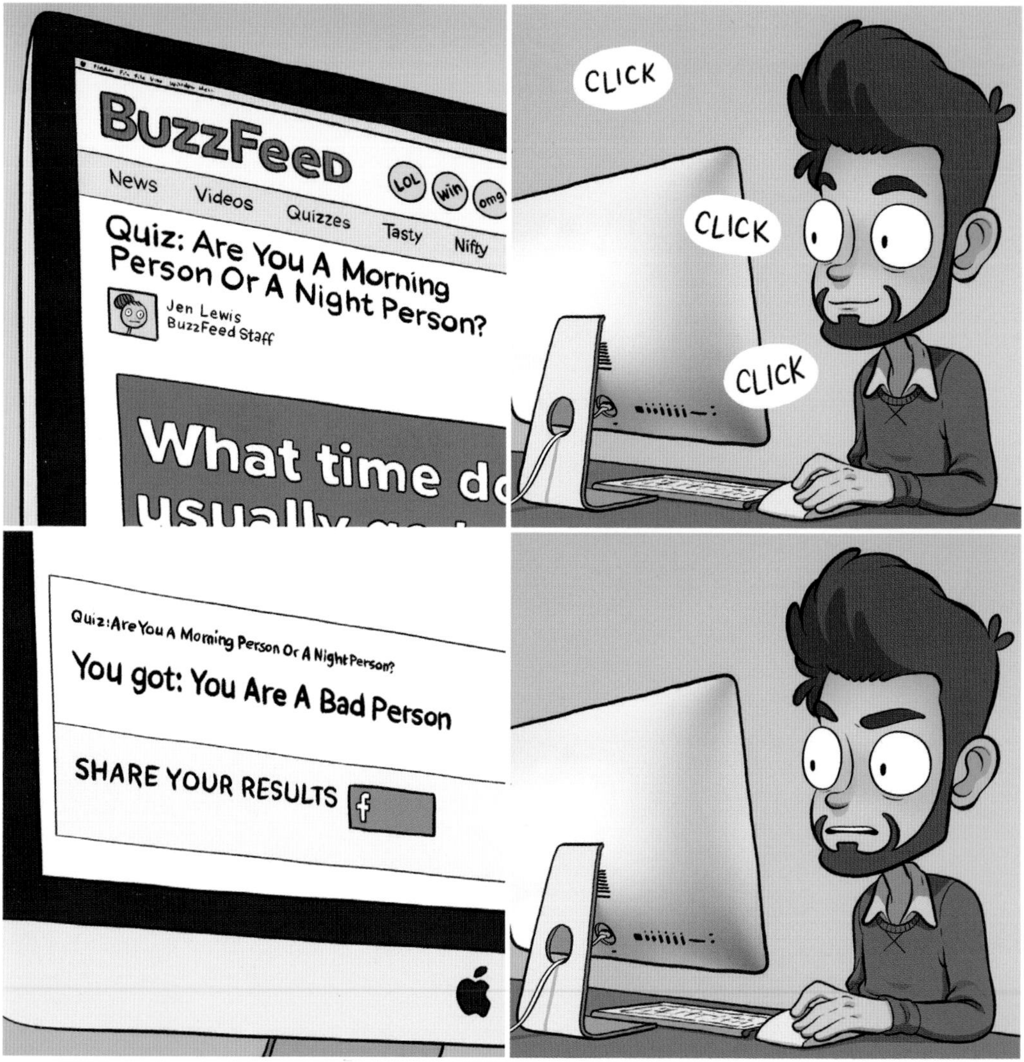
BuzzFeed
News
Videos
Quizzes
Tasty
Nifty
LOL
win
omg
Quiz: Are You A Morning Person Or A Night Person?
Jen Lewis
BuzzFeed Staff
What time d
CLICK
CLICK
CLICK
Quiz: Are You A Morning Person Or A Night Person?
You got: You Are A Bad Person
SHARE YOUR RESULTS
f

NEW FRIEND

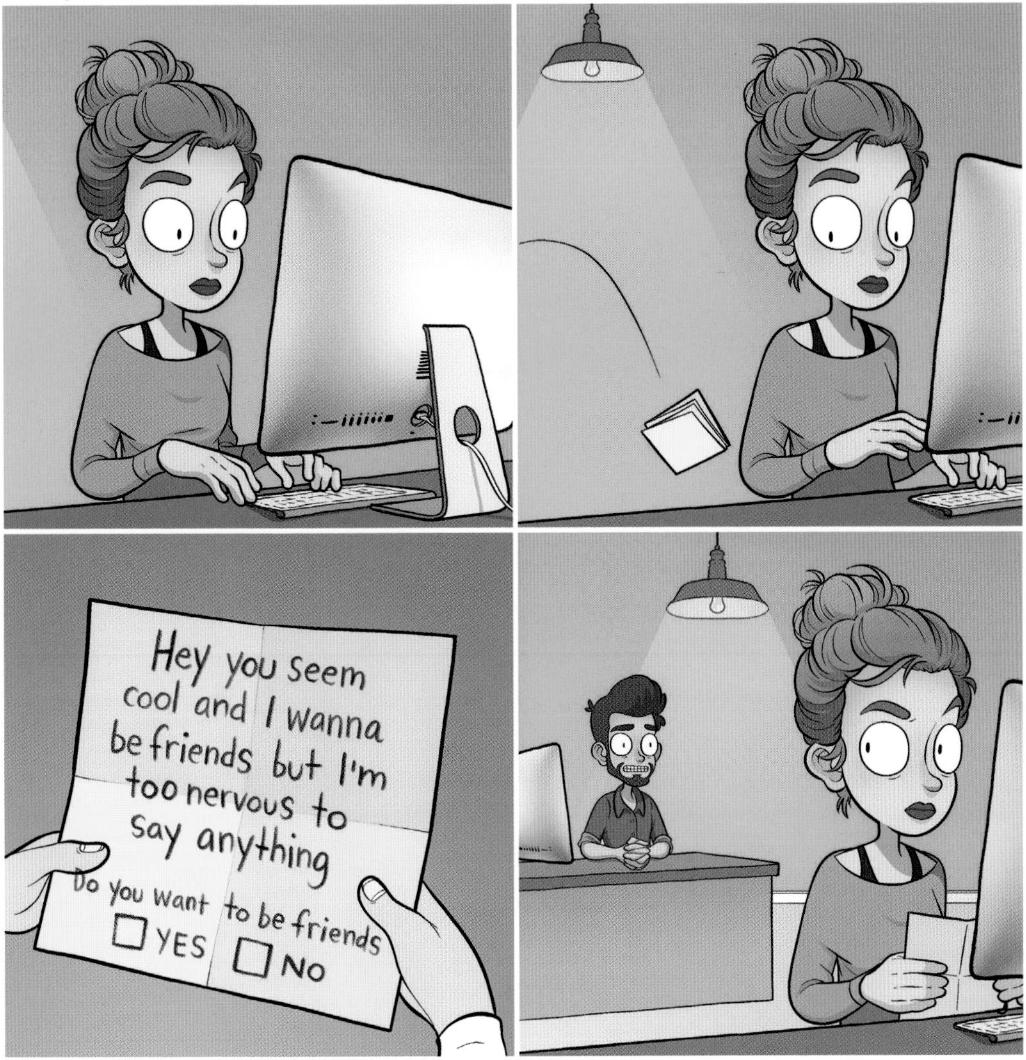
Hey you seem cool and I wanna be friends but I'm too nervous to say anything
Do you want to be friends
YES
NO

SMALL TALK

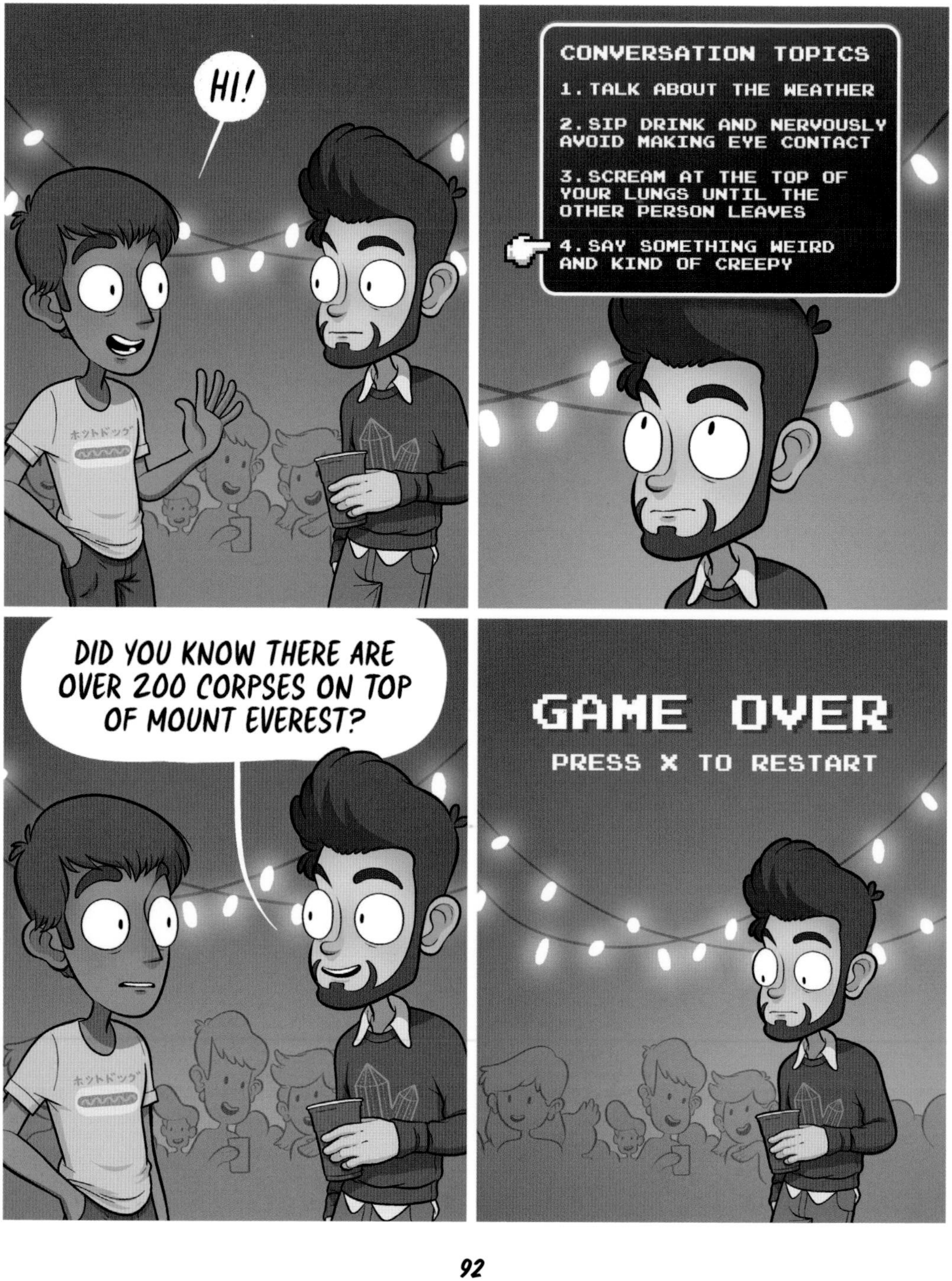

HI!
ホットドッグ
CONVERSATION TOPICS
1. TALK ABOUT THE WEATHER
2. SIP DRINK AND NERVOUSLY AVOID MAKING EYE CONTACT
3. SCREAM AT THE TOP OF YOUR LUNGS UNTIL THE OTHER PERSON LEAVES
4. SAY SOMETHING WEIRD AND KIND OF CREEPY
DID YOU KNOW THERE ARE OVER 200 CORPSES ON TOP OF MOUNT EVEREST?
GAME OVER
PRESS X TO RESTART

MAGIC 8-BALL

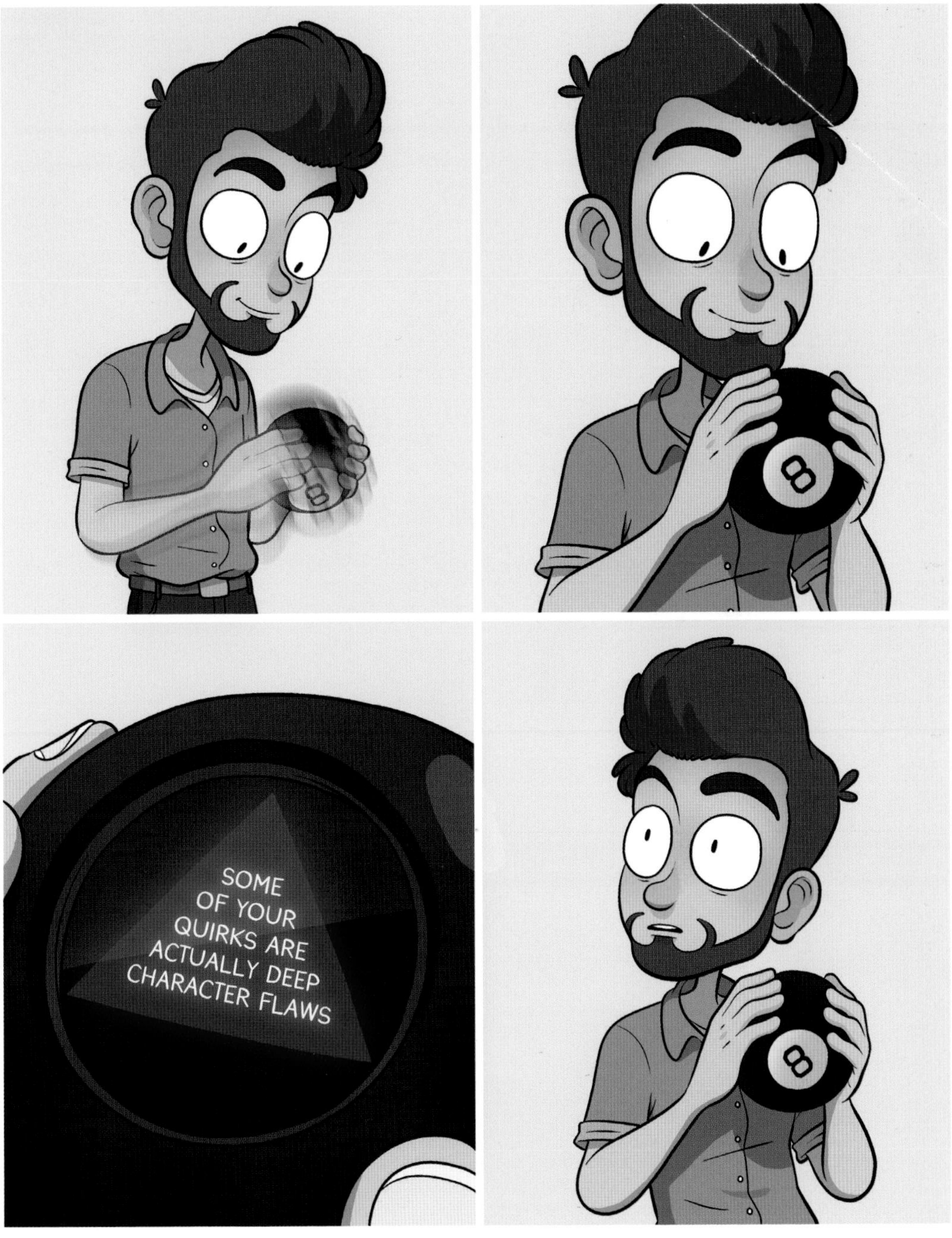
SOME OF YOUR QUIRKS ARE ACTUALLY DEEP CHARACTER FLAWS

YEARLY CHECKUP

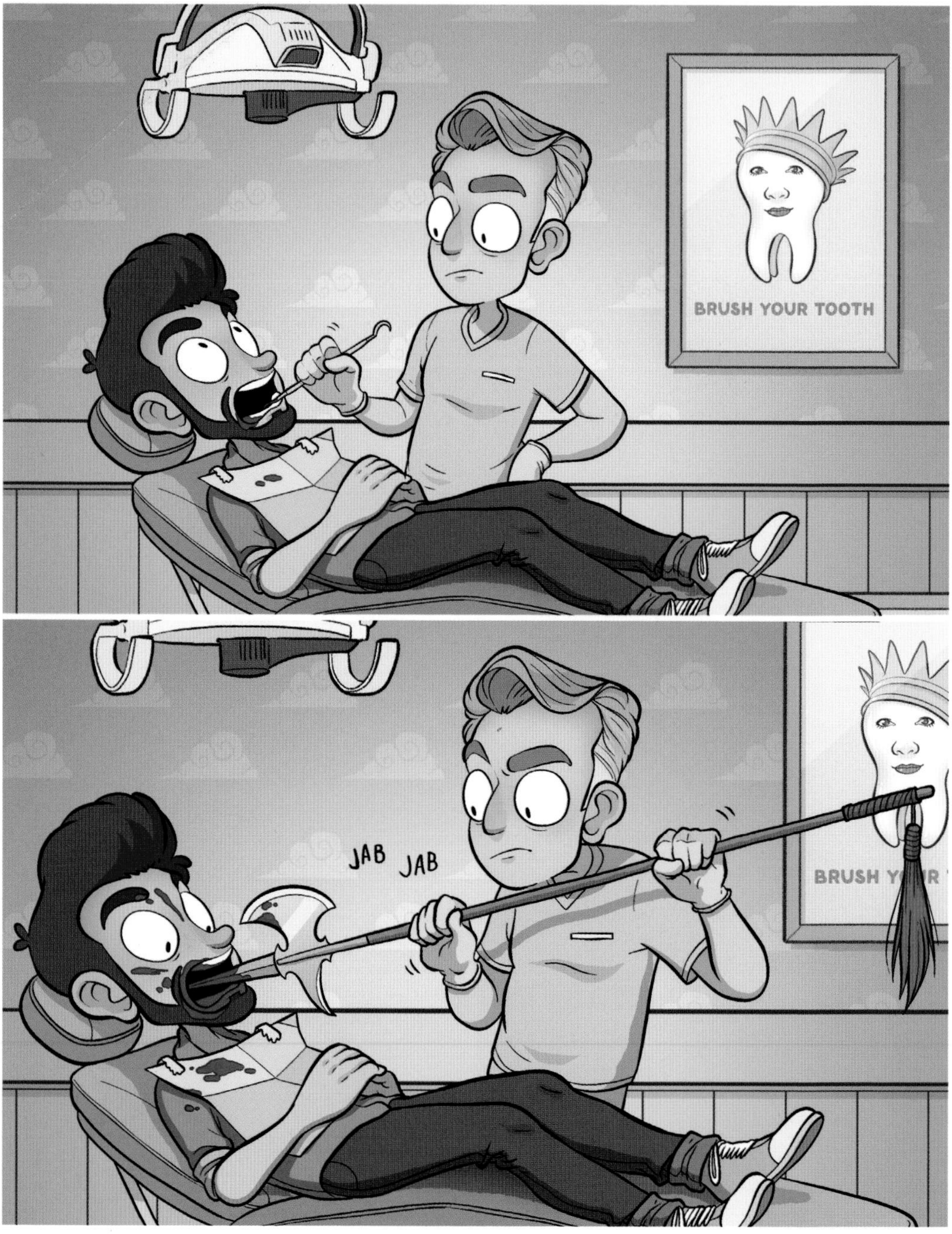
BRUSH YOUR TOOTH
JAB JAB
BRUSH Y

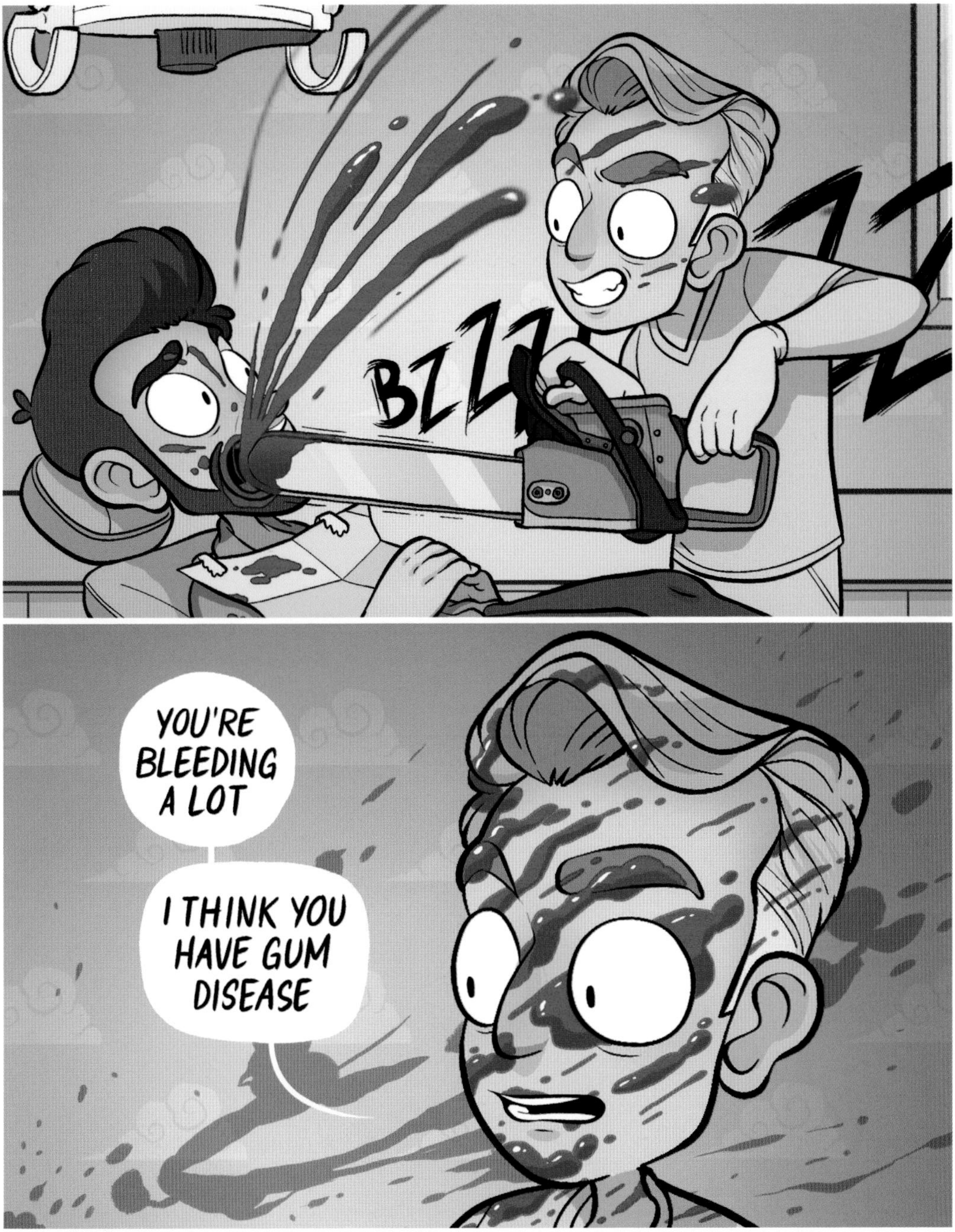
BZZZ
ZZZ
YOU'RE BLEEDING A LOT
I THINK YOU HAVE GUM DISEASE

NEW BEGINNINGS

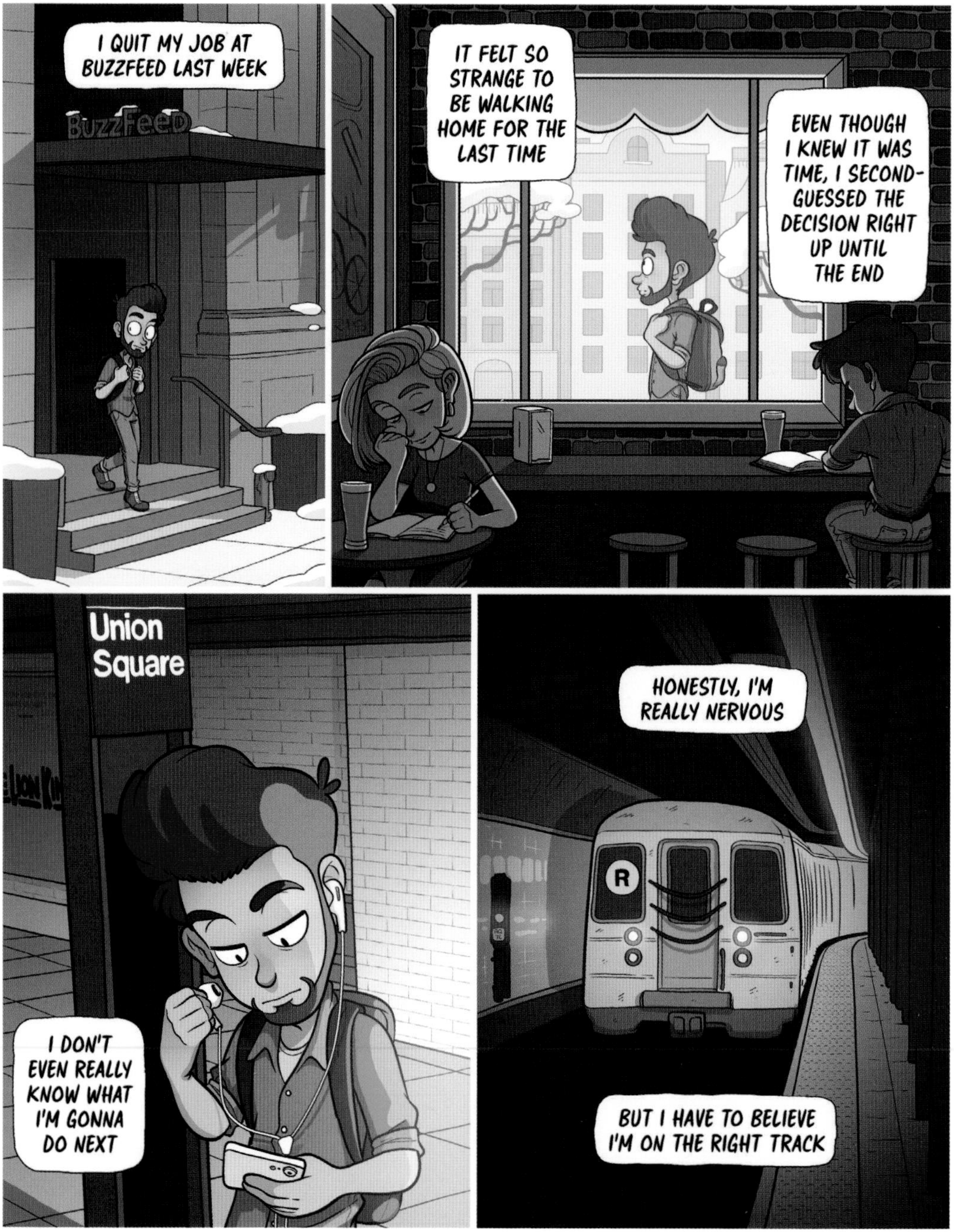
I QUIT MY JOB AT BUZZFEED LAST WEEK
BuzzFeed
IT FELT SO STRANGE TO BE WALKING HOME FOR THE LAST TIME
EVEN THOUGH I KNEW IT WAS TIME, I SECOND-GUESSED THE DECISION RIGHT UP UNTIL THE END
Union Square
I DON'T EVEN REALLY KNOW WHAT I'M GONNA DO NEXT
HONESTLY, I'M REALLY NERVOUS
R
BUT I HAVE TO BELIEVE I'M ON THE RIGHT TRACK

GREY GARDENS

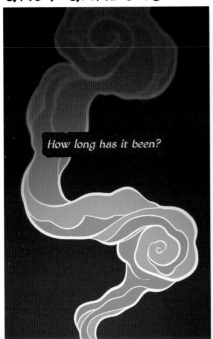

How long has it been?

I barely remember the outside world any longer.

I can't even recall the last time I saw another human...

Perhaps it's better this way, cut off from the outside wor—

OK, YOU LITERALLY QUIT YOUR JOB **THREE DAYS AGO**

STOP SMOKING WEED IN THE DARK AND GO DO SOME WORK

FLICK

HISSSSSS

WORK OF ART

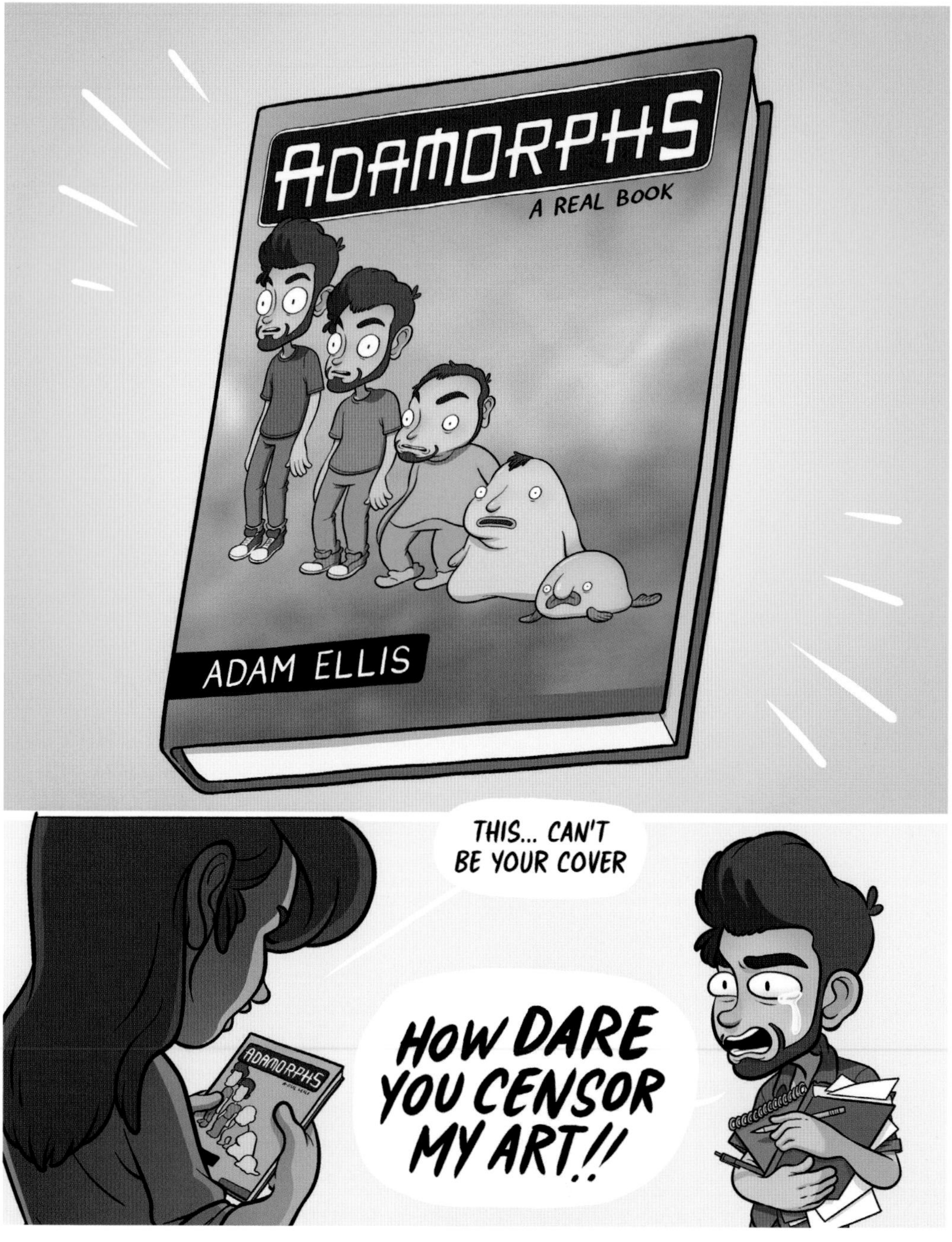

ADAMORPHS
A REAL BOOK
ADAM ELLIS
THIS... CAN'T BE YOUR COVER
HOW DARE YOU CENSOR MY ART!!

AUTUMN LEAVES

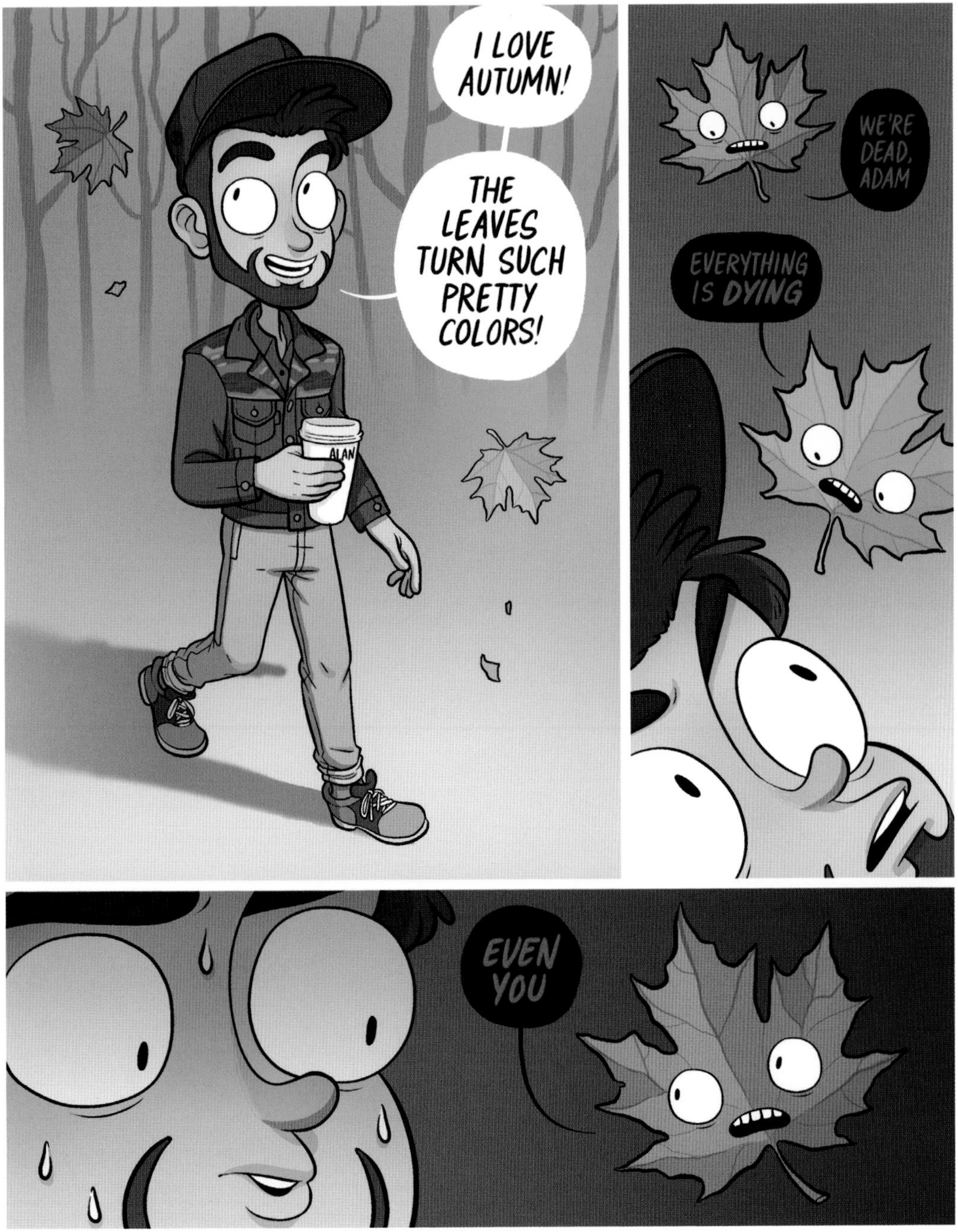
I LOVE AUTUMN!
THE LEAVES TURN SUCH PRETTY COLORS!
ALAN
WE'RE DEAD, ADAM
EVERYTHING IS DYING
EVEN YOU

BEST TIME OF THE YEAR

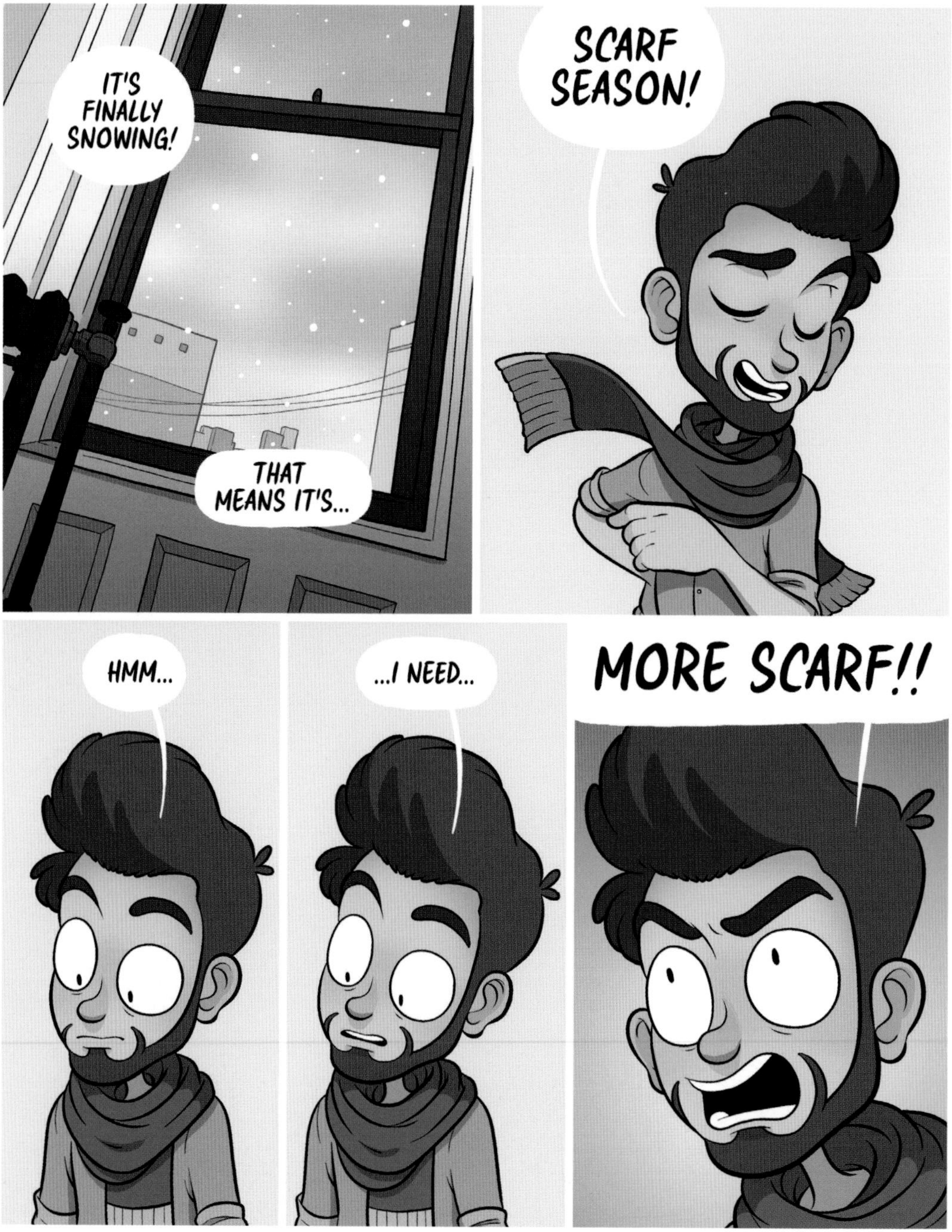

IT'S FINALLY SNOWING!
THAT MEANS IT'S...
SCARF SEASON!
HMM...
...I NEED...
MORE SCARF!!

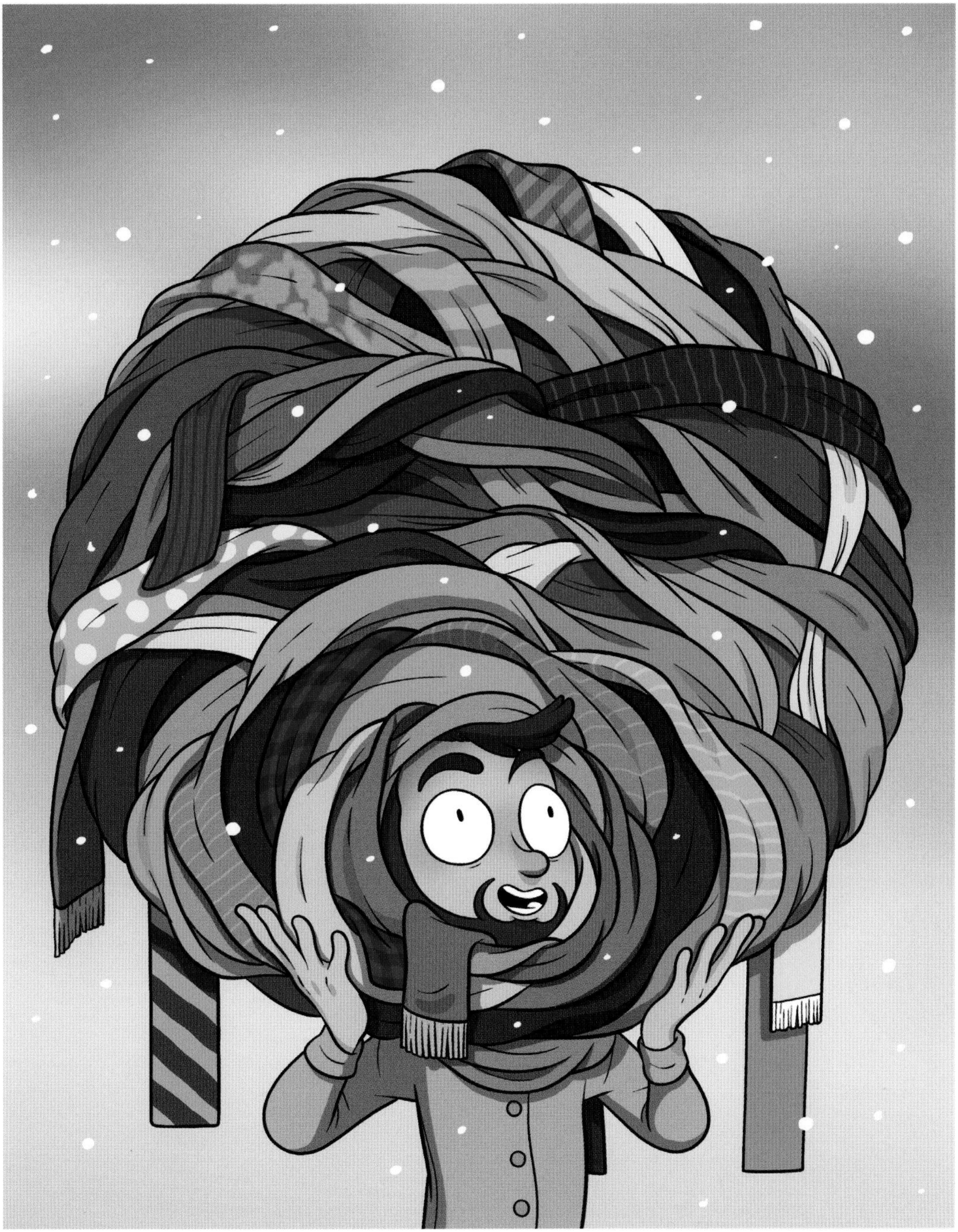

LIL' TREAT

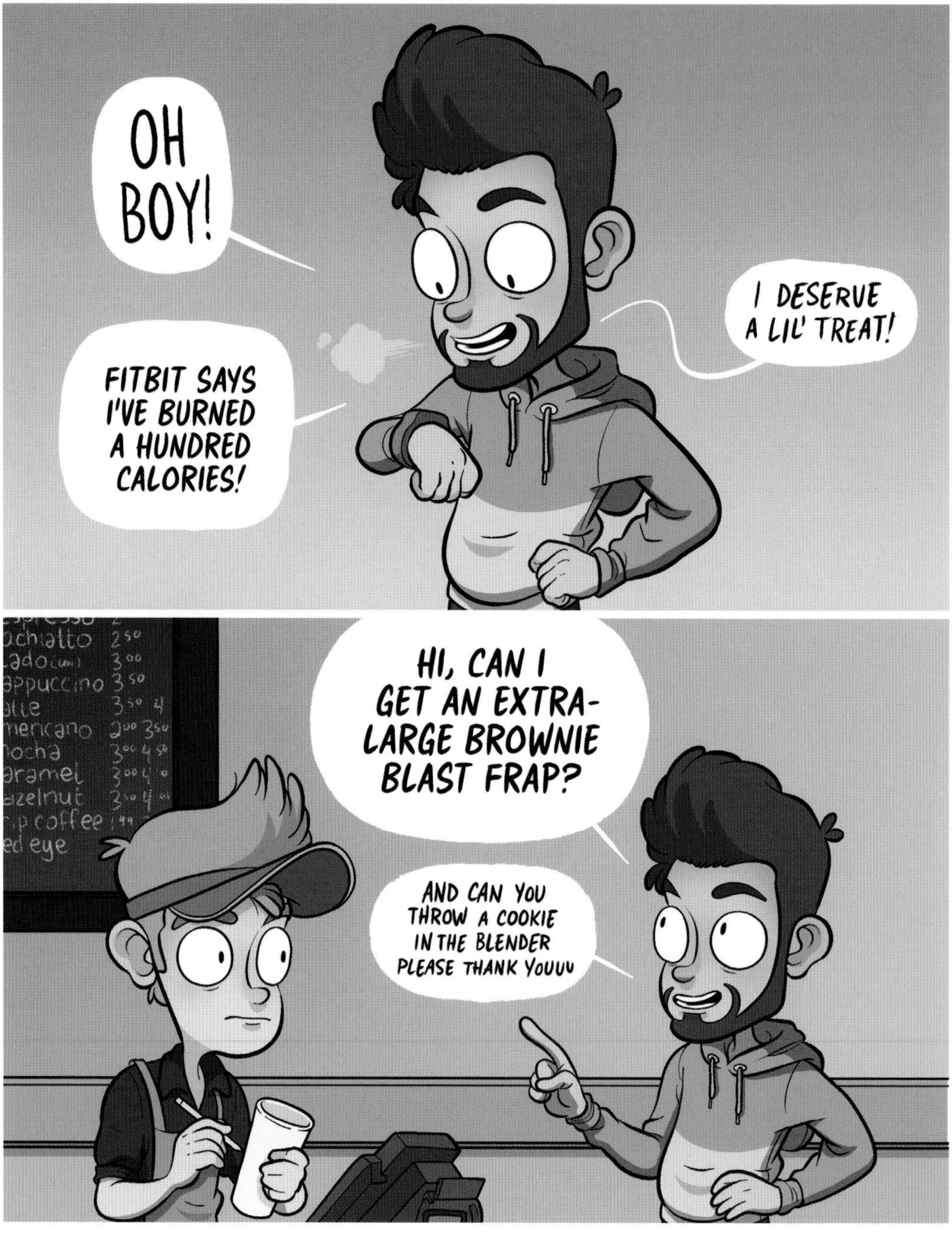

OH BOY!
FITBIT SAYS I'VE BURNED A HUNDRED CALORIES!
I DESERVE A LIL' TREAT!
HI, CAN I GET AN EXTRA-LARGE BROWNIE BLAST FRAP?
AND CAN YOU THROW A COOKIE IN THE BLENDER PLEASE THANK YOUUU

WHAT, LIKE IT'S HARD?

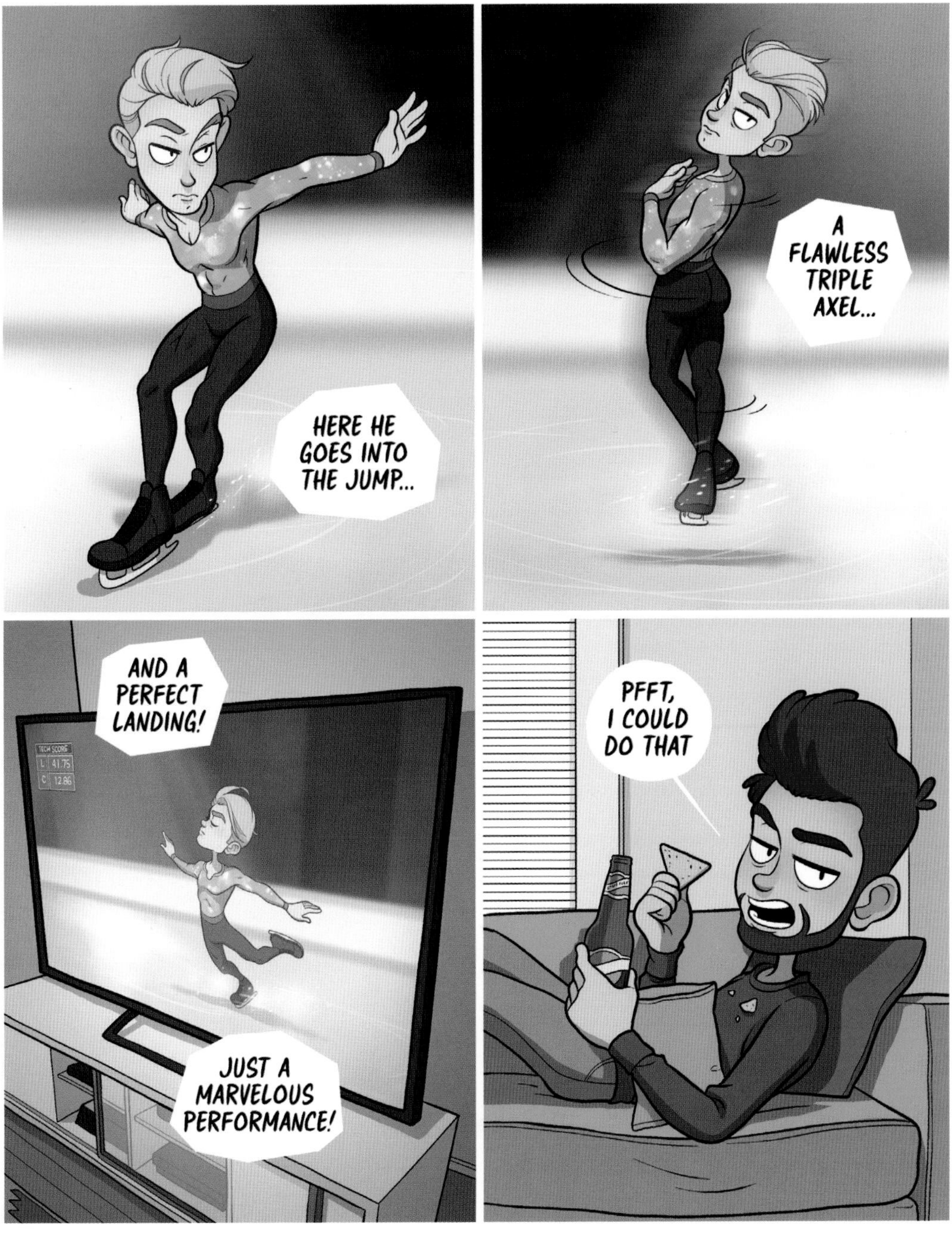
HERE HE GOES INTO THE JUMP...
A FLAWLESS TRIPLE AXEL...
AND A PERFECT LANDING!
JUST A MARVELOUS PERFORMANCE!
PFFT, I COULD DO THAT

LONG JOURNEY

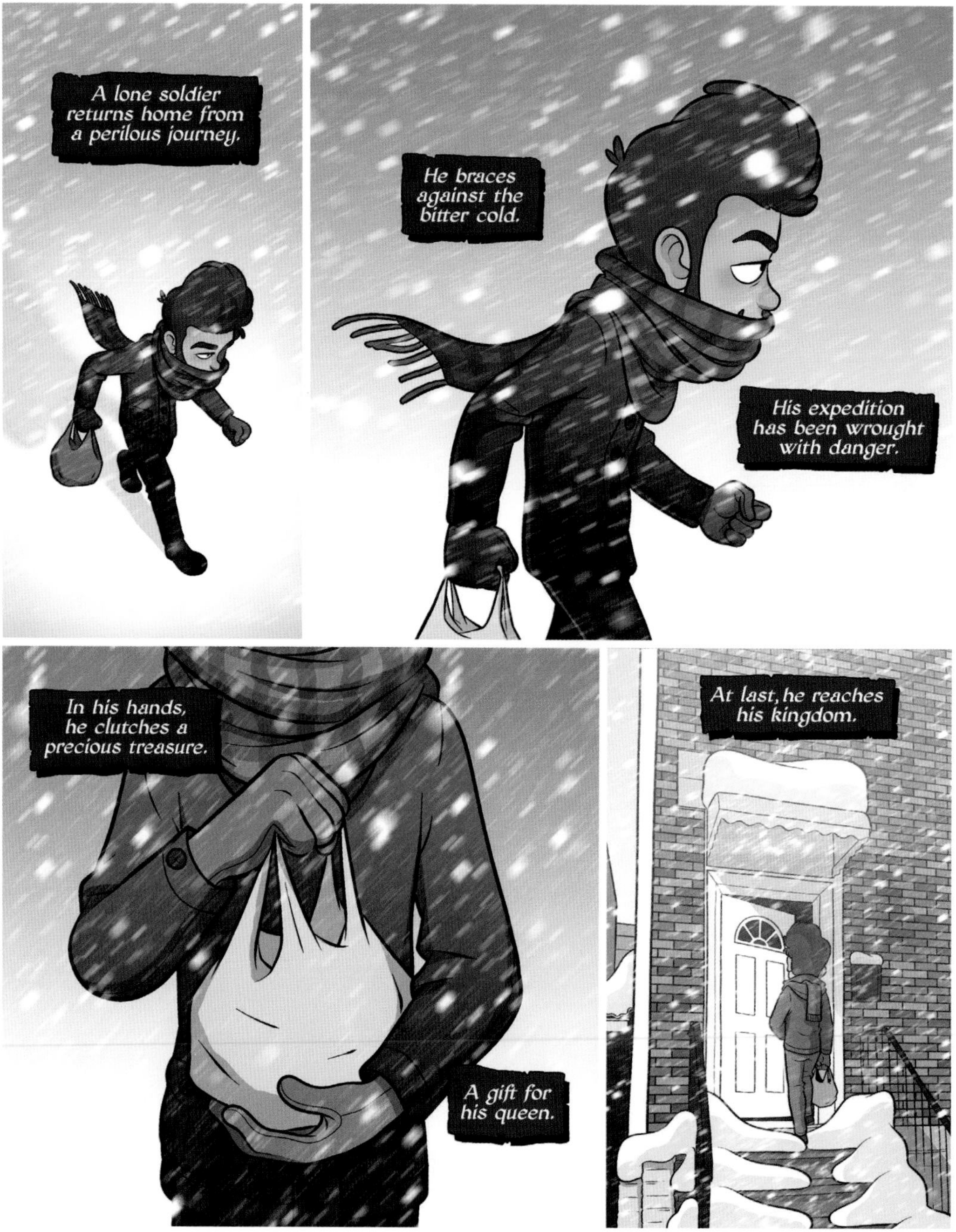

A lone soldier returns home from a perilous journey.
He braces against the bitter cold.
His expedition has been wrought with danger.
In his hands, he clutches a precious treasure.
A gift for his queen.
At last, he reaches his kingdom.

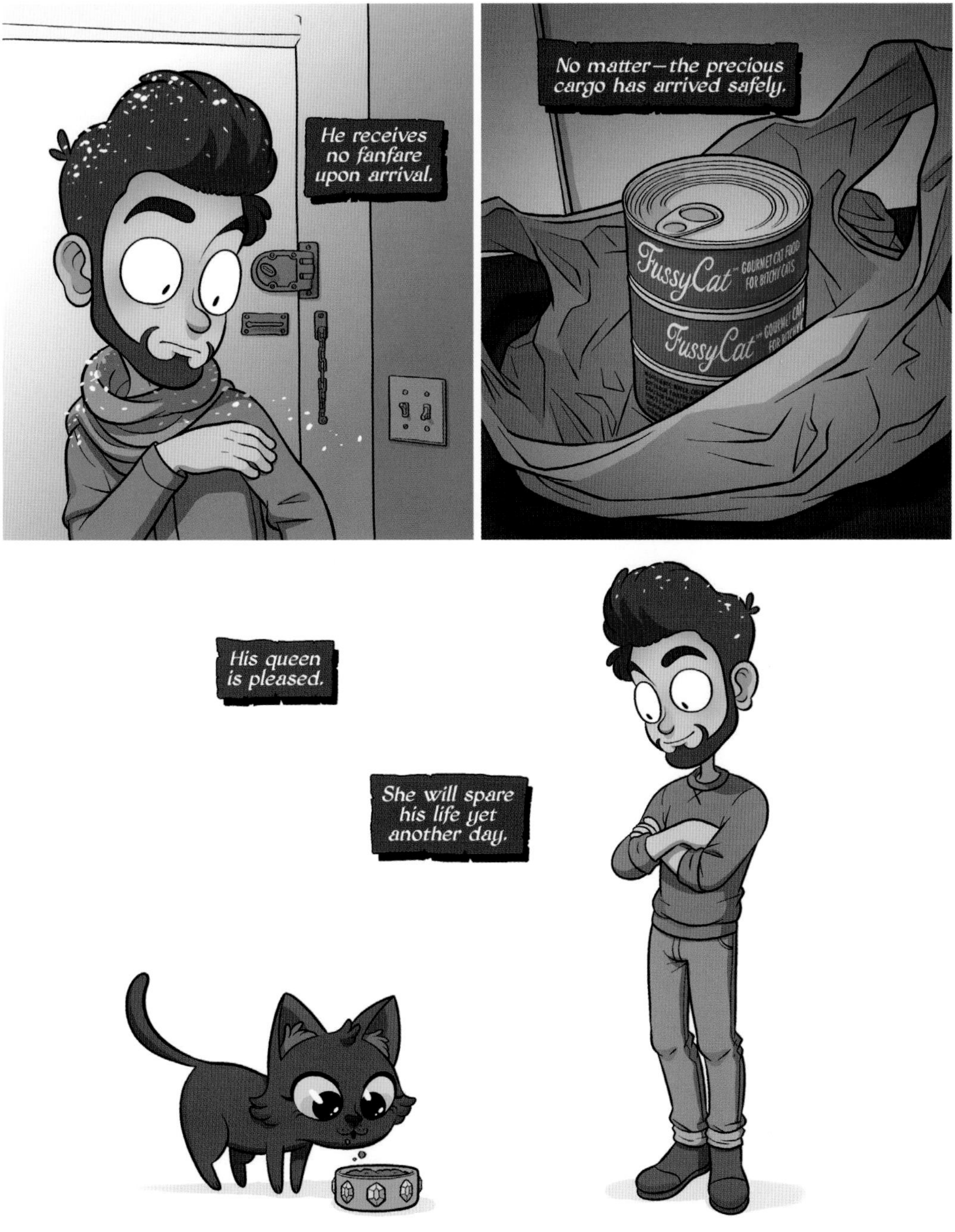
He receives no fanfare upon arrival.
No matter—the precious cargo has arrived safely.
FussyCat GOURMET CAT FOOD FOR BITCHY CATS
His queen is pleased.
She will spare his life yet another day.

MONTANA · CHRISTMAS MORNING

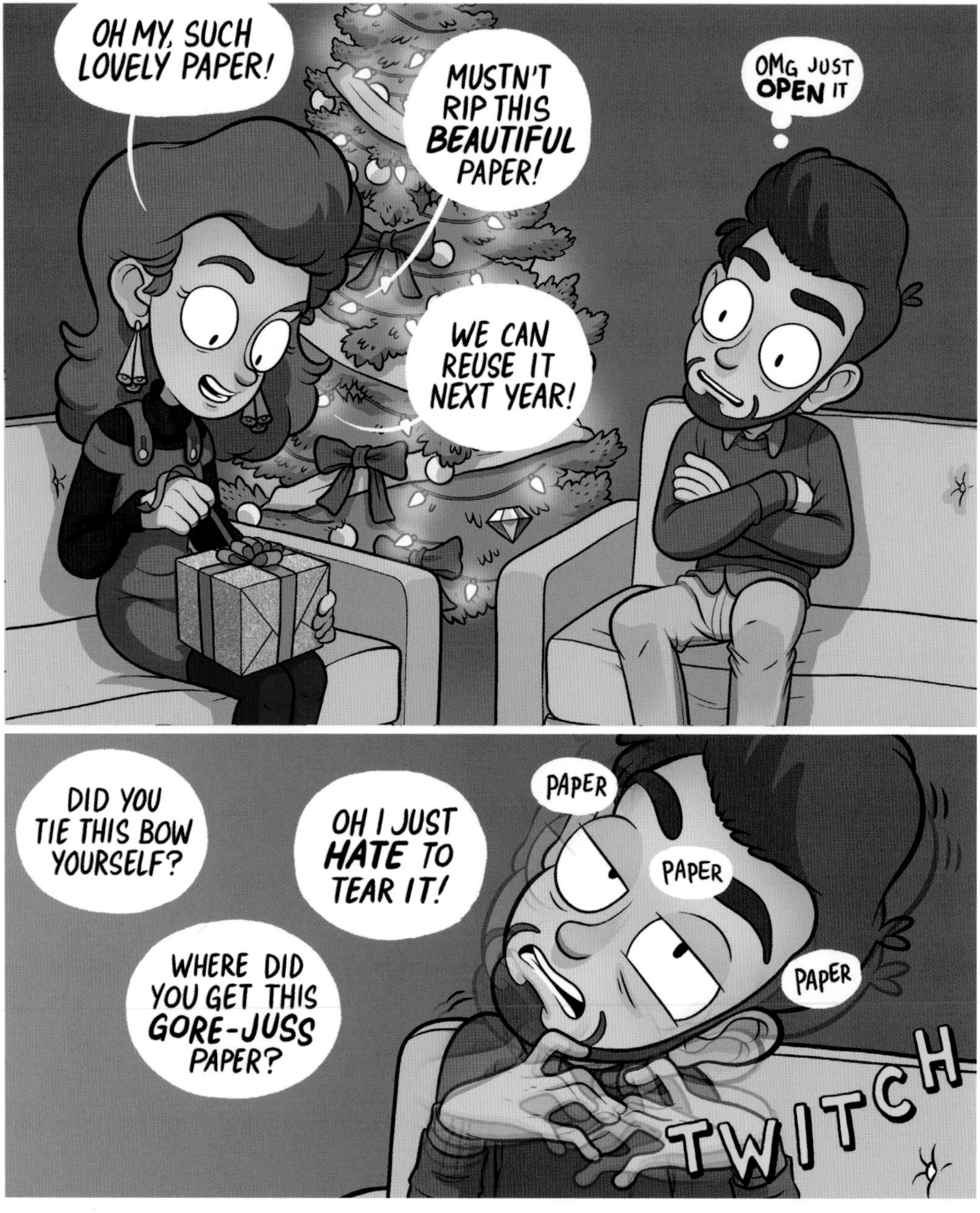
OH MY, SUCH LOVELY PAPER!
MUSTN'T RIP THIS BEAUTIFUL PAPER!
WE CAN REUSE IT NEXT YEAR!
OMG JUST OPEN IT
DID YOU TIE THIS BOW YOURSELF?
OH I JUST HATE TO TEAR IT!
WHERE DID YOU GET THIS GORE-JUSS PAPER?
PAPER
PAPER
PAPER
TWITCH

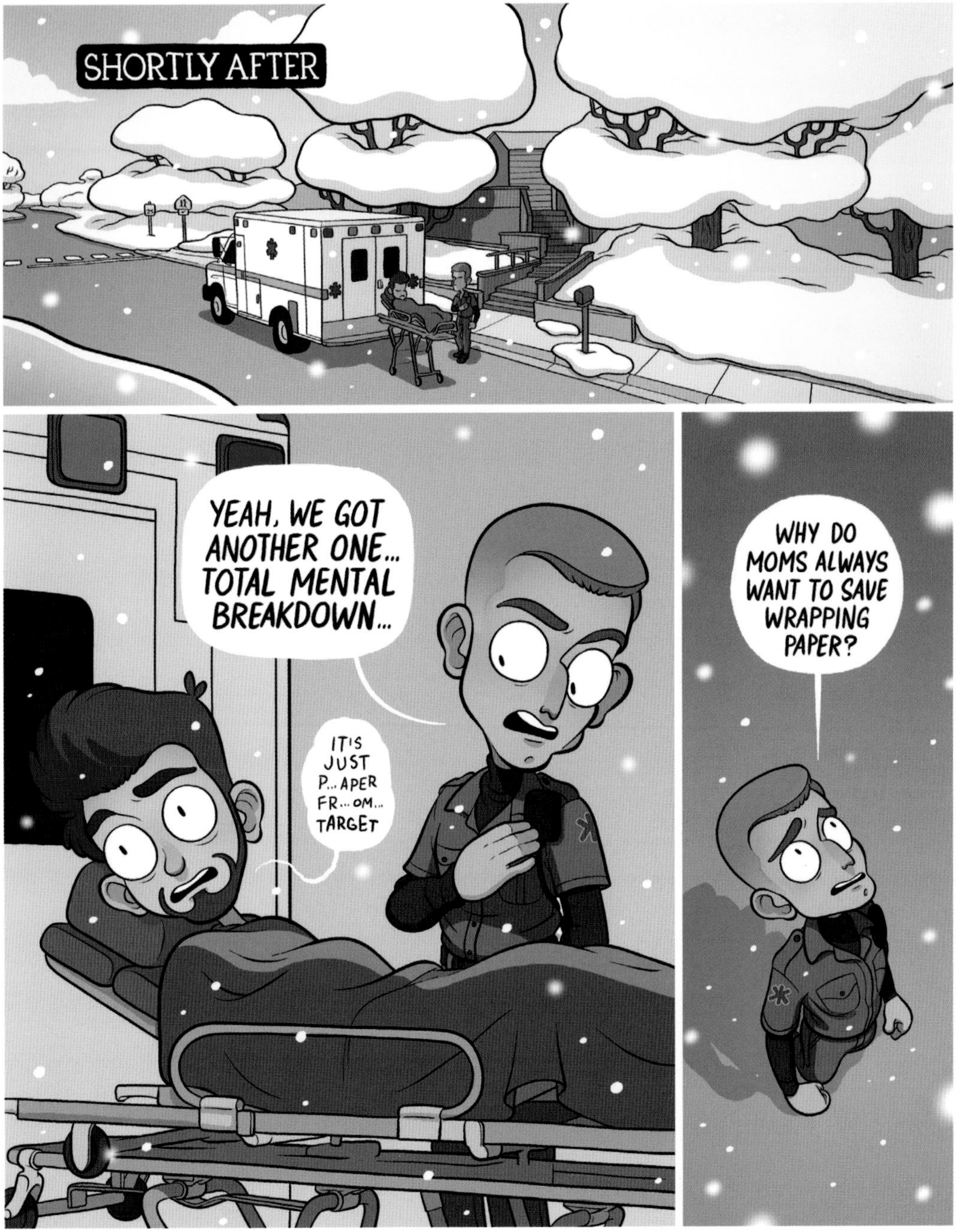
SHORTLY AFTER
YEAH, WE GOT ANOTHER ONE... TOTAL MENTAL BREAKDOWN...
IT'S JUST P...APER FR...OM... TARGET
WHY DO MOMS ALWAYS WANT TO SAVE WRAPPING PAPER?

NINTENDO

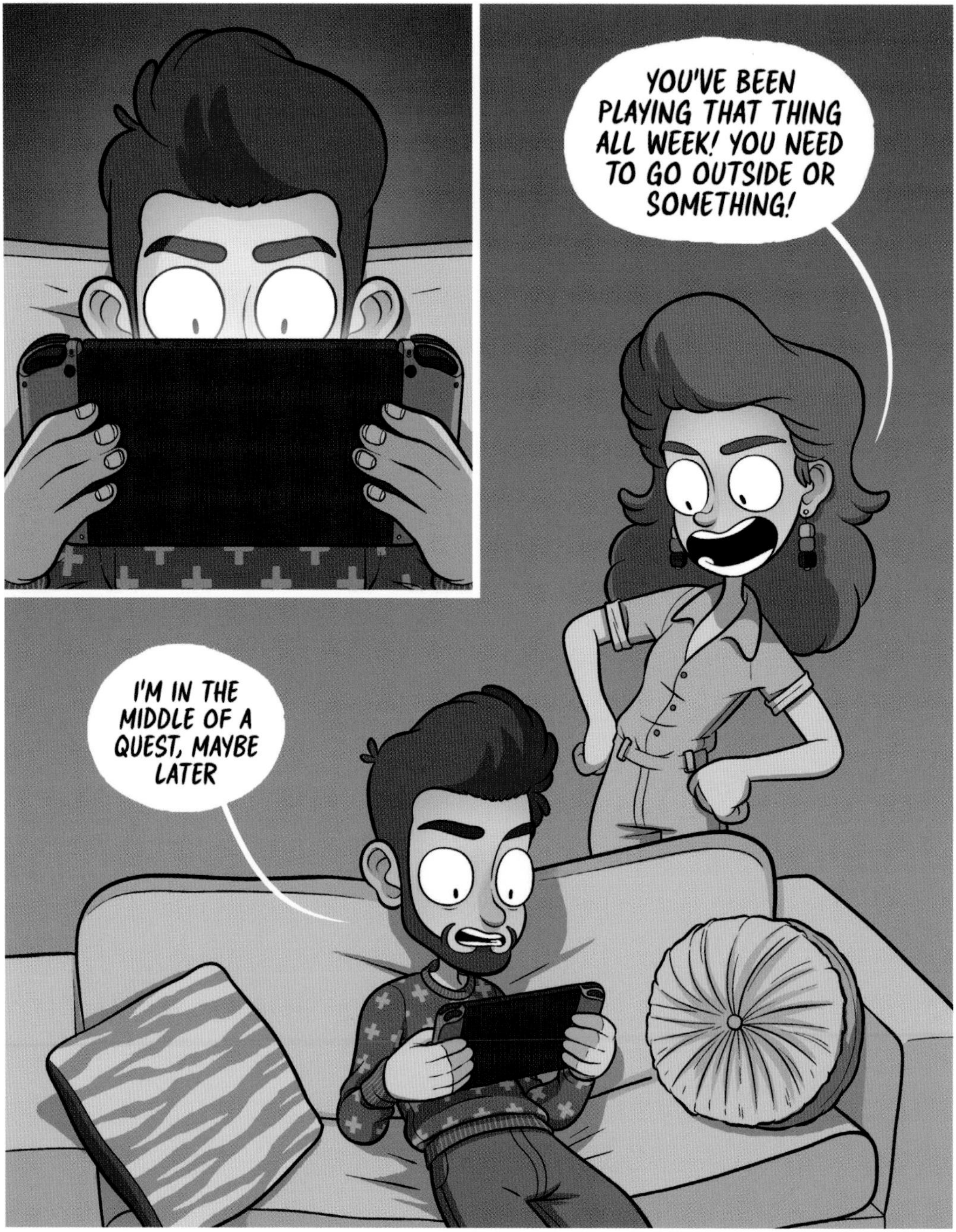
YOU'VE BEEN PLAYING THAT THING ALL WEEK! YOU NEED TO GO OUTSIDE OR SOMETHING!
I'M IN THE MIDDLE OF A QUEST, MAYBE LATER

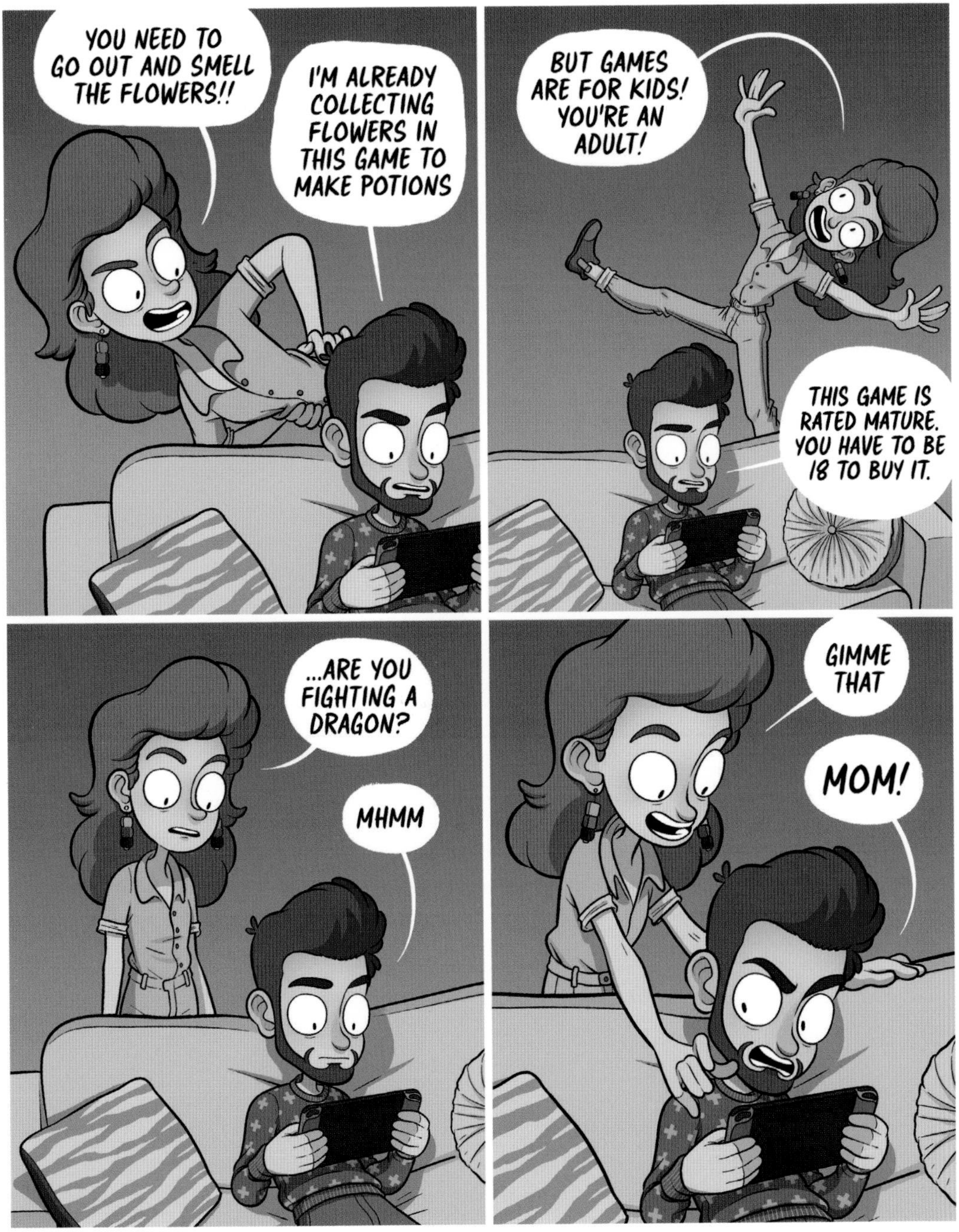
YOU NEED TO GO OUT AND SMELL THE FLOWERS!!
I'M ALREADY COLLECTING FLOWERS IN THIS GAME TO MAKE POTIONS
BUT GAMES ARE FOR KIDS! YOU'RE AN ADULT!
THIS GAME IS RATED MATURE. YOU HAVE TO BE 18 TO BUY IT.
...ARE YOU FIGHTING A DRAGON?
MHMM
GIMME THAT
MOM!

ORIGIN STORY

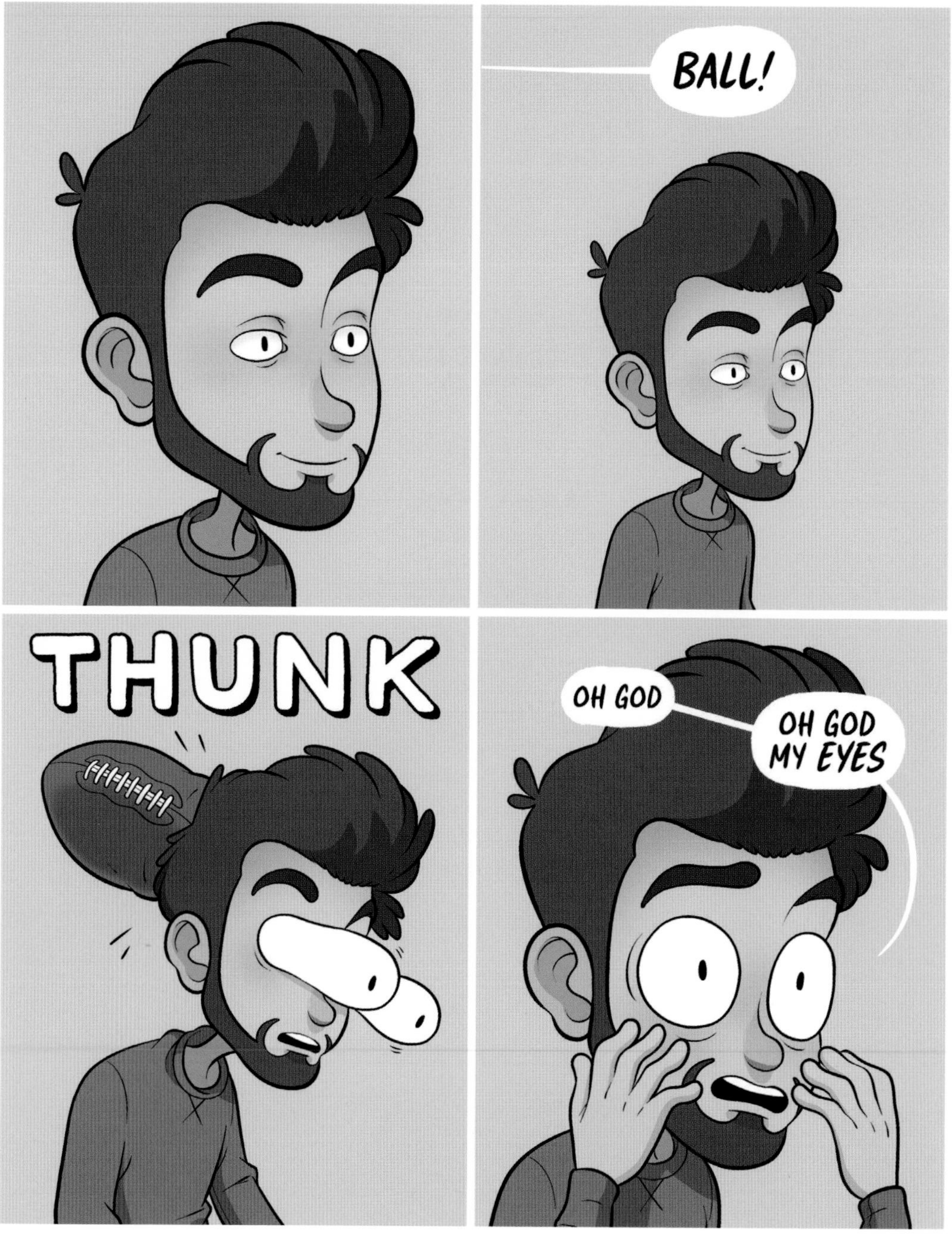

BALL!
THUNK
OH GOD
OH GOD MY EYES

FOURTH WALL

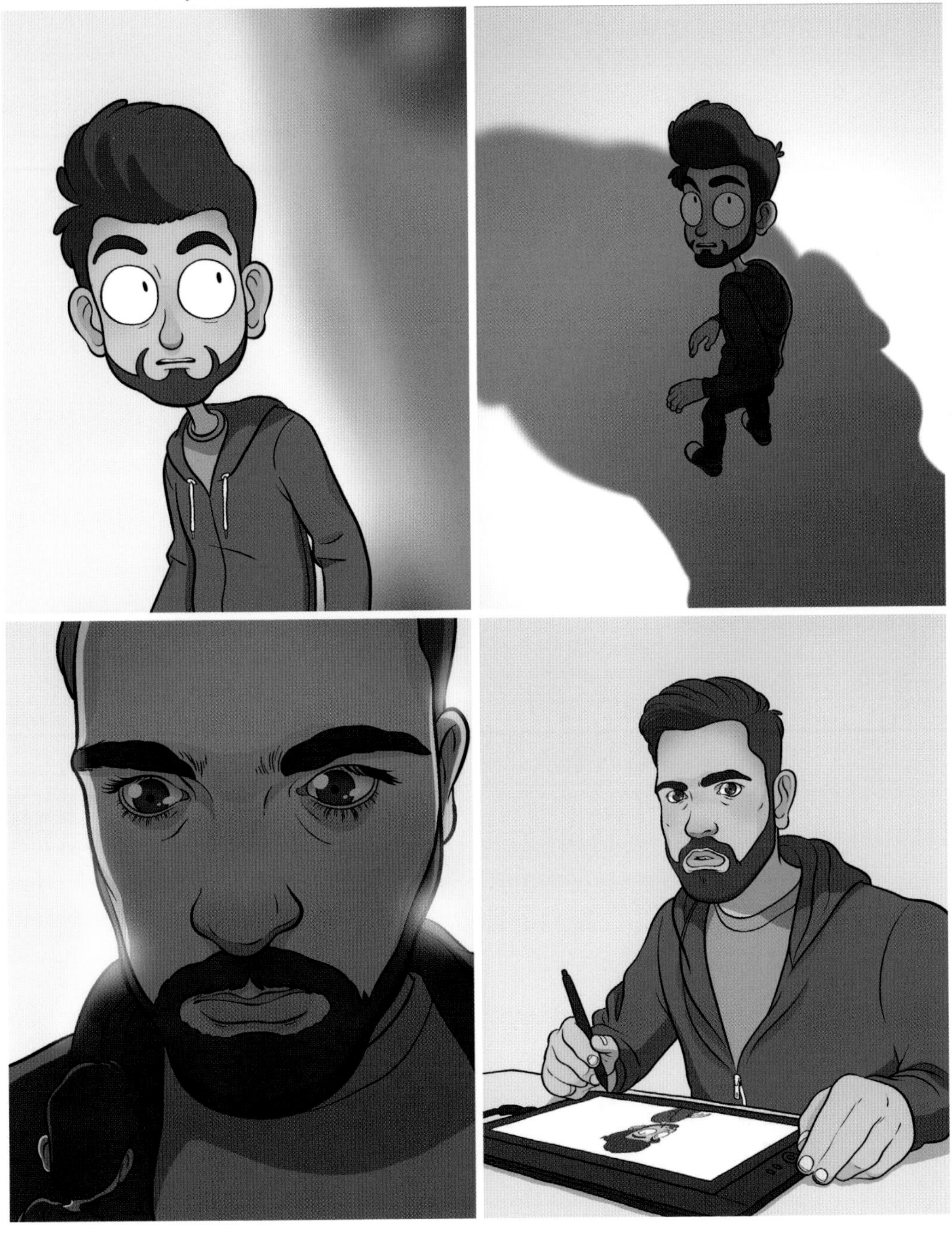

KNOCK IT OFF

CAN YOU QUIT SHAKING YOUR LEG? IT'S MOVING THE WHOLE TABLE...
I...
CAN'T...
STOP...
RRRRRRRRRRRRRRR
RRRRRRRRRRRRRRRRRR
RRRRRRRRRRRRRRRRRRR
KRAKOOM
fin.

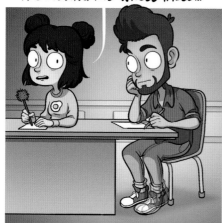

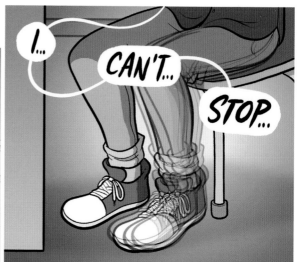

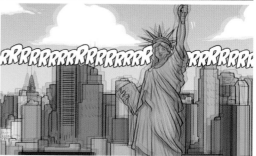

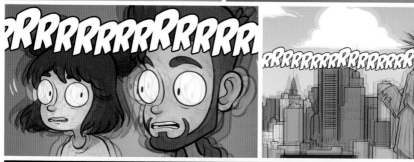

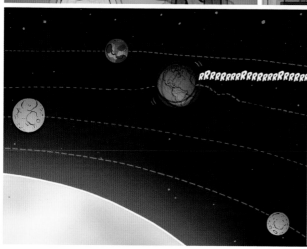

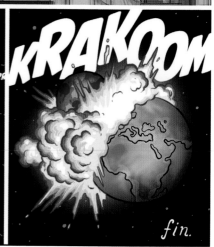

follow me!

 instagram.com/adamtots

 twitter.com/moby__dickhead

 facebook.com/booksofadam

 Books of Adam

 adamtots.tumblr.com